See pg 63 for how to
use MR volunteering
and farm sitting
as biology/Animal
science.
MR also includes
interacting with
special needs
riders.

Ages and Stages: Teen & Beyond.....................7

Beginning Independence in Middle School.........................9

Creating Socialization Opportunities for Teens 15

Teaching Your Teens to be Independent Learners.............19

High School Extracurricular Activities and Electives...........31

Fun With High School Electives 45

Career Exploration Ideas for Teens 53

How to Assign High School Credit to Life Learning
Opportunities 61

How to Summarize High-School Learning on a Transcript:
Creatively Combining Academic Studies *and* Life
Experiences 67

Using Dual Enrollment for College Credit........................73

The Nervous Mom's Guide to College...............................81

Homeschooling to College...89

General Homeschool Helps....................................97

Homeschooling: The Good, the Bad and the Unnecessary.99

The Best Curriculum Recommendations from iHomeschool
Network Bloggers..111

Ways to Make Back-to-School Time Special.....................127

How To Incorporate Extracurricular Activities 139

How Learning Styles Can Help Your Homeschool...........149

Have Fun with Board Games in Your Homeschool.........159

How to Stay the Course (or Not) When the School Bus
Looks Tempting..165

Model Lifelong Learning and Inspire Your Children........173

Making Flashcard Learning Fun 181

Determining How and When to Outsource Homeschooling
Subjects...187

Homeschool Educational Methods to Consider...............193

Learning Resources: Language Arts and Literature.207

Finding and Fostering Your Child's Reading Interests 209

Homeschooling through the Library 217

Family Literacy: The Secret to Raising a Writer 225

How to Teach With Living Books 231

How Memorization and Narration Benefit Your Child 251

Forming a Family or School Book Club 257

Learning Resources: STEM 263

Hands-On Homeschool Geography 265

Homeschooling Digital Natives 271

Nature Study Opportunities for City-Dwelling
Homeschoolers 279

Incorporating Fitness and Health Into Your Homeschool
Routine 285

Making Science and STEM a Priority 293

Incorporating Living Math Books into Your Homeschool 305

Learning Resources: Training Hearts 309

Life Skills for Kids: What You Need to Know 311

Helping Your Children Become Entrepreneurs 317

Raising Tomorrow's Thought Leaders 323

Stop Counting Raisins: Cultivating an Attitude of Gratitude at
Home (Advice from the Trenches) 329

Ten Ways to Volunteer Without Leaving Home 335

In But Not of the World: Helping Our Children Develop
Strong Character 341

Learning Resources: Unique Needs 351

Adapting Your Homeschool for Your Sons 353

7 Things I've Learned from Raising A Gifted Child 365

Homeschooling Worriers 371

Homeschooling with Chronic Illness.................................379

Learning at Your Child's Pace 385

Homeschool Planning Based on Your Kids' Personalities
(and Your Own!) 393

Incorporating Special-Needs Therapies Into Your
Homeschool..399

Synchronizing Curriculum for Asynchronous Learners.....405

When Your Child Doesn't Understand a Subject.............413

Homeschooling Your Child with ADHD 419

Managing Your Life: Unique Homeschool Situations...425

Family Learning: Combining Ages with a Multifaceted
Approach..427

Co-Parent Homeschooling..435

Homeschooling in Small Spaces..445

Academic Acceleration: When Your Child Moves Faster
Than the Curriculum 455

Homeschooling When You Have to Work.......................461

Dealing With Anti-Homeschooling Family 467

Involving Dad and Extended Family Members in
Homeschooling..475

Ages and Stages: Teen & Beyond

Beginning Independence in Middle School

Sara Jordan

You have successfully gotten your homeschooler through elementary school. Congratulations!

Now you have middle school to look forward to. It is during this leg of the homeschooling journey that many parents start having doubts again about whether they will be able to continue.

After all, the sixth- through eighth-grade years are a time of many changes. However, I am confident that you can do this. You just need a bit of preparation. This article will cover some of the things you should take into consideration when preparing for middle school.

Transitions

The middle-school years represent a time of change and growth for many children, not just academically, but also physically and emotionally. Because of the changes that come along with adolescence, you will likely find that the homeschool environment will change. Let's be honest – adolescence can be prickly. It can come with behavioral and mood changes. Your child may suddenly prefer to work, learn or study in a different way, which means you might have to be flexible in the "classroom." You might have to provide your middle-schoolers with a new workspace, change your schedule a bit and present information to them in new ways. They will also likely become more independent during these in-between years.

Teach Them to Learn

As your child enters the middle-school years, the subjects will become more and more complex. This is why it is important that you move from teaching your child information to teaching your child how to learn. The ability to seek out, learn, retain and apply information is a skill that will serve your children well – not just academically, but as they navigate life. This is also a great opportunity to truly reinforce what they already know and to brush up on any areas in which they show weakness. You could also start asking them how they feel about their progress. The ability to assess one's own progress is definitely a great and necessary skill to develop.

Seek Outside Help When Needed

Along these lines, it is also critical that you be aware of YOUR strengths and weaknesses. Many of us pride ourselves on being our children's educators. However, as the subjects that they study become more complex, you will often find yourself out of your depth. It is nothing to be ashamed of! We can't be experts at everything. As your child's educational needs become more complex, you might want to consider utilizing resources such as textbooks (or living books if you are a Charlotte Mason homeschooler), audiovisuals, co-op groups, tutors or even classes that your child can take at local institutions or online.

Skills to Focus On

Some of the basic skills that you should really focus on in the middle-school years are reading (and reading comprehension), writing and mathematics. This core group of subjects is one that will present itself in a wide variety of forms, not just through the rest of your child's academic career, but in life. You want to ensure that your children have a solid grasp of the following skills and subjects before they enter the high-school years:

- reading comprehension
- grammar
- composition (including self-editing)
- algebra
- geometry

This is also a great time to focus on the non-academic skills (also known as life skills) that your child will need to navigate not only academia, but the real world. Two main skills to develop during this period are independence and responsibility.

Hobbies and Extracurricular Activities

As mentioned previously, this is also a time when your child will likely want to explore more interests. You should not only support your children in this endeavor, but encourage them and provide them with opportunities to try new things. One of the best things about homeschooling is that you do have the flexibility that enables your child to pursue a variety of interests. Who knows, something they start doing during these years might lead them down the path of a future career. Give them the chance to explore various things and develop their passions and interests.

High School Prep

The middle-school years are a good time to start preparing for high school. As your child enters eighth grade, you might want to consider incorporating some high-school subjects so that the transition into high school runs more smoothly.

Although this is not a definitive guide to navigating the middle-school years, I hope that I have given you some things to think about.

Sara Jordan is a homeschooling mom to three girls. She has been blogging about homeschooling, faith and purposeful living at EmbracingDestinyBlog.com since 2008. She is also the owner and editor of hsbapost.com.

Creating Socialization Opportunities for Teens

Mary Wilson

Socialization: It can take a different turn when our kids become teenagers. When the kids were young, a simple day at the playground with children in the same age range was the perfect socialization opportunity. As they enter their teenage years, things begin to change, and socialization often has to become more organized, purposeful and frequent to help our older children make meaningful friendships.

There are all sorts of opportunities we can create or find for our teenagers. Here is a list to help you get started brainstorming with your child.

Five Socialization Opportunities for Teenagers

Local Classes. Begin with a Google search, check out your county parks and recreation guide, or ask your local library. Classes for teens can be found in all sorts of places. Local businesses, such as paint-your-own-pottery studios and art studios, host events open to teens. Of course, it can be awkward to make new friends at events like this, so your teen will need to visit consistently and/or bring a friend.

Game Night. Invite a group of teens over to learn the rules, and then play a specific game. Card games are fantastic with this age group, and many can incorporate more than four players. Learning a large-group game like Bunco works well for a game night! Board games are often limited to smaller numbers, but would work well with a more intimate group of kids. Start by giving a quick lesson and playing a round or two with the kids, and then let them keep going on their own!

Book Club. A great monthly book discussion is a perfect way to make new friends and/or to see good friends on a regular basis. Titles can be selected by the participating teen members or the organizing parents. Meeting locations can include homes, bookstore cafes or the local coffee shop. Having a book title as the topic of discussion helps spark conversation as kids are growing up. A regular meeting will help everyone involved get to know one another and feel more comfortable as a group. Of course, if you are up for it, you can create book clubs around a theme and have a blast with decor and food. While this can be fun, it certainly isn't necessary!

LAN Party. Everyone can bring a laptop and play online together! Depending on the space you can access, this can be as large or as small of a group as you can manage. Online games have a way of bringing teens together easily. This is a great way to host a co-ed get-together without too many awkward feelings. Throw in a little food, and you have a great night ahead of you! If you need a little help, you can find guidance online, or just ask your teenager for some help.

Activity-Based Evening. Host a group of teens and teach them a skill or create a product together. This could take the shape of a cooking class, sewing class, crafting night or even an archery night in the backyard! The options are endless, but the goal is to provide a focus for the group to interact around. Of course, off-site activities such as bowling are perfectly acceptable!

The options are endless and can be as unique as your teenagers. It only takes a few other interested teenagers, and you can build a group from there. If you want to branch out to new members, talk to your local homeschool group. Find another group of moms with teens who are interested in the same sort of group socialization time. It might take a little planning and effort, but it will be worth it for your teenager!

 *Mary Wilson is a homeschooling mother of four children, ranging in age from 7 to 14 years old. She loves to share her experiences of homeschooling, parenting and adventuring on her blog, NotBefore7.com. When she isn't blogging, you can find her hosting book clubs, traveling and running.*

Teaching Your Teens to be Independent Learners

Heather Woodie

Most of us know that entering high school is a game-changer for the homeschool. Many families feel the pull of the increased workload, and the way we approach homeschooling might need some adjustment. We recognize the need for our teens to become more independent, but maybe we are unsure of how to do this, especially if we haven't already been building up to it during middle school. Let's start by taking a look at what it means to be independent. Then we'll talk about strategies for helping our students to practice independence.

Defining Independence

According to the Merriam-Webster dictionary, independence is the state of being independent. So, what does it mean to be independent? This is the exact definition in part:

1 : not dependent: as

a (1) : not subject to control by others : self-governing (2) : not affiliated with a larger controlling unit <an independent bookstore>

b (1) : not requiring or relying on something else : not contingent <an independent conclusion> (2) : not looking to others for one's opinions or for guidance in conduct (3) : not bound by or committed to a political party

c (1) : not requiring or relying on others (as for care or livelihood) <independent of her parents> (2) : being enough to free one from the necessity of working for a living <a person of independent means>

d : showing a desire for freedom <an independent manner>

Healthy Independence

For our discussion, we'll focus on not requiring or relying on others, and perhaps showing a desire for freedom. In our homeschools, working independently means students working on their own without relying on others - whether it's Mom, Dad or a sibling.

The truth is we need to be somewhere in between totally dependent and too independent. We want our teens to be able to work well on their own and with others. What does healthy independence look like? Teens need to be:

Self-Starters. This means they're able to follow the directions and get started on an assignment without a lot of hand-holding. Sure, it's OK to clear up questions and make sure our students know the job, but once that is complete, they need to get going and make progress on their own without a lot of adult intervention.

Task-Finishers: Students need to be finishers. That means allowing enough time for our students to finish well, and it means they need to be able to observe a deadline and eventually do that without a lot of reminders.

Focusers. They should work on tasks without interruption on their own. Whatever challenges our kids have in this area, we need to give them coping mechanisms to do this well in a variety of settings.

Independent Thinkers. Our students need to formulate their own ideas and opinions and express them well without a lot of influence from others. I'm not talking about large worldview issues here. I'm talking about even the everyday moments when they are asked for their thoughts. There are lots of ways to work on this, but it is important.

Problem-Identifiers. Can your students sit down and make sense of what they need to do? Can they identify the essential problem and begin to work on it? It's a good skill.

Problem-Solvers. Developing problem-solving skills in any subject area without tons of input is a goal to work toward.

Decision-Makers. This is not a problem I struggle with, but I see it a lot in adults. Our kids need to be able to make decisions and move toward their goals. Making too many decisions for our kids will interfere with helping our students get better at decision-making.

Copers. If our teens struggle in any of these skill areas, then it is our responsibility to teach them coping skills. None of us are 100 percent on our game 100 percent of the time. Whether or not we have diagnosed special needs, we all need to be able to function at less than 100 percent. What strategies can we teach our high-schoolers that will keep them in the game of life when they struggle?

They do not need us to do these things for them. What a tragedy life would be for our teens, who are also our students, if we did not allow them to become proficient at these skills on their own! That is not to say we should never step in. But, if we are doing a lot of hand holding during the process, they will not develop these skills as easily, if ever.

There are a multitude of ways to help your students develop healthy independence. Consider how your student thrives and work from there.

The Downside of Independence

The critics of independence will remind us that homeschooling shouldn't occur in a vacuum. And they're right. The goal for us should not be a completely hands-off education – at least, not in the sense that we no longer connect with our students during the day.

Here are some things to watch for as your teens become more independent.

We need to check in on progress to keep tabs on learning. It's easy to let workbook pages get filled in or the next lesson finished without really going over the work with your student.

Misconceptions are uncaught if we go too long without checking in. When we aren't connecting with our students often enough, things get missed that we thought they understood.

It might require backtracking when we do discover big mistakes. This is frustrating for the student and the parent when it happens.

When students are too young for independence, they can develop poor habits. Getting work done quickly but not accurately is a good example.

Independence can lack the connection piece of homeschooling. This is true both with siblings and the parents. One of the advantages of homeschooling is the opportunity to connect one-on-one and in small groups together. There are a lot of benefits to learning with others.

Does that mean we shouldn't work on independence? Does it mean we look for any and every opportunity to work with our students? My answer is no. There is such a thing as too much dependence in learning.

Expectations for High School Students

Many people wonder what to expect from a high-schooler. We also approach our homeschools with varying degrees of independence. So here are a few things to keep in mind:

Typically, younger high school students will need more guidance as they learn to manage their time, especially in light of the new workload that high school can demand.

Older high school students need to be managing their studies and schedule on their own. That is not to say we never interact with our high-schoolers, but micromanaging their time management and assignments is not helping them get ready for what's next, whether that is college or the workplace.

Age might not be the guiding factor if your student has learning issues or other unique circumstances making independence difficult. The key is to keep working with your students, giving them coping mechanisms to help them to manage on their own more and more.

Our goal is to put our high-schoolers in the driver's seat of their own education. Start working on this before high school!

High school is the time to transition from being a direct teacher into a mentoring role, making sure your students have the tools they need to be successful and having discussions to help them form and own opinions.

Teaching high-schoolers is a busy affair, but not in the same way teaching younger children demands. If you find yourself responsible for a lot of instruction, take a step back. If your students are capable of learning the material on their own, then let him them it. Your job is to make yourself available and to lead discussions about the work to help them hone it, if necessary. Help them to make connections and present their best work. This requires knowing the work as they go, reading what they are reading (or skimming to get the general idea), and throwing resources their way to expand what they know on a topic. Be prepared to challenge them with questions and discussion.

A Quick Note about the Unmotivated Teen

By high school, we're really transitioning our parenting and likewise our schooling strategies. I am always keenly aware that my 14-year-old freshmen only have about three more years until they are completely responsible for themselves, their education and their future. The time-consuming task of early parenting has been replaced with an equally arduous goal of making doubly sure they are ready to be on their own. This chapter would not be complete without acknowledging that some teens take the long way to this goal.

For us, making sure our students know that they alone are responsible for their actions is so important. When an assignment is completed haphazardly, it is so easy to place the blame on others - whether it is a sibling, a chore you asked them to complete, or that they simply forgot. At the end of the day, they have to own their part in whatever happened.

There are many strategies we can employ as parents with students who lack the internal motivation to succeed.

Tools for Organization

There are a variety of tools out there for your high-schoolers to use to keep track of their days and their coursework. Have your students help to choose the one that fits them the best. I have high-schoolers who do well with technology and prefer it, and some who prefer a paper calendar. They certainly don't have to be the same, so make it a good match. The goal is to use a tool for fostering independence.

Student Planner: We have two kinds. One is a student planner from Mead that has a monthly calendar followed by a weekly view in a list format for each day. The other is a spiral notebook that has blank pages where daily work is listed. This is great for a new high-schooler still gauging how long to work. Day-by-day planning is helpful for younger high-schoolers, allowing them to focus and not get overwhelmed.

Online Programs: There are many that can deliver email assignments to students, or the student can log in. This is especially handy for high-schoolers with mobile devices. Put them to work for you! Over the years, I've tried lots of these.

Google Calendar: No membership cost necessary. It only requires a Google account and a shared calendar. This one works well for kids who like to be on their computers.

Email: Just a simple email from the teacher will do for many kids. The disadvantage with both the calendar and email methods are that they are great vehicles for delivering assignments, but they do not offer record-keeping.

Whatever method you and your high-schooler choose, make sure it is sustainable. I have found long-term that electronic methods are harder to keep up with, particularly those which require grades.

At the start of each school year, I sit down with my high-schoolers one-on-one to discuss their coursework and other activities. Then together we form the template they will use to guide them through the year. It's important to keep in mind the whole picture when you are working with your high-schoolers to form their schedules. When it's time to sit down and hammer out the schedule, we always put certain things down first. Pay attention to things like course load, co-op classes, other outsourced courses, part-time jobs and other activities. Fill in a schedule grid with all the non-negotiables and see what is left. Is the schedule a realistic one? If so, it can serve as a guide for your high-schooler to follow. It will detail the things they must remember and it will help to see how much time they will spend on any given area compared to everything else they have to do.

Remember that it is OK to reevaluate as time goes on. Six weeks into the year is a good time to asses with your teen how things are going. As a mentor, I can plainly see what's going well and what is not. This process gets your teen thinking about how the work is going and what needs to be tweaked for success. This is all part of the process in developing independence. It's also a good lesson in flexibility, letting them know it's OK to make adjustments.

If you would like to know more about how to schedule high school in a way that keeps the big picture in mind and allows your high schooler to thrive, please see the post at Blog, She Wrote titled Strategies for Scheduling High School.

Mentoring High School Students

When our children are young, the teaching portion of our homeschool is very demanding and teacher-oriented. As our children grow, our role as their teacher will change as we allow our kids to take on more responsibility. Sometimes this comes naturally to parents, and other times it does not. The goal is to give them ownership of their learning over time and to develop our role as mentors in our teens' lives. How do we go about this transition? Here are a few tips:

Help with Goal-Setting. Bring your older kids to the table and let them take the lead in their own learning.

Model Lifelong Learning. Keep up with your learners so you can discuss topics with them and continue learning yourself. Reading what our kids are reading helps a lot in this area if nothing else.

Provide Time. Give the space in the schedule for your kids and teens to explore and find their niche.

Make Space Available. This way, your students can continue learning and not have to find the spot to work.

Provide Materials and Resources. Make sure items are available and ready for use. Taking your teens to where the resources are located and generally helping them to get what they need to work needs to be a priority. I try to just anticipate what they will need at the start, or, as I see things that might be useful, I leave them out. This is a tried-and-true method.

Collaborate. Meet with your kids as they work and see where they are and how they are doing.

Be Available. Being a mentor doesn't mean disappearing. It means being available while your students are working and consulting with them.

Also, remember that as parents, you can choose to find other mentors for your teens based on interest. Mentors come in the form of online classes, local opportunities, family members and other trusted adults.

I've written more about transitioning from teaching to mentoring in this book's predecessor, The Big Book of Homeschool Ideas: volume one.

Offering More Independence

The last thing I want to talk about is the need to give our teens more independence at the same time we are requiring it. We cannot constantly require independence in their academic world without offering them more in the rest of their world. This could mean meeting milestones like working toward a driver's license or otherwise allowing them the room to grow as young adults.

At the time of this writing, our two oldest (18 and 16 years old) are still working on getting their driver's licenses, but while they practice and get closer to the goal of driving on their own, we have also given them bus passes to get around town. We encourage them to head out and study at the local campus or public library, meet friends for lunch, or to make a trip to the mall for supplies. The bus system allows them some freedom while still home with us, and it develops skills they need to get around on their own. We live in a unique university community, but consider how you can do the same for your teens.

Finally, as your teens take on more responsibility, give them more freedom to grow and the privileges that come with being successful at living up to those responsibilities.

Teaching teens to be independent is more than just requiring that their schoolwork be done on their own. Engaging the whole person with regard to increased independence is key. Enjoy the process of working with teens and seeing them through to adulthood. It's not the for the faint of heart, but it is rewarding!

 *Heather Woodie is a homeschooling mom to her own fantastic four - three in high school and one in middle school at the time of this writing. Heather, a former middle and high school biology teacher, has embraced the independent nature of homeschooling and mentors her children through authentic, student-driven projects and learning adventures. Find her at BlogSheWrote.org.*

High School Extracurricular Activities and Electives

Meg Grooms

High school is a time of exploration, a time to learn who you are and the principles for which you stand. Many people assume kids who are educated at home miss out on all of this, but just because your children learn at home doesn't mean they won't have the same opportunities as their traditionally-schooled peers. Elective classes are the key to giving your children the power to explore their world while providing an important piece of education.

Why Are Electives So Important?

While it's true that portfolio evaluators and colleges like to see that your child has experienced a well-rounded education, what matters more is the personalized education electives provide. Electives allow children to explore careers, learn more about their interests, discover new interests, determine what topics they don't care for and take the time to specialize in topics they already know a lot about. Most importantly, electives allow your children to take real control over their education, giving them total freedom in a safe manner.

Electives can be confusing and seem overwhelming, but it doesn't have to be like that. In fact, your child is probably already an expert in picking electives. Let's take a look at some of the most common questions I've been asked about electives and break down the process of picking and recording electives into easily digestible steps.

What Are Elective Classes and How Do They Work?

Electives are non-compulsory classes your child chooses to take. Electives are often classes outside of the typical reading, writing, math, science and social studies one takes in a traditional school setting (but they can be related to those subjects). Elective classes can include foreign languages, art, music, home economics, occupational education, advanced math and science ... the list goes on and on.

What is the Difference Between Extracurricular Activities and Electives?

The line between something being an extracurricular activity and an elective is often fuzzy. Generally speaking, extracurricular activities fall outside of an academic pursuit and electives add to academic pursuit.

Clear as mud, right? I asked my 18-year-old son how he would define both terms and he replied, "Extracurricular activities are more for fun, and electives are academic classes that you can choose." He went to on explain, "Extracurricular activities are optional while electives are not, though what elective you choose is up to you."

The fact is, most homeschooled kids excel at participating in extracurricular activities and taking electives. While it's true that most homeschooled kids are exposed to far more elective content than kids who attend a traditional school, that doesn't mean everything your child does should qualify as an elective credit. There is a difference, for example, between taking a few art classes at the museum (extracurricular) and studying art (elective).

Also, remember that an elective needs to meet credit requirements to be counted as an elective, which generally means 120 to 180 hours for a full credit. This doesn't mean that those art classes aren't important, it just means that you need to be intentional in determining what is best listed on the transcript as an extracurricular and what is best listed as an elective.

Now, there is no rule saying you can't turn your child's extracurricular activities into electives. In fact, this is a popular way for parents to beef up their child's elective credits if needed. For example, for a student who loves to cook or travel, you can create a Cuisines of the World elective in which your child studies a culture in depth each month, preparing a full meal using traditional foods and customary cooking techniques.

You can both visit local ethnic restaurants and maybe you even schedule a tour or cooking techniques class. Add in some videos and books about traditional food and compare them to modern-day meals in that country and your own. The possibilities are endless.

Word of caution: It is possible to turn your child's love of an activity into dread by making it too academic. Most homeschooled children have no problem finding enough elective classes to put on their transcript, so it really is OK to allow your child to participate in an activity just because they love it. I learned an important lesson very early on in our homeschooling career that not everything has to be educational. When you "over-educationalize" something your child loves, you run the risk of burning them out.

Be aware of the signs of burnout (resistance of a beloved activity, for instance) and know that you can always list these activities as extracurricular on the transcript if you would like them to be recognized.

In the end, you get to decide where the line between extracurricular and elective lies. As you create your child's high-school transcript, continually ask yourself the following questions: Did my child complete enough hours to make a full credit? Was this experience varied enough to qualify as an elective class? Is this experience more of a hobby than an academic pursuit?

Are Some Electives More Important Than Others?

Yes, in the eyes of college admission recruiters, anyhow. There are four electives that I recommend to everyone, especially those who will be pursuing post-secondary education at some point in their lives.

First, it's recommended every child take two consecutive years of a foreign language (three is even better). While many states no longer require foreign language for high school graduation, nearly every university requires two (and sometimes three) years. Generally speaking, most universities don't care which language you pick (keep in mind that not all universities accept American Sign Language as a foreign language) and your credit hours should include reading, writing and speaking to basic proficiency.

Note that many colleges and universities will allow you to skip this requirement if you were raised in a bilingual home, though they may ask you to take a language proficiency test.

Second, I recommend one total high school credit in PE/Health, which would include half a credit of physical education and half a credit of health. Half a credit is roughly 60 to 90 hours, or the equivalent of one semester. Furthermore, some states require an extra half-credit in health occupation for graduation.

PE and health are another requirement of many colleges because they want to know that their new students are going to be able to care for themselves with minimal intervention once they are on campus. And let's face it, none of us were ever at a disadvantage because we had a good education in personal and reproductive health.

A good health curriculum will include alcohol and drug education, reproductive education (including how both male and female bodies operate, pregnancy and STD prevention, and rape education for males and females), basic first aid, CPR, how to stay healthy through proper nutrition and exercise, and self-care (making doctor appointments, recognizing illness).

Two full credits of some kind of fine art are also recommended. Preferably one of those credits will be in a performing art. Why? Part of having a well-rounded education means being able to present your ideas to people of different backgrounds.

Some universities see that as a challenge homeschoolers don't always meet. Despite the fact homeschoolers have outgrown the days of hiding at home, the myth prevails that homeschooled children are sheltered from the world and those with different views.

There is nothing that shows how well-rounded a person is more than a knowledge of the arts, and performing arts (dancing, theatre, music lessons with recital) give your child the experience of presenting themselves to others in a professional manner. Oh, and many colleges require a credit of performing arts for admissions.

The fourth elective I recommend is a half-credit in driver education using a program that includes drug and alcohol awareness. One-quarter of the credit should be classroom learning (online classes are particularly popular for driver ed) and one quarter should be behind-the-wheel training.

Why? First, it makes financial sense, as most insurance companies will offer a discount to children who have taken a verified driver education program. Second, in some states it's required to obtain a driver's license before the age of 18. It's important to include the drug and alcohol education because it's something your child will eventually have to make a decision about, and education is key to preventing tragedies.

In all of the planning, don't forget that your children still have control over the electives they take, even the required ones. Let them pick which foreign language to take, which arts to pursue and which health program to complete. High school is the perfect time to start handing over the reins to your child, as every choice they make now will prepare them to make decisions when they are an adult.

How Many Elective Credits Does My Child Need?

The answer isn't going to be the same for each student and will largely be dictated by where you live and your child's post-secondary education plans. The first thing to do is determine if your state has a number listed in the graduation requirements. Next, look at some of the universities your child is considering to see what they require. If your child doesn't think that college is the right choice or is taking a few gap years, take a look anyhow because it's better to have the credits than not. Admission requirements vary widely, but it's pretty common for universities to require a minimum of eight elective credits, including two foreign language, one PE/health and two art.

Once you've checked into any state and college admission requirements, have your child start researching scholarship and grants. Sometimes these opportunities have specific credit requirements as well, and you'll want to find a way to include them.

Once you know the requirements, the rest is up to you and your child. I'll say again that it's my experience that homeschooled kids get considerably more elective credits than their traditionally schooled peers because they simply have more time to pursue their interests, so let your child guide you!

What Kinds of Electives Have Your Kids Taken?

When I start talking about homeschooling high school, I'm often asked what electives my kids have enjoyed. I've graduated a daughter and a son, and I have another daughter currently in the high school years (and three more kids coming up through the ranks!)

While we have made sure all the kids have the "big four" (foreign language, art, driver education, PE/health), the rest of their electives were totally up to them.

They've taken some really great electives over the years, including business math, costume design, special effects makeup design, art in advertising, Japanese, drama and musical theater, study skills, entrepreneurship, historical fiction writing, newspaper writing and Icelandic history.

When Should My Child Start Taking Electives? Do We Have to Wait Until High School?

I think it's great to start the process of picking electives in the middle-school years. It allows your children an opportunity to try things out without the pressure of having to complete enough work to make something into a half-credit or full credit. If you start introducing electives in middle school or even sooner, your children will be prepared to pick formal activities when they enter their ninth-grade year.

If you're already past the point of middle school, however, don't worry! High-schoolers and electives go hand-in-hand. Kids of this age are exploring their world in a whole new way. They're considering job prospects, figuring out what they are passionate about, and making a lot of little (and big) decisions that will frame the rest of their lives. High school is when electives really start to count.

Can I Count Electives in the Middle-School Years as High School Credit?

Yes! Also no. It's complicated. It all depends on the level of work completed. Introduction to Spanish, for example, is a popular class taken in middle school. It doesn't quite have enough work to qualify as a credit, but while you probably won't want to count it as a high school-level elective, it is still a very valid middle school-level elective and will help when your child enters high school and takes Spanish 1.

That said, there are plenty of middle-school-aged students who are able to complete high-school-level work, but that doesn't always mean you should list it on their transcript as a high-school elective. Most colleges are only interested in the classes your children took once they were of ninth-grade age, but as with everything else there are exceptions.

I generally suggest to have your child take the electives of their choosing when they are ready but keep anything before ninth grade (age-wise, not grade level) off the transcript. Why? Well, if you listed every elective your children took between sixth and 12th grades, their transcript might be 17 pages long!

We are homeschoolers, so there is some wiggle room. Let's take Spanish as an example again, assuming that the university your child is interested in requires two consecutive years of foreign language as an elective.

If your child takes Introduction to Spanish and Spanish 1 in middle school and continues to take Spanish 2 and 3 in high school, I would only count Spanish 2 and 3 on their transcript. If, however, your child takes Introduction to Spanish and Spanish 1 in middle school, Spanish 2 in high school and nothing further, I would list Spanish 1 and 2 on the transcript along with the school year in which the course was completed.

How Do We Decide What Electives to Take?

Your local law, graduation requirements or college admission requirements may answer this for you, so start there. Once you've met all requirements, turn to your child for guidance.

Ask your children if they would like to explore any careers. Examples of occupational education electives can include military history, political science, veterinary science and computer programming.

Choose electives that teach skills that are valuable to independent living. Examples of these sorts of life-skills electives could include CPR/first aid, cooking, money management, car maintenance and public speaking.

You can also ask your child to go more in-depth with something they already love. Movie buffs might enjoy a course about women in film, while avid readers might enjoy a course in 19th century poetry or Norse mythology.

Another option would be to ask your children if they have any activities they'd like to try. Photography, sewing, animation and songwriting are good examples of electives based on an interest.

Where Do I Find Elective Classes?

Homeschooling parents are a resourceful bunch, and if you do a little digging, you'll find lots of options for electives. I can only cover a few of those options because there is no way we could cover them all, so I've elected to list some of the most popular methods in which homeschooled students can obtain elective credits.

Option 1: Go to School

Many states now allow homeschoolers to take extra classes at their local public school. This won't be the best option for everyone, but is a very viable option for courses like organic chemistry (the schools have lab equipment) and band.

Online classes, both through the public schools and independent, are another wonderful option. Online classes are especially popular for the classroom portion of driver education and other subjects like health and advanced math. Similar options that might be available in your area are homeschool charter schools and local co-ops that split the cost of hiring a teacher for individual subjects.

Option 2: Go to College

Every state in the US has some sort of dual-enrollment or early-enrollment policy for their community colleges, though the policies vary widely. My children were able to start on-campus college courses at 14 years of age, though 16 seems to be more common.

Dual enrollment allows high-school students to earn college credit, often for free, while fulfilling their high school requirements. Dual enrollment is a good way for homeschoolers to take core courses, but it's also an excellent way to take electives like design, creative writing and theater.

Option 3: Find a Local Expert

Some electives are best taught by the people who know the subject matter best, the people who work in the field every single day. Woodworking, glassblowing, vehicle maintenance and coffee roasting are all wonderful elective choices that can be taught by a local craftsman.

Option 4: Buy Curriculum

I know this seems like a no-brainer, but don't forget to hit up your favorite (and some new) curriculum stores or websites for elective choices. There are hundreds of curriculum providers out there, don't be afraid to branch out to find exactly what you are looking for.

Option 5: Watch Television

Don't forget to include streaming media and educational DVDs. Thousands of educational videos are out there waiting to be watched. My two favorite sources for educational viewing are the Howard Hughes Medical Institute, which will mail you DVDs and virtual labs on CD at no cost, and The Great Courses, which offers educational DVDs, online streaming and a monthly subscription service. *not sure what this is — might like*

Both (HHMI) and The Great Courses offer high school *two* and college-level courses and materials that can *they* become the base of a fantastic elective.

While planning your child's high school education can seem daunting, you can relax when it comes to electives. Electives are easy to plan for, easy to find, and, because your children get to pick what they take, they'll be happier to complete the work. Now that you're armed with the information I've just given you, get out there and start planning those electives.

Meg Grooms is a Floridian living in the Pacific Northwest, a long-time homeschooler of six, a grandmother of almost two, an eater of all the foods and an admirer of goats. Meg blogs at HomeschoolGameschool.com and runs a small business providing discounts to homeschooling families at HomeschoolGroupBuys.com.

Fun With High School Electives

Tatiana Adurias

When I think of high school electives, I can't help but remember senior year ceramics class. The only thing I managed to accomplish was a weeklong detention after repeatedly hiding a classmate's lunch in the kiln. My graduation credits had nearly been met, and though I had no interest in ceramics, my guidance counselor thought that some form of art would look great on my transcripts. I admit that I was not very nice then, but I'll also say that I was extremely bored. This class was anything but fun.

High school electives are courses outside the required curriculum. They are not required, but can be chosen to meet specific college requirements, to reflect interests or to challenge your high-schooler by teaching a new skill.

My first high-schooler had a passion for writing, so he spent a semester writing a novel and another writing short stories.

My second high-schooler was interested in art and engineering. She took an engineering course that allowed her to build pretty amazing things, like a roller coaster powered by marbles and a working model of an earthquake-proof building. She even sat in on university lectures before she realized that, though she enjoyed building the things she did, engineering was not for her.

As fall was fast approaching, and we had not decided on a traditional elective for high-schooler number three, we finally started thinking out of the box. I nervously put together a YouTube course for my YouTube-crazy girl. She created storyboards for all her videos and we went over filming, lighting and editing techniques. She learned about copyright laws, plagiarism and YouTube monetization. Best of all was that, since she was already making videos in her free time, it made for an enjoyable class.

The Benefits of High School Electives

Did you know that as many as 16 U.S. states don't have specific graduation requirements? And according to GreatSchools.org, many high school requirements are "not rigorous enough to satisfy college admissions officials." However, if you happen to live in a state with no elective credit requirement (California, Wisconsin, Wyoming) and your high-schooler does not plan to attend college, why bother with the extra work?

The simple benefits of high school electives are that, since these are courses outside of the core curriculum, they give your high-schooler the opportunity to:

Try Something New

There's nothing to lose. Taking a semester of engineering helped my daughter to discover she had great problem-solving skills and resourcefulness.

Pursue an Existing Interest

Let's face it, chances are good that your high-schooler will put more effort into anything they are interested in than they will in something you assigned.

Explore Possible Career Opportunities

Take the opportunity to expose indecisive teens to different fields of study. Eventually, that semester in engineering allowed my daughter to move on and pursue art full-time.

Express Their Unique Personalities to College Recruiters

Yes, colleges are interested in grades and core subjects, but they are also looking to see who your child is. Electives in a high school transcript will allow colleges to see the continuous pursuit of a specific interest, as well as the ability to balance a well-rounded education.

How Should You Choose Elective Courses?

Because homeschool laws and graduation requirements vary by state, the best place to start is by finding out what your state requires.

Arizona, Delaware and Kentucky require a career focus or college-prep elective. Louisiana requires an elective in language arts, while Minnesota requires two units in resource management and New Mexico wants high-schoolers to complete one unit in communication skills (how great is that?).

A good starting place for your state's specific requirements is the National Center for Education Statistics website, but verify with specific state education department websites for the most current information.

After the required courses are met, get creative and have fun.

Elective courses don't need to have a high academic focus. If your high-schooler plans to attend medical school, an anatomy class could be good; an elective could also allow that student to relax by taking a dance class. Look for elective courses that will allow your high-schoolers to pursue a hobby or learn new skills, or that are related to their academic focus.

If college is part of their plan, be sure to also consider your desired school's individual requirements.

Not Your Typical Courses

Growing up in a relatively small town (by California standards) my high school course selection left much to be desired. I enrolled myself in French and journalism every semester of every year - not very exciting. Given the opportunity, I would have loved to take something like sailing, flight training or skydiving.

My favorite perk as a homeschooler is having the ability to choose. We are never limited by the course selection of a high school catalog!

As I was preparing to write this chapter, I came across some unusual electives. Here are some that are pretty out of the box in my opinion:

- Animal Husbandry
- Appliance Repair
- Battle Re-Enactments (in the South)
- Cooking (meal-planning, cost of food, nutrition, dietary guidelines)
- Cooking Outdoors (when camping)
- Equine Science
- Equestrian Training

- Life Skills (preparing for adult roles)
- Marathon Training
- Medieval History
- Mythology
- Pilates/Yoga
- Political Process (campaigning)
- Winter Camping

I'm really loving the ideas of meal-planning and preparing for adult roles. Just. Plain. Genius. When you think about it, the possibilities really are endless.

Issuing Credit for an Out-of-the-Box Elective

As I nervously created my first course, I searched the internet for assurance that what I was trying to do was both acceptable and accurate.

- How do I give credit?
- How many hours should we dedicate to this course?
- Should I create tests?
- Will it really count?

These are questions that, as homeschoolers, we've all asked ourselves at one point or another, especially when dealing with high school.

Thankfully, HSLDA.org had clear and simple answers to my frantic questions:

"For an elective course (such as physical education, art, music, or other course that lies outside of the core courses), log 120 hours for a one credit course or 60 hours for a one-half credit course... Some integrated curricula pull from many different resources such as real books, websites, articles, and primary source documents. For this type of curriculum, logging hours is a good method to determine the actual high school credit earned in each subject discipline."

I'll admit that since we were not used to it, logging hours was a bit stressful in the beginning. Now that we've established the importance of keeping clear and accurate records, logging hours has become second nature.

Get Creative and Have Fun

As a new homeschooler, my approach with my first two high-schoolers was pretty conservative. I purchased curriculum with detailed instructions, materials and hour requirements, and we followed it to a T.

When it came to kid number three, we took more risks and got creative, and though in the beginning, I felt somewhat queasy and nervous, the end result was fantastic!

Tatiana Adurias is a momma to five girls and one boy, married to her best friend, a homeschooler, a lover of books and a follower of Jesus. Find her at TheMusingsofMum.com

Career Exploration Ideas for Teens

Adrienne Bolton

"I have no idea!"

That's what my high school senior would tell you if you asked him what he wanted to do with his life.

Maybe that's not a good thing? Maybe it's a perfectly normal thing? I don't know, but I think that the majority of teens struggle with the decision of choosing a college and career path.

It's not as if he's completely without a plan. He's currently dual-enrolled in college courses and working on his general education requirements, but his ideas on a career path are still broad and need a plan of execution.

For some teens, especially those with a clear passion or interest, the question "What's your plan after high school?" isn't tough to answer, but for the teen who is still so undecided, it's a tongue-twister. Just ask my son!

Start with Self-Discovery

Help your teens learn more about themselves and what they want out of a career. Personality tests are a great way to explore interests and abilities. Look for free assessments online. Be sure to select a variety of styles, and have fun with the activity. You'll find that some tests are engaging and interesting, while others leave teenagers scratching their heads. Remember, these tests are not definitive, but they can be useful tools in sparking interests and conversation about the direction your teens would like go.

Things for each teen to consider:

- What are your skills and interests?
- What are your favorite subjects?
- Where do you plan to live?
- How much money do you need to make?
- What kind of work environment do you like best?
- What kind of schedule do you want?
- How many years of school will you need to start out in your career?
- What colleges, universities or trade schools offer programs in your field of choice?

More self-discovery activities for your teen:

"About Me" Project. Write a report about yourself. Use your life as a timeline. Birth, elementary years, middle years and now. Go a different direction and write about your passions or interests.

Create a Vision Board. Fill it with pictures and images of things that interest you. It could be anything. People, places, things. Use corkboard so you can pin small items to it. Includes pictures of places you'd love to visit or live.

Make a Career Collage. Look for images of people in the workplace. What work environments attract you? What type of area do you want to work/live in? Get creative! Include your favorite colors or dream office space. Do you want co-workers or solitary space?

"Phone a Friend." Conduct a reverse interview and ask friends and family to answer some questions about you. You could even send out an email letting loved ones know you're working on a project and need their help. What qualities and abilities do they see in you? Don't worry what others think about you! Just have fun hearing the responses.

Once you teens have had a chance to learn a little more about themselves, it's time to dig into some career research! Here are some career exploration ideas.

Interviews

Have your teen arrange some interviews with professionals currently working in the fields they're considering. Keep in mind, you don't have to know someone personally to land an interview. Look on corporate websites for contact information. Remember, an interview can be done by phone, email, FaceTime or Skype. You'd be surprised how many people are willing to answer a quick email or take a few minutes out of their day to encourage our youth.

Questions to ask an interviewee:

- What educational path did you take to accomplish your career goals?
- What are the pros/cons of the job?
- What's your daily work environment like?
- How much money does someone typically make in this career?
- Is there room for advancement?

- What is your schedule like?

Speakers

Like interviews, speakers are an excellent way to give teens a real-life perspective of someone's job. Look for events in your area with speakers of interest. Better yet, form a group and invite speakers to come to you! Maybe you're part of a co-op or youth group? Ask around and see if other parents/teens would be interested in forming a study group and hearing from professionals in your area.

Job Fairs and Career Expos

Job fairs an excellent way to give your teen a "one-stop shopping" experience. Search for job fairs in your area that welcome students. Have each teen prepare questions for exhibitors in advance. Be sure to map out the exhibit hall the day before, to save time hitting the booths that are most important to your teen.

Job Shadowing and Internships

Seek out professionals or companies that will allow your teen to spend a day or two on the job. Perhaps a local doctor's office, private attorney or real-estate office might be an option. Get a real-life look at what their day-to-day is like, and observe their interactions with clients or customers.

Volunteering

Is your teen working on those community-service hours for a scholarship? Instead of volunteering just anywhere, seek out companies and organizations of interest. You never know what future opportunities could come from a volunteer position.

Write a Research Report

A research report is a great place for your teen to really dig into a specific career of interest. Include statistics about job security in her chosen field, potential income and the history and future of the industry.

Create a PowerPoint

For the teens who can't stand the thought of writing one more paper, a PowerPoint presentation is the perfect alternative. Remember that study group I mentioned earlier? Have your teens compile their research in a presentation that can be shared with a group of peers or even family and friends.

Read Up!

Have your teen read books, magazines and blogs pertaining to their career interests. Select biographies about people who have succeeded on a path that interests them. Choose books that inspire, educate and help your teen discover new and exciting interests and possibilities.

Keep a Career Research Notebook

Be sure to have your teen keep track of all the research that's done throughout the career exploration journey! This isn't just for fun and games. In many states, courses in career and college planning are worthy of a high school or college credit. Be sure to keep good records of the research your teen completes.

What should be put in a career research notebook?

- Research notes
- Written reports
- Transcripts from interviews
- Brochures from job fairs or career expos
- Printed results from personality assessments
- A reading log
- Printouts of important email correspondence
- Grade reports or certificates of completion from online courses

Tips For Your Teen

DON'T stress. Think of career research as just that: research. You're not selecting the job you will have for all eternity in this very moment. You're just exploring ideas and gathering information. Who knows? Maybe you'll find your passion in the midst of the journey. Maybe you'll just have a more articulate answer for that dreaded question, "So, what's your plan after graduation?" Either way, don't stress about the final decision. Just have fun exploring ideas and get to know yourself a little better in the process.

DON'T be afraid to ask. So much of your research will involve interacting with others, asking questions and putting yourself out there. You may have to send emails, make phone calls (shudder!) or meet with individuals in person to accomplish your research goals. Just remember, it can't hurt to ask. Even if someone turns you down, at least you tried and you gained the skills it took to even ask in the first place.

DO be professional. If you attend a job fair or career expo, dress appropriately. Take the time to make sure emails are grammatically correct. Show up on time, be dependable and make a positive first impression.

DO be confident. You're awesome! You're already thinking about your future, gathering a plan, and putting yourself out there. Be confident in the abilities God has given you and the plan He promises. (Jeremiah 29:11) Every person has unique gifts. Give yourself time to discover yours!

Adrienne Bolton is a Florida homeschooling mom of two boys - one teen, one tween. She writes at her overly neglected blog, TheMommyMess.com, when she can. You can expect find her there "coming clean" about homeschooling, parenting and more!

How to Assign High School Credit to Life Learning Opportunities

Pat Fenner

High school is such a wonderful time for homeschooling!

The early years of teaching the "basics" – reading, writing, primary math facts – are over. The seasons of seemingly endless repetition, review and drills have come to an end. The kids have most of their facts and phonics down and are usually smooth readers; independent learning is a concept that is at the very least understood, even if it's not exactly embraced.

Your children's learning style is well-established by this time, and they may finally have found their stride in terms of future focus. Even if they don't yet have a career choice, at least your children *do* know where their interests lie!

With a more specific range of skills, talents and goals, this is the time you want to hone in on meeting them; yet, far too often, this is the time when parents are most worried about "accredited curricula." This is the time when the fear of college readiness rears its ugly head, often resulting in pulling away from experiential learning and moving toward standardized studies.

So we as parents/teachers succumb to the familiar. After all, it's easier to find pre-packaged curricula than to find programs that can bridge academics with life learning; it's easier to assign grades with a standard curriculum; it's easier to "check off the boxes" in order to file an application to that perfect college, right?

An Alternate Approach

Let's look at it another way. Let's consider high school as a preparation for life-in-action. Let's consider high school as an on-ramp to two distinct highways: one being further academic studies, and the other being a hands-on career and/or entrepreneurship. Then let's look at how we can apply non-standard approaches to *both* highways.

Mentoring and/or apprenticeships are learning formats that can most directly lead straight to a business or career transition after high school. This method of learning is a practical approach in this season of your child's life. For example, in the technology-driven society we live in, it's easy for our kids to pick up a computer-related skill and run with it as a career. And, these days, it might be a genuine reason to put off or even avoid college-type studies until later.

Even so, you might want to ensure that your child is at least *able* to attend college after high school. We'd always told our two older children that college attendance was not optional, and they should plan for it! That was 10 years ago. It's a bit different, however, with our three younger ones. These days, it's totally a possibility that one or more of them takes a gap year, for example, or enrolls into a trade or tech school, or starts a job that might very well develop into a full-time career, sans college.

That being said, there is still value in creating a transcript that will pass muster as part of an exceptional college application!

How to Summarize Life Learning into "Education-ese"

Contrary to popular opinion, there is nothing magical or mysterious to putting together a high school transcript. You just have to translate learning into "education-ese."

This is the language that teachers, principals and administrators use to understand and process every student's educational history. It's a combination of grades, credit hours and averages that yield what is termed a GPA (grade-point average). This is utilized, along with standardized test scores such as the SAT or ACT, to predict the success your child will have in college.

That's it, pure and simple.

It's easy enough to figure out how to assign credit to "regular" courses. Most of the time, when your student finishes a book or program of study, you give him a grade and a year's worth of credit. When he finishes a life-learning event, however, things get a tad more complicated.

It's for these cases that you need a bit more backup. Here's what to do:

Definitely plan ahead. Have a game plan for the activity/opportunity. Is this potential career training? A life skill? Something that could be applied to a standard subject? For example, a "junior zookeeper" position that included animal studies could be applied to a biology/life sciences credit. Keep accurate records of activities, time spent and contact info of supervisors.

Make sure the program is well-rounded. Ensure your teens read relevant books (and keep track of them, of course), and complete at least a research paper or two. Writing is a skill that is uber-useful in both career *and* college. Definitely arrange some sort of final project where they can present summaries of their experiences and learning, as well.

Create a grading rubric and use it as a class "contract." A rubric is a description of what standards need to be met to achieve each grade. If you present it at the beginning of the experience, your children will know what your expectations are in terms of their efforts and will be able to adjust accordingly.

Assign credit as follows: Generally speaking, we award half a credit after 75 hours of study, and a full credit after 150 hours. Determine the amount of time spent, the level of expectations met on the rubric, and voila! You have a grade and credit amount to add to your transcript and include in figuring a GPA.

If college is in any way a short-term possibility, **consult with an admissions counselor at one or two colleges that your child might be considering** to see what kind of admissions requirements they have. Don't be afraid to call the counselor; a discussion over the phone in no way commits you to anything!

See? That wasn't so hard, was it? Here's the best thing about it all: With these tools, you can use myriad electives, jobs and extracurricular experiences to craft a robust and relevant high school program of study for your child. For further direction on how to put all this information together for college applications or post-high-school studies, read the chapter "How to Summarize High School Learning on a Transcript."

No longer will you hear your children pose the "Am I *really* gonna use this in life?" question, *and* you'll be able to include valuable and worthwhile non-traditional learning experiences into your child's educational and academic history.

Pat Fenner has been homeschooling her brood of five for more than 20 years. With a passion for encouraging moms as parents and home educators, she shares experience -inspired wisdom with her friend Candy at PatAndCandy.com. Sign up at their site for immediate access to free printables to help you find joy and creativity as a mom and in your homeschool.

How to Summarize High-School Learning on a Transcript: Creatively Combining Academic Studies *and* Life Experiences

Pat Fenner

I'd be a millionaire if I had a dime for everyone who contacted me with fear in their eyes and panic in their voices because... *it was time to do a high school transcript!*

OK, to be fair, I once felt the same way. As a matter of fact, when we first started homeschooling, I had no idea I'd ever be *considering* teaching high school.

Nevertheless, as I write this, I am in my fourth round of working through high school with our young 'uns. Despite the many mistakes I've made along the way, the two eldest seemed to have survived pretty well, and our two current teens are holding their own, too. So I offer the following insights not only based on my own experiences, but also on the experiences of dozens of friends and colleagues who have walked the same road. I have full confidence that your children are resilient, and just the fact that you're reading this chapter means that you have the desire and drive to craft a high school experience in which they will not only blossom, but also grow and thrive!

Some Principles to Consider

Get organized. I'm saying this to you with as much kindness and empathy *and firmness* as I can convey! This is NOT the time to repeat the mantra you might have been saying over and over again throughout your life: "Oh gee, I'm so unorganized!" or "I'm just not the organized type." I'm not saying that you need to become a Type A personality, or that you must develop organizational skills in <u>every</u> area of your life. But if you're committing to homeschooling through high school, you *have* to develop some type of filing and/or record-keeping system that will keep your student's information together during this time!

Create your transcript with the reader in mind. College admissions departments can get hundreds of applications over the course of their enrollment periods, and *somebody* has to go through them. Unless the admissions department asks for extra information or a portfolio of work, your final transcript should be two pages long: one page of courses and grades in transcript form and, if necessary, a second page listing awards, activities and achievements. That's it!

Don't over-inflate your student's experiences. Think about it: When an admissions counselor sees an application that includes a 4.0 (or higher!) GPA, multiple awards and pages of flowery descriptions of positions held and extracurricular achievements, *written up by Mom*, what is she going to think? Does the phrase "If it's too good to be true..." perhaps apply here? These may be hard words to read, but they're the truth and it's better to hear it from a friend. Keep it simple, sister - overselling your student might backfire in the end.

Be able to document any claims you make. Don't include it in your standard transcript, but *do* have a document available that lists the books used in your coursework, especially if the course was parent-created and not a standard published product. Also include hours worked or served if you're including a work-study program or volunteer work, or if you need to substantiate self-study hours for parent-awarded credit. You can use our self-study tracking sheet, found in PatAndCandy.com's free Homeschool High School Planning Package, or a piece of notebook paper. The important thing is that you use whatever works for you.

Don't overthink it. Seriously, the best way to prepare to do a transcript is to start out with one! As your student approaches high school, use our High School Planning Chart that doubles as a resource for your final product. After freshman year, when you as a teacher/counselor/administrator have gained some experience and confidence, transfer the information to your actual transcript, or use our template. Work from there for the remaining years, making adjustments and notations as needed.

Documenting Traditional Subjects

Traditional subjects are probably the easiest thing to document, as each one most likely has its own textbook or scope and sequence of materials to complete and pass in order for your child to receive credit.

Required subjects such as math, English, science and history most often are awarded a full credit; fine arts, speech, government/civics, or less-traditional classes and electives are usually awarded a half-credit.

If you're feeling a little unprepared or unable to meet the challenge of teaching some of those subjects, or you're not sure how and what to outsource, please read the chapter "Determining How and When to Outsource Homeschooling Subjects."

Documenting Life Experiences

Life experiences can and should be incorporated into your student's high school education. Of course, I'm talking <u>serious</u> life-preparation activities, and this is the best time to get creative and forward-thinking in this area.

Our eldest child provided me with tons of experience from the get-go. Most definitely not a "book learner," he developed a serious fascination with cars as he approached the time to get his license. Always having been a kinesthetic learner, he became intrigued with the functioning of an automobile. However, my husband and I didn't really see him pursuing a career as a mechanic, so while we remained firm that he would be college-bound, it was apparent that, at least during his high school years, we'd have to come up with a more creative way to further his education. This became a wonderful blueprint for a high school application of unit studies!

He became a voracious reader about anything auto-related, and I asked him to maintain a reading list. This began with magazine articles, but grew into all sorts of books – autobiographies, car-related inventions, histories of his favorite makes/models and more science-focused books on the actual workings of engines and systems. All these covered relevant studies in science and history. Periodic reports developed his writing skills. At times we'd go down to the shop where he would show us, with the aid of "props" and other appropriate visuals, what he'd been learning; other times he'd share at the family dinner table. Both situations were opportunities to develop presentation skills. Working on a project with dad helped him learn and then hone newly developed mechanical skills, too. He kept records of time spent on all his shop and study time, and at the end of the year, he was able to receive a full credit, two years in a row, for a life-skill course we called Auto Mechanics I and II.

Documenting Honors, Awards and Extracurricular Activities

Depending on how many and what kind, you could divide this list into categories, or simply format them in a bulleted list. The easiest and probably most clear way would be to present them as you would a resume: most recent first, and including dates of involvement. Include a *short* description, but only if necessary. It also bears repeating here that you do not want to oversell your child's successes. Yes, put the best foot forward, but don't contribute to the idea that homeschool moms can't or don't accurately portray their children's achievements.

Some Final Thoughts

While it does take preparation, planning and follow-through to craft a practical and useful high school experience for your teens, as you can see, it's not rocket science (although you *could* have them study that and receive a full science credit). With the information and tools presented here, it's entirely feasible that your high-schoolers will receive a fulfilling and rigorous four years of high school at home, which will more than adequately prepare them for a wonderful future!

Pat Fenner has been homeschooling her brood of five for more than 20 years. With a passion for encouraging moms as parents and home educators, she shares experience-inspired wisdom with her friend Candy at PatAndCandy.com.

Using Dual Enrollment for College Credit

Shannen Espelien

Dual enrollment goes by many names depending on where you live, but the idea is the same: Your students can earn high school and college credit with one class. While dual enrollment has been around for decades, with the skyrocketing cost of college, it's become an increasingly popular option for students.

Dual Enrollment vs. Credit-by-Exam

There are two main ways to earn college credit at a great discount, and in untraditional ways: dual enrollment and credit-by-exam.

Dual enrollment is limited to high-school students (as determined by state), often only juniors and seniors, who are awarded college credit at the successful completion of a class. These students will be awarded a grade that will affect their GPA and be reflected on their official transcript. In some cases, there is no out-of-pocket cost for the family; in others, the cost is greatly reduced.

Credit-by-exam is a term that describes a handful of tests: AP, CLEP, DSST and, less commonly, TECEP. You can find classes to teach you the material on these exams, and some may be used to earn high-school credit (especially AP classes).

The big difference from dual enrollment is that with credit-by-exam, you only earn college credit if you pass the test at the end. Since the college credit is awarded because of one test, you do not earn a grade, and it does not count toward your GPA. Additionally, you pay somewhere in the ballpark of $60 to $100 per test, and classes can be an additional cost, depending on where they are being taught.

Dual enrollment is easier to fit into a busy lifestyle and a typical high-school schedule. CLEP and DSST exams, though, do not have any age limitation, so you can do them both before and after you would have the opportunity for dual enrollment.

Highly motivated students can get a bachelor's degree for a tiny fraction of the total cost by taking advantage of both dual enrollment and credit-by-exam. No matter what level you want to take it to, both are fantastic opportunities to be wise with your money and time while earning a college degree.

How is Dual Enrollment "Free?"

Dual enrollment is often paid for with the tax dollars that would otherwise pay for your student to take classes at their local public high school. Most dual-enrollment programs have limitations on what classes are included within the program, such as only allowing 100- and 200-level classes, but most will include all necessary costs for approved classes, such as books, lab time and the like.

At our local community college, each credit costs roughly $180. At 15 credits a semester, that equals $2,700 a semester, or $5,400 a year. It's quite the savings for you, and surprisingly it's a very comparable price to how much is spent to educate your child in a public high school. If your student is willing to give it a shot, there are very few reasons not to give it a try!

Preparing for Dual Enrollment

My advice is only on how to prepare for dual enrollment generally. Ensure that you are familiar with the laws of your home state so that you are always in compliance. In order to make sure you're ready to apply for dual enrollment, the first and foremost priority is keeping good records.

After scouring the Internet for years (seriously) for the best way to keep track of assignments and grades, I fell in love with Homeschool Planet. It's worth far more than they charge, and they do offer a free trial to test it out. Plus, you can cancel and then open the account back up without losing any information.

Regardless of what tool you use, you want to make sure you are putting together a transcript and, just as a precautionary measure, keep your book lists and a description of what you covered, just in case there are added questions.

Second, encourage your child to get good grades, as many schools require a minimum GPA to apply as a dual-enrollment student. Working hard to achieve good grades is also an important aspect to being emotionally and mentally ready for the rigor of college.

As a side note, I want to encourage parents to start keeping grades at some point in middle school, at the latest by eighth grade. Our family learned the hard way as we transitioned from a pass/fail system to formal grades in my daughter's ninth-grade year that there's a bit of a learning curve for both parent and child.

Again, I highly recommend Homeschool Planet for keeping track of assignments and grades. With starting a year earlier than necessary, the bumps in the road of deadlines and formal grades should be smoothed out before it is being recorded in their high school transcript.

Third, I find it extremely valuable to sign your children up for a class outside your home so they can get exposure with communicating their needs or questions to a stranger, and being responsible for their work to someone else. Some great resources for classes are:

- classes at the local public school (call the district to see if this is something they can accommodate)
- local homeschool co-ops
- local nature centers or museums that offer classes for older students, including homework and assignments
- online classes, from places like: Currclick, Institute for Excellence in Writing, BraveWriter, Well Trained Mind Academy, and Pennsylvania Homeschoolers (AP classes available for all homeschoolers)

How Do I Know They Are Ready?

As a homeschooler, you see your kid working on their schoolwork day in and day out, so you would think that's a good indicator on how they'll do at college, but I want to say that it might not always be the case. How your children work with you might be very different than how they work with an outside teacher. I've seen many families that really struggle with their child following through with deadlines on their assignments to Mom, but who are ultra-organized and on top of their assignments to their online teacher.

As long as they are academically ready, meaning they would generally test no more than one or two grades behind the academic year they are applying for, then give it a shot! Worst-case scenario is they come back home after a semester having learned some lessons about college, and likely they will have passed at least one or two of their classes, earning free college credits.

How Do I Sign Up?

Dual enrollment is conducted in vastly different ways depending on where you live. Some states have you take courses at the college that will be awarding credit, while other states offer classes within the high school, then will award college credit when successfully completed.

In our state, the requirements for students applying for the dual-enrollment program differ from college to college. Some require a 3.5 GPA, while others require a 3.0. Each place has their own deadline and possibly their own intake exam.

Personally, we've found schools to be very welcoming of homeschool students. Some colleges have asked for homeschoolers to complete an intake exam since they do not have a class ranking, while traditionally schooled students could use just their transcript.

Basically, you just have to call and find out. With homeschooling becoming much more popular recently, colleges are pretty familiar with their requirements and how they may differ for homeschool students.

Supporting Your Dual-Enrollment Student

Finding your student a great planner is key to set the stage for college success! We really like the Well

Planned Day College Planner because it has checkboxes for the assignments, a spot for the due date, and, one of my favorite things, a worksheet to plan out your days by adding in how many hours you spend on various activities like work, homework, class hours, sleep, etc. I know my daughter sometimes plans her days as if she has 36 hours to get everything done!

The logistics of college might also be an area where your children need a little guidance.

As an outsider, you might be able to observe their peak times (especially as a homeschooling mom, you probably know this already!) and offer advice on best times to do homework. If your children are open to it, you can still offer to look over their papers before they are turned in to give any tips you might have.

I found my favorite role as a homeschooling mom with children doing school elsewhere is to help them find resources to make their first steps easier. Looking around for the perfect planner or finding an app to help them with making a bibliography are areas where I can lend a helping hand without being too overbearing.

While this is a time where your children are usually ready to run out on their own, feeling like the adult they are growing to be, it's a great balance of them still being at home so they can have that support from their parents while they are starting on this new journey. I hope you find it to be an exciting journey together!

Shannen homeschools her teen daughter, focusing on earning college credit while in high school, and is getting ready to start the homeschool cycle again with two little ones. You can find her blogging about how they homeschool high school and everything that goes along with it at MiddleWayMom.com.

The Nervous Mom's Guide to College

Betsy Sproger

Do you have teens who are college-bound? Do they want to go to a four-year college after graduating from homeschool?

When we were in the middle-school years, my husband and I, along with our daughter, began thinking about college. Our daughter was interested, and we knew that scholarships were more available for college freshman than for community college students who transferred in as juniors. But I was more than a little nervous.

How would I, as a homeschooling mom, help her get there?

The idea of knocking on the college door with a homeschool transcript in hand was more than a little daunting for me. I knew the homeschool transcript was being widely accepted by colleges all over the U.S. But the colleges seemed so big, and I, in contrast, felt so small.

Do you ever feel that way?

I wanted more information, so I began to research college admission for homeschoolers. I found out that there were many homeschool-friendly colleges out there that wanted the type of kids that homeschooling produces - motivated, independent learners. And ours was one. So throughout her high school years, we helped her to prepare and apply to college.

It worked out well. My teen was accepted to all of the colleges that she applied to, with scholarship offers. She is now studying at her top-choice university and is a happy camper, thriving there. As a mom, that was so good to see. And I found out that the whole process of applying to college was really not that hard!

We were able to keep our nurturing homeschool style while going through the college application process at the same time by following six key steps.

Research

Our first step was to research the college websites. We needed to know what our daughter's college entrance requirements would be at her preferred colleges.

Each college will show its entrance requirements with just a click of the button. This information was easy for us to find, just by looking at college websites for the freshman admission requirements.

We found that they were similar from college to college, but not consistently the same. For example, some colleges asked for specific courses for social studies, and others gave a wide range of choices. Some asked for four English courses, while others only asked for three.

I looked up the most likely colleges that my daughter would attend. Some of the colleges had extra requirements for their homeschooling applicants, to validate the homeschool transcript. But some didn't. Through my research, I came up with a list of what high school courses would be required overall.

Starting this research early was a help, but it is still possible to do this any time in high school, by just recalling info from your child's previous studies and going from there. And you can always add in an extra quarter or two to make up for any requirements that you might have missed.

Once we had this important information, we made note of it, and kept it handy when planning our high school years. In fact, we used it to make an overall high school plan. That was our second step in our process of aiming towards college.

Making an Overall High School Plan

As homeschoolers, we are already experts in planning. We have searched for and chosen curriculum for our kids each year.

Planning for high school with college in mind is really no different, except for the entrance requirements. Looking at the whole list of requirements can be overwhelming at first. What I did to combat this was to lay out a tentative overall plan for high school.

We just sketched out a plan for all four years, with our best guesses of what we wanted to do. Our overall plan was flexible, and was revised and reworked every year as life happened. With this plan, we were less likely to forget a requirement or two. And we kept it handy each year when it was curriculum-purchasing time. Once we had this plan, we used it each time we chose high school curriculum, and that became our third step in this process.

Choosing Curriculum with College in Mind

We explored our favorite sites and catalogs as usual, choosing the textbooks, living books, and/or online courses that would a good fit for my teen. We worked to meet our teen's entrance requirements, but did not forget to focus on her special interests as well. Getting the college entrance requirements done still left lots of time to do electives.

All of our electives were teen-led. My daughter's interests focused on filmmaking and political science. We made our own courses in these subjects and also did a dual-credit course in state government. If she majored in either of these areas in college, the college entrance requirements (language arts, social studies, math, foreign language and science) would be the same.

We kept in mind any specifics that her colleges were requiring while we planned. For example, does the college ask for labs to be done with each science course? Do they require two science courses, or three? What do they ask for in math?

Keeping track of what credits were earned was key to making our homeschool transcripts. That was our fourth step.

Making Your Teen's Transcript

As you know, homeschool transcripts are being accepted widely by colleges all around the US. Colleges are used to seeing them, and sometimes even are recruiting homeschoolers.

The homeschool transcript serves as a clearinghouse, and should include all the courses taken, either in your homeschool or completed outside.

Be sure to include your grading scale and your student's GPA on your transcript. If you have any special courses, such as Advanced Placement or courses from a community college, just note them with an *, and mention that at the bottom of your transcript.

Course descriptions are separate from the transcript, and are easy to do with your record-keeping that you have done each year. And the good news is, homeschool transcripts are requiring less validation from homeschoolers these days. That is the trend. Some colleges don't even ask for course descriptions.

Besides the homeschool transcript, another important part of applying to college is the college entrance essay. That was our fifth step in going from high school to college.

Writing a Winning College Essay

Do the words "college admissions essay" make you cringe? I was feeling more than a little nervous about this task, and my teen was, too. So we began with brainstorming. As it turned out, the essay was not nearly as hard as I thought it would be, and my daughter was able to write one essay to use for multiple colleges applications. That's because all of her colleges happened to use the Common Application.

The college essay is actually a personal essay based on the essay prompt that your student chooses. By Googling the Common Application, we found the current essay prompts for my daughter. Some colleges use their own application, and that is where you will find their essay prompts as well.

Nancy Burgoyne, from Fat Envelope Essays, says:

"Choose a topic that allows your student to shine. Think of the essay as kind of an interview with college admissions. Pick whichever prompt will help the college to get to know your teen better. "

Editing, essay structure, spelling and grammar are all very important as well. The colleges will be looking for these factors as well as the substance of the essay.

Did you know that your teens' activities and electives can also help them get into college? Sharing our teen's activities and electives with the colleges was our sixth step in this process.

Sharing High School Activities and Electives

Having the time to delve deeply into my teen's interests was one of the reasons that we homeschooled all the way. Isn't that one of the reasons that we all chose to homeschool, anyway? So I encouraged my daughter to explore her interests and to try out different activities.

Colleges are looking for self-motivated students with special interests and a desire to develop their talents. They want to see the activities and electives that your student has completed. Whether it is in music, art, drama, web design, etc., you will want to share these with the colleges. This can be done on the application or in the college entrance essay, if it coincides with the chosen essay prompt.

Many colleges are looking for leadership skills in their applicants as well. Aiding at Girl Scout camp, volunteering to lead a class at co-op, or participating in TeenPack are all ways to develop leadership in your teens.

We have now covered all six key steps for applying to college. If you are looking for more detailed information on the subject, including how to assign high school credit and compute the GPA, with tips for transcripts, the college entrance essay and more, I invite you to check out my new e-book, "Homeschooling High School," available through Amazon and CreateSpace, which includes printables and serves as a guide to college for homeschoolers.

- Printables included in the book are:

- College Entrance Requirements Form
- Overall High School Plan
- Curriculum Planning Sheet
- High School Credit Record Form
- Sample Transcript Form
- Blank Transcript Form
- Activities and Awards Form
- Homemade Course Form
- Writing the College Essay Form
- Course Descriptions Record-Keeping Form
- Reference Letter Request Form
- PE Record Form

 *Betsy is a veteran homeschooler who writes about high school, college, and the early years on her blog at betsyhomeschoolconsulting.blogspot.com. Her daughter graduated from homeschool and is now a junior in college, studying at a tier-two university. Betsy offers homeschool help at BJ's Consulting and loves doing photography when she is not writing words on paper.*

Homeschooling to College

Shannen Espelien

College: The place that has become almost the only socially acceptable way to enter adulthood. Even if we don't believe everyone *needs* to go to college, as homeschoolers we want to make sure we aren't closing doors for our kids with their education at home.

It would be a hard pill to swallow if our children wanted to go to college but couldn't because of their homeschooling experience. (By the way, that's highly unlikely to happen. Colleges want students. There are always options.)

So how hard is it to prepare a child for college? If you ask me, there are far harder things to do in life, but it does takes a little forethought and planning.

Get an Early Start on Planning

If you want to ease into college work, it can be a good idea to start gathering information and taking steps as early as middle school. A few questions to ask yourself as you are exploring the idea of college:

- What are my child's interests?

- Do those interests point to a particular field of study that would require a college degree for job opportunities?

- Do my state and local area have opportunities for dual enrollment (taking college classes during high school years)? If so, what are the requirements (GPA, testing, etc.)?

- What is my child's interest and motivation level in credit-by-exam (taking a college-level exam to earn college credit)?

- Does this child envision being a future college student?

These questions will help you gauge how to approach college with your child.

Not everyone has to go to college, but many would argue that it affords you more security in your adult life through the ups and downs of the economy and job market. At the very least, as parents we should encourage the option for college and provide opportunities to get there.

Planning for the High School Years

If you don't plan anything else in middle school, at least do one thing to get started toward college readiness: Keep track of grades by eighth grade.

Going from a pass/fail system, as some homeschoolers use, to a fully graded system is a big learning curve for both parent and child. Give yourself a year of working out the bumps before you have to keep track of grades for a high school transcript. We'll touch on what things to keep track of in a bit.

Also of great importance is getting familiar with your state laws and any graduation requirements you might need to comply with. In our state, we don't have to follow high school graduation requirements like the public schools do, so I checked what both the public schools and colleges require to get a feel for what classes would be necessary to have a college-ready transcript.

All high school graduation requirements include room for electives. Use some of those electives to get your students ready for the career path they are passionate about!

Don't know what career path they want? Neither did my daughter, so we barely used any electives during her freshman and sophomore years at home, and left them for choosing both career-centered classes when she entered dual enrollment. It also afforded her some easy credits in the first years of her college journey. For instance, in her senior year, she was taking Law and Contracts as one of her electives, and yoga as another.

If you haven't started planning early on, don't worry! There are so many paths to success. Getting started with the planning process in middle school only helps stretch out the time to consider options and get started. It is not essential to getting college-ready.

Record-Keeping

Again, your requirements for record-keeping vary by state. The Home School Legal Defense Association is a great place to learn about your state requirements. Our state is pretty relaxed in this area, but I decided for high school I wanted to keep more thorough records so we could address any questions if and when they came up when applying to colleges.

Surprisingly, the transcript can be very easy to compile. We use Homeschool Planet, a gradebook, calendar, lesson planner and transcript generator, and while there are only a few competitors to match all the features they offer, it is just one of many tools to make your own transcript, including just creating a transcript yourself in Microsoft Word.

Worried about colleges taking a transcript made by Mom? The transcript is just one piece of the puzzle. As long as it jives with the other information they have (not having low-end test scores, but an A in Honors Algebra, for instance), it shouldn't be a problem.

To be on the safe side, we chose to also keep a list of resources we used for each class as well as any notes useful to further describe the class. These are not included in the transcript; they are more just notes for me to use rather than counting on my memory to serve me if the time comes where I would need those details.

Additionally, it's a good idea to keep excellent work in a portfolio to add to a college application and keep a log of volunteer work. Never count on your memory to keep track of everything! Even better, put your children in charge of keeping these documents; then, check in on them from time to time to make sure they are keeping up on it.

Keeping track of routine work plus extracurriculars doesn't need to be done in a fancy program. If you're not the most organized, keep this information in Google Drive or Dropbox so it can't be lost. If needed, you could also set up a recurring reminder on your calendar each month reminding you to update your files, with a link to where you are keeping it.

Academic Readiness

Before we start homeschooling high school, it's the academics that rack our brains. How are we going to teach math? How will we grade book reports properly? How will we do labs for science?

First, homeschooling high school seems much harder than it is. When you realize how many resources are available, you quickly realize that you don't have to teach everything! When you start searching for "homeschool high school science" or "homeschool high school literature" you'll find more websites than you know what to do with!

Sit down with a cup of coffee and get comfortable as you peruse your way from one site to the next, exploring online classes, fully packaged curriculum with teacher guides, books that the public schools use and distance-learning programs.

If you are part of some in-person homeschool groups, these can also be invaluable in helping you find curriculum as you page through books they already have on their bookshelves.

In order to lay the first foundation blocks for college-readiness, I highly suggest using at least one teacher-led class, either online or within a traditional classroom setting. Some states allow homeschool students to take classes at the public school, an option that may be worth exploring.

Another possibility for academic readiness is credit-by-exam, the option to take a test (AP, DSST, CLEP or TECEP) and earn college credit with a passing score. Giving one of these tests a try while your children are in high school is a great way for them to see what a college-level exam will feel like, and the rigor needed to pass.

Standardized Testing

Most schools list a certain SAT or ACT score as a requirement for admission. You can easily sign up online to have your student take the SAT or ACT at a location near you, just like a traditionally schooled student.

You'll be able to send all their test scores to a college of your choosing or choose have them submitted at a later date.

SAT and ACT prep options are widely available online, through tutoring centers, books and any other way you can imagine learning. Some schools may also have their prep classes available to homeschool students as well. Call around and find an option that will work best with your schedule and the way your child learns.

What if your child normally struggles with big exams, or you personally don't see the value in them? There are a growing number of "test optional" or "test flexible" colleges around the country! Some will use test scores just as a tool, while others will allow for other forms of academic proof (and here's where your file of projects, volunteer work and class descriptions comes in handy!) to fill out your application.

Even if your preferred institution isn't on that list, you can always call and see what an advisor has to say about test scores below their cutoff, or if they allow for other forms of academic proof.

Don't Forget Your Tribe

Academics and record-keeping are important, but the secret to success in many homeschool parents' lives is having a tribe they can go to when in need.

Our tribe has come from our involvement in various groups throughout the years. Some groups have been more informal, like play groups, and others have been more formal classes offered through a homeschool co-op. Both types of groups enriched our homeschool experience at the time and filled a need, while allowing both my kids and myself to meet other like-minded homeschoolers.

When I have had curriculum questions, sometimes I can find another family with the books at home I can thumb through. We've even set up a small class with three families to address our need for a high school biology course.

With all the preconceptions people have about homeschooling, especially in the upper grades, it's important to have people who know what it's like and can offer relevant advice. Plus, it can be lonely without a tribe! If you don't live close to other homeschooling families or have not found a group that you jive with, there are hundreds of online groups that can be your sounding board on a bad day, or your cheer team on a good one.

There are many paths to adult success, and college is one used by many. Most homeschool moms who have been through the high school years can tell you that it's a lot harder in theory than in practice. Getting your class list laid out and selecting resources is the most time-consuming piece. Find college-ready resources like credit-by-exam or classes with another teacher as it fits for your family.

And finally, remember that even if your children aren't ready for college straight out of high school, it is not necessarily a direct reflection on you as a homeschooling mom. Maybe they want to have some school-free time for a bit, or maybe they have other aspirations. Relax!

Shannen homeschools her teen daughter, focusing on earning college credit while in high school, and is getting ready to start the homeschool cycle again with two little ones. You can find her blogging about how they homeschool high school and everything that goes along with it at MiddleWayMom.com.

General
Homeschool
Helps

Homeschooling: The Good, the Bad and the Unnecessary

Adelien Tandian

Many people are still cynical about the home education system, or homeschooling. Apparently, although there are some burnt-out homeschoolers, homeschooling has grown significantly over time.

I am not sure about the exact statistics, but in Indonesia, where I live, a ministry regulation regarding homeschooling has been published. Although the law itself is still not clear, my conclusion is that it exists at all because of the increased numbers of homeschoolers in existence.

We started our homeschooling five years ago without any help from people around us. We just thought about the happiness homeschooling would bring at first. As time went on, we experienced the bad things about homeschooling that many homeschoolers, especially new ones, should know about.

Here are the loves and hates of homeschooling that I have experienced.

The Good of Homeschooling

The Freedom of Learning Anything, Anywhere, at Any Time

Once we decided to homeschool our children, we enjoyed the feeling of freedom in learning. It is hard to answer questions about how long we learn each day. We learn any time that we want to and can.

There is a school time, but it is hard to keep the learning time limited to "school hours." The flexibility to learn and school might make people think we are not disciplined. We might learn until 10 p.m., when we have a bright sky to observe with a telescope.

We have a school room, but it is hard for us to answer questions about where we learn. We might spend our time in the garden when the topic is about plants. We do our science experiments in the kitchen most of the time.

We use textbooks for some lessons, but we will tweak the lessons when we want to know other things outside the curriculum.

Customization

Another fact that make us love homeschooling is the ability to customize the lessons for each child. For example, both of my elder sons have used different math resources. I help them in different ways, since they have different ways of learning math.

At first, we used the same curriculum for both of my children, but it didn't work well. I can't imagine how my friends who had difficulty in learning did with following the school's curriculum when I was at school. No one gets to go at their own pace.

Deal with Real Things

Homeschooling children have a chance to experience real things in learning. Children socialize in a real society. They face people with different backgrounds, ages and characteristics.

Children have more chances to apply knowledge in real-life situations. For example, learning about plants can be applied by planting and taking care of plants naturally, without any time and space limitations like might happen at school. Children learn naturally, not in an artificial or made-up condition.

Get To Know Each Other Better

I became aware that I hadn't known my children as well as I thought when we started homeschooling. I had a guilty feeling at that time. I felt that I had neglected them a lot. Homeschooling has helped me know my children so much better. I find out new things about each of them every single day we spend together.

Thus, I feel very grateful that we have a chance to homeschool. I know that this period of homeschooling will not be as long as I imagine. All too soon, this phase will have passed and we will be remembering it. You might think that I am too self-centered for being afraid of missing the time with my children. However, later, my children will also remember our family getting to know each other in homeschooling. Family relationships should be more everlasting than friendships.

More Time To Explore Interests

I wonder what children in public school are able to do in a day, other than the school's assignments. Before our children were homeschooled, they spent the whole day for school things. They woke up at 5:30 a.m. Their school went from 7 a.m. to 1 p.m. at that time. They had tests and homework almost every day, so they still had to learn and do the same things they had done at school when they were home after taking a nap in the afternoon. Other schooled children might have extracurricular activities, often also related to academic things.

We feel that the routine is tiring, and children have too much to do related to purely academic matters. There isn't any chance for them to take part in activities related to their interests and talents while they are still young.

The Bad of Homeschooling

Divided Attention for Moms

Homeschooling my children, I have to be able to multitask. I know that this is not a good idea, as I would lose my focus a lot of times. I also cannot do things my best when working in that way. However, the more frequently I multitask, the more I am getting used to it, and I can do it much better. It is kind of a habit right now. Every day, I always think of writing a blog post for 30 minutes without disturbances, but it rarely happens.

The Uncertainty of Law

This is the hardest part of homeschooling so far. The Indonesian regulation for homeschooling is still not settled yet. One officer in the education department will have different interpretations about the idea, the law and the regulation of homeschooling from other officers. For us, the problems will be dealing with exams and other requirements, mostly. Therefore, we need to be proactive in our approach to the government.

Other countries should have better homeschooling laws. In the USA, I found that each state has different laws or rules for homeschooling children. HSLDA is a great place to find out more clear regulations about homeschooling, especially in the USA. Once you clearly understand the laws that apply to you, it won't be a problem anymore.

Negative Opinions and Attitudes from People

There are a lot of negative opinions and concerns that I'm honestly just bored of hearing. Every time people find out that we homeschool our children, there are a lot of the same questions that I'm sometimes tired of answering. I consider it lucky when the questions don't lead into a debate, which I try hard to avoid. People have a right to choose how to learn and how to educate their children, and as long as parents are still meeting their responsibilities to their children, it is fine.

More Responsibility for Parents

During the four years we've been homeschooling, my husband and I have come to feel a huge responsibility toward our children's education. We feel we should not make any mistakes in our decisions and actions. The administration work is hard for me, honestly. Then we need to register and prepare our children for the required exams. Whether I agree or disagree, those exams are something unavoidable for homeschoolers in my country.

Parents whose children go to public school can have the school do this work. However, the academic things are not the main goals and purposes of our homeschooling. Character education is much more important than all of those things. Even when the work is hard, we are not alone. As the Family Toolbox says, God will be with us in educating the children. Children are not ours only. God has created them among us for a purpose.

Impatience

Every homeschoolers will know about this. Impatience is a big temptation, especially as we begin to adjust to homeschooling. I have never claimed that I am a patient and capable homeschooling mom, but my children have taught me a lot about being patient. Although I still have to work hard at this, I think I have improved a bit at being patient.

The Unnecessary of Homeschooling

Homeschooling doesn't always start smoothly. I have some homeschooling regrets that I would change if I could turn back my homeschooling time.

Homeschooling has changed my life completely. I was very busy with my multi-level marketing business while my children attended private school. I enjoyed going to the gym regularly in the mornings when they went to school. But now, I have to stay and work completely at home. I cannot grow my network as fast as I was. I cannot go to the gym as I was before. I am still lucky that I can work out at home.

There were other sacrifices I made to homeschool, too. At first it seemed everything was better when I sent the kids to school, but as time went on, I started to get used to our new life, and learned a lot of lessons that caused me to reflect. I wish no one had to make some of the mistakes I made.

Here are my 10 biggest unnecessary mistakes, some of which I still deal with.

Not Distinguishing Homeschooling from School at Home

Our official "first day of homeschooling" was so horrible. I still remember that we sat nicely at a table in the middle of the living room with my mom spying on us. It was really not comfortable. I worried so much what others would think about us. We were very stressed, I can say.

Although I was the teacher, I should not have thought homeschooling was like doing school at home. I should not have even compared them at all, the way my mom does. At school, we sat nicely in our chairs with textbooks on the desk, listening to the teacher. Everyone did the same lesson at once. In our homeschool, I have a couple of different-level students who need similar, but not the same, attention. I made the mistake of putting them together and trying to do the same thing with both. I should have seen to their specific needs personally and in a more comfortable way.

Not Joining Virtual and Real-Life Homeschooling Communities

At first, I didn't join any homeschooling communities via social media. I was actually very poor at social media use. This was a terrible mistakes of me, and I'm very sure nobody reading this would make the same one. I could use the internet when I started homeschooling, but I could not use social media, and I even thought that people who did so were fools.

I am very sorry about that now. It is social media that can connect me to other homeschooling parents around the world. They are my buddies, from whom I have been learning a lot. We have shared our sorrows and encouragements together. Getting together with both virtual and real-life homeschooling buddies brings a positive atmosphere to our homeschooling and makes me feel so much less lonely.

Not Having a Vision and Mission for Homeschooling

When people ask me why I homeschool, or what kind of abnormalities my children have that led to me homeschooling them, I used to be very annoyed. I would not be so annoyed if I had a simple answer prepared, right? I even ask myself the same questions sometimes, wondering if things are worse because of homeschooling.

That makes me aware that I have forgot all the motivation, vision and mission of our homeschooling that I had when we first started. Having a written vision and mission for your homeschool is important, and helps when you reach a point of uncertainty. Not writing down your mission and vision can make it too easy to forget our motives and then we too easily give up.

Purchasing Too Much Curriculum

I think this happens to many new homeschooling moms when we're either too excited or too worried about our homeschooling. It was very hard for me to stop my "homeschooling shopaholic" trend when I started it, but now I have learned a lot about it. It is not even just about monetary purchasing, either. We also have a tendency to collect all the free resources we can until we forget that we even have them. This kind of collecting doesn't spend your money, but it spends your time. The best way to deal with this challenge is to have priorities based on the real needs and abilities of your children, as well as your homeschooling vision and mission. A good plan is to evaluate your children's recent achievements and think about what would (or wouldn't) make sense to add. Keeping a requirement list is also helpful.

Focusing on Academic Areas Too Much

As a homeschooling mom, getting worried about my children's achievement is not really strange. But I often get so focused on planning for this area that I forget the religious and character education. When I think further, I realize I have already passed the greatest time of homeschooling. We can catch up on missed-out-on academic lessons at any time, but the right time to build my children's religious side, their morals and their character, won't ever return. There are many geniuses and clever and smart people. But finding trustworthy, reliable people is very difficult.

Too Much Time on Administrative Matters

In the beginning of our homeschooling, I spent a lot of time doing written planning for my kids, and I had less time to build close relationships with my husband and children. After I changed to using an online planner, I found more time to spend with my family. I still can blog regularly and seriously, and do some business at home. I should have opened my mind to the huge range of planning choices before I started one that was too time-consuming.

Focusing Too Much on Exams

Honestly, until right now, I was still worried if my children could pass their exams. Therefore, we spent a lot of time preparing for them. Now I'm realizing that I should not spend so much time in testing or more exam-preparation memorization. Exam preparation can be done through some focused, serious preparation just in advance. It's useless to spend years ahead of time preparing. It is better to get to know my kids by observing the best way for them to learn, so they can have more time to learn more enjoyable things.

Getting Too Worried About Socialization

I was too worried about socialization before I read The Well-Adjusted Child: The Social Benefits of Homeschooling. I was too busy looking for any chance for my kids to "get socialized." I think it was just a waste of time. We can use that time for doing something more useful. And the kids didn't enjoy it, either. What I can see from them right now is that they just enjoy their lives. The most important thing for them is character education so that they can adapt to the real social situation of society. The socialization process is a natural one, and I shouldn't have worried too much about it.

Comparing My Children to Others

Because of my worry of my children being left out, I often compared them with other kids. Although it is not in front of them directly, I believe that they feel these comparisons. I am so ashamed of myself. A child is a gift from God who is completely unique. I should not put my own children down. It also happens sometimes with other people, who always try to test my children to compare them with others.

I know my children will not win every competition, but I would like to say that it is a shame to compare my own children to others in certain aspects like their intelligence and appearance. It will just make them broken-hearted.

Copying Old-Time Education and Parenting Styles

Well, you should know that I have three sons, which is completely different from my mom, who raised three daughters. Boys and girls are completely different. It also makes me different from my mom in terms of giving them discipline. What I did previously was very stressful, as I tried to apply my mom's methods of disciplining her daughters. Running, shouting, play-wrestling and so on were forbidden. I got so stressed trying to hold my sons to this standard. Even when they were sleeping, they were moving!

This mistake is not only for homeschoolers, but also for most parents. However, as I started homeschooling, the constant movement of my boys was very distracting. What I am doing right now is giving them time to move, but without any destructive action. I get them tired through play, then they start to "get tame" when their energy is almost finished.

Adelien Tan is a mother of three awesome boys and a wife of a great husband. They are a home-education family living in Surabaya, Indonesia, where home education is still very rare. English is her foreign language, but she tries to use it when blogging and writing about homeschooling. You can visit her at BlessedLearners.com where she shares some thoughts, experiences and information about homeschooling, family, parenting, blogging and personal growth.

The Best Curriculum Recommendations from iHomeschool Network Bloggers

Adena Foster

What I love about belonging to a diverse group of homeschool bloggers such as iHomeschool Network is the ability to glean so much wisdom from a variety of homeschool moms – from their level of experience to their teaching style or even the size of their student body. This spectrum of experience is an invaluable resource and one that I accessed to find out more about one of the most important aspects of homeschooling: curriculum choices.

I have just started my 21st year of homeschooling, and I can confirm that the landscape of homeschooling has definitely changed over the years, mostly in the area of curriculum. When I began homeschooling, there were basically two groups, those who taught with textbooks (Abeka or Bob Jones were the most popular) or those who used workbooks (Alpha Omega or ACE). Even though curriculum fairs were growing and showcasing more vendors, it took awhile for homeschool moms to venture out and try new products. Fast-forward to today, where the sheer volume of curriculum choices is so vast you might be tempted to give up before you even begin! Have no fear, I am here to help you as I share some of the top choices.

So, just how did I determine the top curriculum choices? I searched every single blog of my fellow iHomeschool Network group members, yes, all 146 of them. It was the only way I could think to be fair and to account for each one. I have two main categories: elementary and high school. Middle school is calculated with the elementary group as I have found that most homeschool parents do not make a drastic change of course until high school. Also, high school levels will differ more, even with the same publisher, than middle-school levels.

Then, within each academic level, I have listed top curricula by subject. There were some very clear winners and some not-so-clear. I am very aware that what works for one family might not work for another, so I will give other recommendations as well. I will list the curriculum in order of popularity.

Preschool

First things first, let's discuss preschool. While I stress allowing creative play and reading lots of books together for preschool, I know some prefer more structure that curriculum programs can offer. I did have my last child do more structured work, because he wanted to be included in our schooling. There were several preschool options being used:

- Raising Rock Stars Preschool by 1+1+1=1
- Slow and Steady, Get Me Ready by June Oberlander
- I'm Ready to Learn by Winter Promise
- Learn & Grow: Hands On Lessons for Active Preschoolers by Michelle Caskey

All preschool programs focus on establishing some sort of a routine, plenty of hands-on activities, developing fine and large motor skills, and early skills needed for learning, such as counting and the alphabet.

Elementary

Phonics/Language Arts

This is one area where the choices can be overwhelming. Not only are there so many options, but the users often feel very passionate about their decision in what they are using.

All About Spelling/All About Reading: You can use either the spelling or the reading program, or both, as they are designed to work beautifully together. All About Spelling uses the Orton-Gillingham approach, coupled with multisensory activities to help establish encoding skills in the student's mind. All About Reading also uses multisensory activities to teach complete phonics and reading comprehension.

Running a very close second place is Essentials by Logic of English. LOE also has a Foundations program, which includes handwriting instruction. Essentials covers phonics, spelling and grammar and is designed to be used by anyone learning to read, beginners to older struggling readers. This is my personal favorite because it was the program that helped my son who had language delays that caused multiple problems in reading and speaking. I have used Foundations and Essentials. I highly recommend for anyone who has a child going through speech therapy to use Foundations! As the child learns the sounds each letter makes, they use a mirror and learn precisely how to move their lips and tongue. If this had been around when my oldest son was younger, I would have used this program before going into speech therapy and could quite possibly have skipped that altogether.

Brave Writer is the most popular writing program. I admit that this program is new to me, but after seeing its popularity and how it has helped so many resistant writers, I contacted them, downloaded samples and am now getting ready to start with my own copy of *The Writer's Jungle*. They offer a wide range of products, and you can download samples from their website. Their products embrace their "Brave Writer Lifestyle" approach, making writing a natural experience.

There is such a huge gap between those that use the above programs and everything else without a clear order of preference. Some programs that have been around for a long time and still being used are Alpha Phonics, Explode the Code, Abeka, Learning Language Arts Through Literature, and Rod & Staff. A few use spelling programs like Spelling Workout, Sequential Spelling or Building Spelling Skills. You might also want to consider Memoria Press, Writing Through History, or First Language Lessons.

Handwriting

Three handwriting programs were evenly popular – Logic of English's Rhythm of Handwriting, Handwriting Without Tears, and A Reason for Handwriting.

Math

Math does not have to be a feared subject. It can actually be fun. Choosing the right math program in the early years is important to create a love, or at least a good respect, for this subject.

Life of Fred has become the most popular choice and, as a user of this wonderful program, I can confirm that it actually makes math fun! I love that it has a funny story and gives real-life application for math. The elementary level begins with Apples and continues through Jellybeans. (There's a text for each letter of the alphabet). Then you continue through the intermediate level with Kidneys, Liver and Mineshaft. Educents often offers bundle deals. Some might be concerned that it is not enough to be a full curriculum, but I believe that it can be, especially if you can incorporate some of the ideas given on Layered Soul's blog. I have also found it helpful to incorporate more living math books. You can learn more about living math from Loving Living Math by Cindy West. Many homeschoolers will still add a few extra problems for reinforcement by using Math Mammoth or Math on the Level.

Math-U-See came nipping on the heels of our first choice. If you have a child who just doesn't get math, this is an excellent curriculum. This program uses manipulatives that the student uses to build out every math problem and is an excellent choice for kinesthetic learners.

Teaching Textbooks: This was a close runner-up, and it's no wonder why. Teaching Textbooks provides complete instructions on DVD and, if the student makes a mistake in their workbook, it is very easy to go back and watch how the problem can be solved correctly. An independent learner could use this to really help free up mom's time. This is why Rebecca, from Line upon Line Learning, loves it: "He loves that he can do all of his work on the computer. I too love that he can listen to the lecture and do the work on the computer!"

Singapore: Bethany, former math teacher now turned homeschool mom, blogs at Math Geek Mama. She continues to use this program because she "saw such tremendous strides in (her daughter's) understanding and number sense." Her daughter likes the fun workbook pages.

Saxon: This has been a staple in homeschool families and private schools for years. There's a reason it has stood the test of time. If your child does best with textbooks and needs plenty of practice to master concepts, this is one text you should definitely investigate.

Some other math curriculums being used are Horizons by Alpha Omega Publications, Shiller, Rod & Staff, Murderous Math Series (this one I had to check out because the name intrigued me. It's based out of the UK but you can purchase the ten book set on Amazon. I consider it more living math, not a textbook. You can see the author do math tricks on his YouTube channel. There is also Right Start Math, CTC and Math Mammoth.

History

By an overwhelming majority, Mystery of History is the top curriculum. We used this last year and loved it. There are many fun activities and if you need any inspiration, do a search for "MOH" on Pinterest and you will be busy for days!

Notgrass: This publisher offers several products depending on whether you are teaching American history, world history or even state history. Their textbooks offer the most beautiful photographs and use real historical documents and speeches. They also include great literature suggestions to accompany the time period being studied. I gave my son the option to choose what curriculum he wanted to use this year, and he choose From Adam to Us.

Story of the World by Susan Wise Bauer: This is a popular choice among classical homeschoolers. History is taught in short, engaging chapters. I highly recommend the activity guide if you choose this one.

For those teaching multiple children, My Father's World and Tapestry of Grace are popular options, although you can adjust almost any curriculum to use with multiple levels.

Other excellent choices in studying history include Heart of Dakota, any of the products by Golden Prairie Press (written by homeschool graduate Amy Puetz, who makes history fun in a way I've seldom seen), Homeschool in the Woods and Sonlight.

I have used Homeschool in the Woods and I have to agree with the sentiments of Rebecca (who blogs at Hip Homeschooling), who states, "This is a new Social Studies for us, when I first pulled it out the kids thought it was art because we were making our own passports and postcard racks and timelines! It combines notebooking, time lines, lapbooking, mapwork, and more! It is hands on and the most fun we have EVER had with Social Studies, we do this with all the kids."

Geography

Geography seems to be one of those subjects that is often forgotten or incorporated in with studying history. If you are looking for a geography specific curriculum, Galloping the Globe (for world geography) or Cantering the Country (for USA geography), and Little Passports (also available for states or countries), seem to be the most used.

Science

Apologia's Exploring Creation series overwhelmingly beat out every other science curriculum. This series has texts to cover zoology, astronomy, chemistry and physics, botany, and anatomy and physiology. There are plenty of fun experiments included, too. I have found it easy to use with multiple kids. We've used lapbooks from Knowledge Box Central that coordinate with each text. I have found this is a wonderful way to review what was learned.

However, there are a few other curricula that are demanding attention and definitely worth looking into:

Christian Kids Explore series: Betsy (who blogs at Family Style Schooling) loves this program because "because it's written from a Christian worldview, it is intended to take two days a week for teaching time, and it works with multiple kids at the same time." In fact, that is why I am trying it out this year. I love that it is designed to be used two days a week.

Real Science 4 Kids: While I'm unfamiliar with this program, Cait (My Little Poppies) swears it's nothing like the old, boring elementary textbooks.

Building Foundations for Scientific Understanding: "I love this curriculum, it covers what science is, explores the history of science and teaches the scientific method. It then moves on to teaching Chemistry, Biology, Physics, Geology and Astronomy! All in an age appropriate but not watered down way." Amanda (Raising da Vinci) makes a good argument for this curriculum.

Sassafras Science Adventures: I love that it is not a textbook, but rather, it's a story where you follow two children on a journey. Pair the story with an activity and logbook to take complete advantage of this program.

High School

Teaching high school can be a little more intimidating, but with the exceptional curricula and support available, it doesn't have to be. There seem to be three options from which homeschool families choose once a student gets to this level: co-op classes, online courses or continuing a traditional homeschool path. There is no right or wrong answer here. Choose what works best for you and your student. I have often used a mix, depending on the subject and what was available to us. Many of the popular publishers now offer online courses.

English

For English, many make their own courses and use a variety of materials. At this stage, it is usually unnecessary to teach the basics such as reading, spelling and grammar. Most high school levels focus on literature and forms of writing.

Institute for Excellence in Writing (known as IEW) is an awesome program that focuses on writing. Most homeschoolers who invest in this program never stray. It is so complete. I did an in-depth review on my blog about it. I refer you to that instead of increasing this chapter by multiple pages detailing the wonders of this program.

Learning Language Arts Through Literature (aka LLATL): While the lower levels use literature as the spine for a fully integrated language arts program, the gold books that are available for high school levels (available in world literature, American literature or British literature) focus more on exposing the student to various types of literature. Texts include studies on ancient literature, epics, novels, poetry, plays, short stories, essays, books and book reviews. (Refer to their website for a complete guide.)

Lightning Literature: This is an excellent literature program that will help your students' reading comprehension and writing skills. There are many choices for your high- schooler: American literature (early to mid-19th century or mid- to late 19th century); speech; British literature (early to mid-19th century or mid- to late 19th century); Shakespeare (tragedies and sonnets, or comedies); British medieval literature; British Christian literature; American Christian literature; World Literature I (Africa and Asia); and World Literature II (Latin America, Africa and Asia). The hardest decision is which one to choose!

Traditional texts for high school English include ABeka and Rod & Staff.

Math

Teaching Textbooks: I remember when I first saw Teaching Textbooks at a vendor fair. It was their first year, and I could already tell they were an answer to prayer for many homeschool moms who fear teaching higher levels of math. The program is easy to follow. The student reads the lesson, watches a lesson on the DVD, and then completes the problems in the workbook. Then the student checks their work. For any problem that was worked incorrectly, they can view the solution on the DVD, which shows how to work each problem step by step. This means no teaching or grading for you!

However, textbooks are not for everyone, and some students just need real-life application to have math make sense, especially those students who complain, "When will I ever use this in real life??!" Enter Life of Fred. Following the same storyline format as the elementary series, more problems are given and, of course, the work is much more challenging. Again, check out Educents for deals. Heather (from Blog She Wrote) has the most convincing argument for this curriculum. Her high school students scored very well on the ACT and the teacher asked what math program they used. The teacher said that some concepts aren't taught in most math books, but the kids who use Life of Fred are the only ones that get that portion of the test correct.

Math-U-See is still a popular choice for those who have used it from the beginning. They offer levels through calculus and even have a stewardship course.

For those who want to take advantage of online courses, Khan Academy (which is free), CTC and Mr. D Math are very popular.

History

History, much like English, is another subject area where many piece together their own programs. However, there are some excellent history sources available.

Notgrass: They have world history, American history, U.S. government and economics available. I have used this program with all of my children. Personally, I love that the questions are thought-provoking and challenging. I know my students have to read the material and really think about what is being asked and not just search for answers to complete a worksheet. Also, real historical documents are used and great literature is assigned.

Mystery of History: This continues to be popular, especially in families teaching multiple ages. There are activities listed specifically to challenge the older student. There are four volumes that teach history chronologically.

History Revealed: Years ago, I heard Diana Waring speak at a homeschool conference. Her passion for history is contagious! This has been the only curriculum that Tatiana (from The Musings of Mum) has kept through her years of homeschooling, sharing that "It begins with creation and it touches on every major biblical and historical event. All four of my girls enjoys nearly every activity, which range from reading, cooking, art appreciation and performing skits."

Tapestry of Grace: This unit study program is used in many homes teaching the classical method.

Beautiful Feet Books: This is an excellent program for anyone who loves to teach by using excellent literature. I know that, growing up, I hated history class because it was only memorizing dates and reading boring texts. Now that I homeschool, I've gained a new appreciation for history, and that is credited to great literature that portrays time periods and historical events. If you have an avid bookworm, check out this program!

Science

While I really want to give you plenty of options to use, for the subject of science, I simply cannot. If they use textbooks, they use Apologia. For high school, you can choose between biology, physics, advanced biology, advanced physics, chemistry, marine biology and advanced chemistry. While these are high school texts, they are written as if the authors are having a conversation with the student. Add in the many experiments, and you clearly have a winner. You can choose between a traditional textbook, the course on DVD or even online. I have also used the textbook and purchased the optional audio CD.

⮕ A video course that is being used is The 101 Series. This digital curriculum is available for physics, chemistry and biology. Each course contains 4 DVDs. The last DVD includes a high school level course booklet and quizzes.

Other options for science include online classes, dual enrollment through a local college or co-op courses.

Electives

There are so many elective options available that it is nearly impossible to offer recommendations. The most popular elective is foreign language. Visual Latin and Henle Latin are used the most to teach Latin, which has gained popularity due to classical education. If your student is interested in another language, be sure to check out the many choices offered through Mango Languages (we took the course to learn Pirate!!) and Rosetta Stone. Be sure to check out your public library. Many libraries now offer free foreign language courses.

Not every state requires economics, so I'm including it as an elective rather than listing it under history. Economics for Everybody is an excellent choice used by many, including me. This is a digital format that combines lectures with funny dramatizations and graphics. There's a homeschool bundle available that includes a textbook.

If you are looking for a full credit for geography, look at North Star Geography. This course is Christian-based and covers not only geography skills but physical geography and human geography.

I have to mention Schoolhouse Teachers. This is homeschooler's dream. You subscribe to the site and then you have access to all of their courses. I cannot give it justice in this chapter but you can read my full review on my blog. Other than the basics, there are many options for electives: music, photography, art, computer and technology, entrepreneurship, leadership, graphic design... just to name a few. They have courses for everyone from preschool through high school and then even options just for Mom and Dad!

Art continues to be a standard. Artistic Pursuits offers several levels and now even has a course dedicated to sculpting and modeling. My family and I have enjoyed another series that is used by many homeschool families: Chalk Pastels. Tricia Hodges has several books to inspire and instruct you in using chalk. I recommend *A Simple Start in Chalk Pastels: Art for All Ages*.

When it comes to deciding on which curriculum is best suited for your family, remember that what works for one family might not be the best option for you. Also, what worked for one of your children might not work for the next one. Be flexible. Be involved. Experience will help you understand whether a child is struggling with a concept or with the curriculum. Be careful not to jump from one curriculum to another too hastily, but do not insist on staying with a program that is obviously not working. There is a delicate balance, but with patience and prayer, I trust that you will find it and be able to make the best decision for your homeschool family.

Adena Foster and her husband have five children with ages spanning from 9 to 27 years old. She began the homeschool journey in 1995 and has graduated the three oldest. Adena believes in lifelong learning and is often enrolled in college courses or online courses herself, ranging from academics to hobbies. She loves to go on last-minute road trips, cook, read and eat anything coconut or lemon. Suffering from MID (Multiple Interest Disorder), a sure sign of ENTP personality types, you can find her blogging about homeschool products and variety of topics on her blog, adenaf.com.

Ways to Make Back-to-School Time Special

Amy Dingmann

Whether you call it "back to (home)school" or "not back to school," there are many ways you can start the year off with a bang. Stumped on how to light a fire under your first day back? Here are some of our favorite back-to-(home)school traditions, in no particular order:

Special Eats

We always celebrate back to (home)school with an ice cream sundae breakfast. Talk about a crazy way to start the day! Everyone gets a bowl of ice cream and we let them go to town on the multiple toppings we offer on the kitchen table. The kids are allowed to create any kind of sundae they want, the only rule being they have to eat whatever they make. We have a great time making the sundaes, taking pictures and eating our way-too-sugary breakfast. It's really become the tradition we can count on every year, no matter what else is happening that first day.

Ice cream not your thing? You could also celebrate the first day back to (home)school with special eats like this:

- Go out to eat. Have breakfast at your family's favorite restaurant.

- Make reservations at a fancy restaurant, dress up, and celebrate the beginning of your new homeschool year in style.
- Maybe you'd rather have a picnic for lunch or a campfire for supper?
- Play short-order cook. Make a Back to School Café Menu, and declare this the ONE time all year that you'll make a separate meal for each child.
- Have a tea party or set up a hot chocolate/coffee bar.

School Supplies

As homeschoolers, we don't generally have a checklist of school supplies we are required to buy. That's another reason to celebrate! Fill a basket with the homeschool supplies you know your kids want and/or need, and present it to them with much pomp and circumstance on your first day back.

If you want to draw out the excitement, wrap up the school supplies individually and set up a scavenger hunt to find each item. It's a great way to get the kids thinking and moving (especially if they've started out with an ice cream breakfast!)

Itching to start up the "school" aspect of homeschool right away? Try making your school supply scavenger hunt into a review game. Using things you worked on last year, relate the information to the clues of where to find their hidden items. For example, maybe last year you did a study on Betsy Ross. Write down a random fact or question about her and hide one of the items by your flagpole.

What should you buy for school supplies? The great thing about not having to go off a checklist is that you can purchase school supplies that truly relate to each of your children. One year my sons were really into drawing manga so, as one of their supplies, I invested in a nice set of manga pens for them. Other ideas include:

- Educational card games they've been eyeballing
- Computer programs they'd like to learn or work with
- Coffee/hot chocolate/tea and a new mug for the year
- Certificate for a class they want to take locally or online
- Is there a shared school supply that they're always waiting to use? In our house this would be the portable electric pencil sharpener! Maybe it's time to buy them their own?
- What are you always running out of? In our house that would be decent pencils and earbuds. Maybe part of their school supply basket can be a hefty stock of each.
- New pajama pants (homeschooler uniform, right?)

Whatever has to do with the passions and interests your kids want to follow—give them the supplies to make it happen!

Coupon Book

Give your kids a coupon book. The coupons you include will be determined based on how your homeschool is set up. What's the favorite coupon that is always included in our book? The one that lets my kids skip math for the day. Other ideas for coupons to include:

- Special school lunch/lunch out

- Ice cream date
- Get out of (history/spelling/math) free card
- Extra field trip of your choice
- I will drive you wherever you want to go today
- Sleep in
- Skip school (snow day, sand day, just-because day)

Depending on how your school is set up, some of these certificates might require 24 hours' notice to be redeemed. After all, the teacher needs to be able to adjust her schedule accordingly! Be sure to clearly print the rules for redemption on the coupon so everyone is on the same page.

Leave Home

Take a first-day field trip to celebrate the fact that from the hours of 8 a.m. and 4 p.m., the world is yours again! Where have the kids have been begging to go? Is there some place awesome the kids don't yet know about, but you know they'd love? Our state's biggest candy shop is a two-hour drive from our house, and as of yet, my kids don't know about it. Wouldn't that make a memorable first-day field trip? Other away-from-home ideas:

- Geocaching
- Hiking
- Movie theater
- Library

Wherever you've been waiting to go without the summer crowds!

School Pictures

What I really love about (home)school pictures is that a child's personality can really shine through. They don't have to be the cookie-cutter school photos that are quickly snapped on picture day in public school. Take advantage of this freedom and create a memorable photo shoot.

When my sons were much younger, they would choose one fancy outfit and one casual outfit to have photos taken in. Those pictures were some of the most fun ones we've ever taken. Imagine 5- and 6-year-old boys working the camera in a button-up shirt, jeans and a tie! Contrast that with their casual outfit photos — my youngest always chose a Halloween costume!

As the kids get older, they can have even more control over the photo shoot. Consider completely stepping out of the way — have your kids take each other's pictures, or have them take their own — homeschool back-to-school selfies! Turn the photo shoot into a contest where family members can vote on which pictures are best to frame and send to Grandma and Grandpa.

Goals and Stuff

What are your goals for the year? What are your kids' goals? The first day back to (home)school is a great time to think on the year to come and then write down all the things you want to make happen.

One year when the kids were younger, we made a list of goals and then, after taking a picture of our lists, buried them under a favorite tree. Another year we burned our lists and talked about the symbolism of the smoke sending our goals out into the world.

Now that the kids are older, we keep our goals right in front of us. Sometimes we have taped them to the ceiling. I find that anything I've ever taped to the ceiling has been paid attention to more than what's on the actual wall!

Other times we have moved the list of goals around — laminate the lists and tape them above the toilet (boy moms!) or inside the refrigerator, or pin them to the backs of the front car seats so your kids can see them while they are riding. Another idea is to put them under a clear tablecloth on your dining room table. Keeping those goals visible really helps them to become a reality!

All About Me

The first day of the school year is the perfect opportunity to fill out an All About Me survey or poster. Things to include:

- Age
- Height/weight
- Grade in school
- Favorite subject
- Career path/plans
- Hobbies
- Pet peeves
- Best friend
- Other favorites (foods, games, sayings, TV show, song, etc.)

What's fun about these is to see if and how the answers change from the beginning to the end of the school year. And if you save all of these surveys throughout the years, you'll have great memories to look back on.

Time Capsule (with Optional Special Reveal)

Goal lists and All About Me surveys can also be put in a time capsule of sorts. Wouldn't it be fun to dig it up (or take it down from the top of mom's closet) at the end of the school year and see how things have changed? To take stock of what you accomplished and what you'll need to tack on to next year's to-do list?

Bonus: If you're going the time capsule route, after the kids get done putting it together, you could hide a little something in it for them to find when they open it at the end of the year. (Or, if possible, just pop the special something in the capsule right before they open it at the end of the year.) How about a certificate to redeem for movie tickets? Maybe you are going to announce a special family vacation? Perhaps you'll be buying a new piece of technology? If there is something you know you're going to be doing or getting at the end of the homeschool year, this would be a really fun way to reveal it. One family I know did this — the parents snuck a picture of a new puppy into the time capsule as a way to announce they'd be adding a four-legged family member shortly after the capsule was opened.

Brainstorm

Sometimes as homeschool moms we spend a lot of time in our own heads trying to come up with ideas and wondering if what we're doing is working. The best way to find the answer for this is to brainstorm with your kids! On the first day of school (and the last) we always do a big survey/discussion about the upcoming (or past) year. I ask things like:

- What did you like (or not like) last year that you want to repeat (or not repeat) this year?

- What was one thing you wanted to do last year that you didn't get to?
- What is one thing you hope doesn't happen this year?
- Do you need to change something about the schedule or the way things are set up? Is there something new you want to try to implement in our day?
- Regarding things we can't change, how can we work together to make those things easier to deal with?
- If it's your first year homeschooling after pulling your kids from public school, your questions might be a little different:
- How do you hope things will be different from or the same as public school?
- What are your fears about homeschooling?
- What are you hoping homeschooling will be like?

Brainstorm! Ask your kids to submit a schedule they'd like to follow or a list of things they'd like to learn. And, since you're spending all day together, you might as well be honest with each other about struggles or challenges. As my sons have gotten older, I find that when I say, "I'm really struggling with how to make THIS happen in our homeschool," they're more than happy to help figure out solutions. Work together to make things happen!

Re-screen Your Digital/Video Yearbook

When the boys were younger, we started saving all the pictures and videos we'd taken over the year to make a digital yearbook. The boys chose the pictures, video and music for the final cut. (As they got older, they were actually in charge of putting together the entire thing.)

While you'll obviously have a screening of this video at the end of the year after it's all completed, you should definitely have a re-screening of this video yearbook a few months later as a way to get pumped up for the new school year to come. Make some special snacks and enjoy the laughter!

Decorate

Decorate! If you're flat-out celebrating the fact you're not getting on the big yellow bus, then back-to-school day should be a party for you. Hang balloons from the ceilings and streamers from the doorways. Write messages on the bathroom mirror or the windows. Make your house come alive with a special way of decorating that is reserved just for back-to-school time.

Relax

If you're the type of family that is constantly on the run and exploring the world, maybe the first day of school is a day to stay home, relax and contemplate what the year holds for you. Are you the family that doesn't buy into the pajamas-as-a-school-uniform stereotype? Maybe the first day of school is the day to let that slide.

Homeschooling can definitely grow more stressful as the year goes on; why not take the first day of the school year to chill out and enjoy each other?

Party as a Group

Check out what the local homeschool groups or co-ops are doing. In some areas, these groups will sponsor "Not Back to School" events for homeschoolers like bowling, roller-skating or a park day. It's a great way to celebrate with a group and meet other homeschoolers who are local to you. Or, be bold and set up your own Not Back to School party and invite others to join you!

Consider what things you can do as a family that will help that first day of school really stick out from the rest of the school year. Give it a little extra oomph of awesome and make it special! Start your own back-to-(home)school traditions that your kids will look forward to every year.

Amy Dingmann lives in Minnesota with her husband, where they have been homeschooling their two sons since 2007. Her hobbies include filling up her sons' bottomless pits, drinking a lot of strong coffee and smiling. Her least favorite subject is math. Her favorite subjects are everything else. She likes talking to other homeschooling parents and assuring them that even though they worry they're totally screwing things up, they actually totally and completely rock. Amy blogs at thehmmmschoolingmom.com, and works as an author/speaker on homeschooling and parenting/family topics.

How To Incorporate Extracurricular Activities

Amy Milcic

One of the biggest blessings of homeschooling is flexibility. As homeschoolers, we have the opportunity to customize our children's education at home. For a variety of reasons, this flexibility can become overwhelming. There is a wealth of resources and activities that homeschoolers have at their fingertips.

No matter where you are in your homeschool journey, extracurricular activities can seem daunting. You might find yourself wondering how in the world you can include "extras" when it is hard enough to cover the basics. Plus, don't forget your numerous day-to-day responsibilities! It can feel like you will either never have time to relax, or that you are not doing enough.

Dear homeschooler, please know that you have this!

Before I share why extracurricular activities are important for your kids and yourself (and how you can fit them in!), take a deep breath and brew a cup of tea (or grab a favorite beverage). Remind yourself that you are doing your very best and give yourself a hug.

What Are Extracurricular Activities?

Extracurricular activities can be defined as anything outside of academic studies. Academic interests (or strengths or weaknesses), however, further studied and pursued, can also be considered extracurricular if not detailed in your homeschool curriculum.

Here is a list of examples of common extracurricular activities:

- Sports
- Music
- Choir
- Art
- Theater
- Cooking
- Scouts or similar service group
- Volunteer work
- Church groups
- Debate team
- Robotics
- LEGO group
- Mentorships
- Hobbies like woodworking or calligraphy
- Chess

Many of the examples listed above might be already a part of your homeschool curriculum.

These pursuits are classified as extracurricular when one or more of your children participate outside of your homeschool.

Why Extracurricular Activities For Homeschoolers?

These additional activities can provide several benefits to your kids and to you. Extracurricular activities allow for kids to develop interests and learn more about their likes or dislikes. Children learn that there is more to life than just academics.

Extracurricular activities help your kids become more well-rounded.

Numerous social, physical and psychological benefits can result from participation in extracurricular activities.

Socially, homeschool kids and their families often are able to develop relationships outside of their family unit.

Important socialization skills can be practiced during these additional events. Also, kids learn about forming relationships and teamwork.

Depending on the type of extracurricular activity, kids can benefit physically from participation in sports, Scouts and band. The building of fine and gross motor skills is often a part of activities like art, cooking and LEGO Club.

Psychologically, children who participate in extracurricular activities have opportunities to increase self-confidence and self-esteem.

Extracurricular activities provide a chance for kids to test out their skills and develop mastery of concepts. Also, they receive the pleasure of partaking in an interest that engages and excites.

Extracurricular activities also offer the chance to gain experience or training for future careers.

Development of basic skills and proficiencies can translate into acceptance for internships, apprenticeships and jobs. For homeschool kids pursuing higher-level education or training, extracurricular activities are an excellent way to demonstrate a more well-rounded student.

Who Can Benefit From Homeschool Extracurricular Activities?

Any homeschool student can gain from extracurricular activities. Opportunities exist within the home and in the community for all ages. Toddlers to teens can find and participate in individual or group activities.

Larger families might find it helpful or necessary to combine kids in close age groups. Babies and toddlers might have the chance to attend library story times. Elementary-level children, for example, might all enjoy a local LEGO group. Middle-school-aged kids might qualify for group participation in youth choir at church. Tweens and teens might find a robotics club that piques their interest.

Families with only one child might find that homeschool extracurricular activities are ideal for providing opportunities to make friends and connections.

Where To Find Extracurricular Activities

Opportunities might abound in your community for additional events or groups for your homeschoolers. Contact your local public and private schools and ask if they allow homeschoolers to participate in clubs or groups. Local churches might also have activities that allow homeschoolers to attend.

Live near a college or university? Find out if any programs for youth exist. Libraries are also great places to find events or start your own meet-ups. YMCAs and similar organizations often have classes, groups and teams to have extracurricular fun.

If you live in a rural area or have limited resources, consider starting some extracurricular activities in your own home. Private tutors can be a great way to help your children further develop interests. Perhaps you have a particular skill or talent that you would like to pass on to your kids? Go for DIY extracurricular activities!

With our modern world of technology, there are a number of ways undertake extracurricular activities online. Using internet safety at all times, look for educational videos and tutorials on YouTube. Find a webinar or online class. Online outsourcing of additional activities is a great way to help your kids gain new perspectives and skills.

How To Determine What Extracurricular Activities To Include In Your Homeschool

Each family will need to take a realistic look at their season in life. Financially, extracurricular activities can add up, and your pocket can take a beating. Schedules need to be coordinated. Transportation is another key issue when considering extracurricular activities.

A few important characteristics of each child also need to be considered. Your children's ages might limit their level of independence with a club, group or skill. Will an adult be available to assist, if necessary? Perhaps an older sibling can help? Age might also be a limitation as far as grouping children together.

Look at each of the personalities of your children. What are their comfort zones? Would you like to help your introverted child find a safe way to develop social skills? Does your outgoing social butterfly require a group activity to flourish?

Another consideration is the types of goals you have for your kids. Perhaps your introverted child needs a gentle nudge to mingle with peers, or your extrovert requires a bit of practice with quiet, focused work? Discuss areas that you feel your kids might need to work on, and seek out activities that can help develop those skills.

Of course, the biggest factor will be your children's interests. Look for ways to cultivate those interests in a positive way. Perhaps your child who loves to run and run and run would love to be a part of a track and field team? Extracurricular activities can channel interests into areas of growth and development, as well as contribute to improved coping skills or a decrease in problematic behaviors.

How To Fit Extracurricular Activities Into Your Homeschool Schedule

Now that we have looked at what, why, who and where, let's look at when and how.

As previously mentioned, homeschooling offers a tremendous amount of flexibility. Homeschoolers are not typically bound by a set schedule. Consider activities anywhere from early morning to late at night. Most importantly, work toward scheduling events when you and your kids function at your best.

As a homeschool soccer mom to five boys, here are my tips to make extracurricular activities work for your family:

Communication: Every family member who is capable of speaking and comprehending needs to learn open and honest communication skills. Kids through adults need to feel comfortable relaying information, facts and feelings. Weekly or daily family meetings where schedules are reviewed alleviate confusion or trouble.

Organization: A family organizational center is a must! This is a one-stop place for schedules, lists, duties and responsibilities, where family members can check for transportation and more. Equipment and uniforms (really, any required items) must be maintained and kept in one place for easy access and use.

Planning: One of the key factors of successful extracurricular activities is planning! At least one member of your family needs to keep track of (overlapping) schedules, sign-ups and practices. Planning can be on paper or digital.

Meal-Planning: It is extremely helpful to plan ahead for your meals, at least for one week. Find simple recipes that are nutritious and affordable. If you have picky eaters, have an acceptable substitute at the ready to avoid last-minute squabbles that can interfere with arriving at events on time. Create a list of go-to meals that you can easily rotate. Crock-Pot meals and casseroles are fantastic recipes to prepare ahead of time or to come home to after extracurricular activities.

Chores: Momma can't do it alone! Assign chores according to age and ability. Thoroughly demonstrate how specific tasks are to be completed. Set realistic expectations and explain why it is vital that every family member chips in and helps.

Outsource/Ask For Help: As much as we like to think that we can do it all, there are only so many hours in the day. It is OK to ask family and friends for help with carpooling or babysitting. Also, getting takeout or drive-through food every now and again is OK, especially if it helps maintain your sanity!

Extracurricular activities are a wonderful way to add to your homeschool. When a realistic approach is applied, these additional activities can benefit your entire family. Take it slow, work as a team, and you will discover the perks of including extracurricular activities in your homeschool schedule.

Amy Milcic is a mental health therapist turned homeschool soccer mom to five boys. She loves to share positive and creative ways to support learning at home on her blog at rockyourhomeschool.net She can be found on Periscope @AmyMilcic weekday mornings for Rock Your Homeschool! She is also co-owner of plannersquad.com, a site dedicated to uniting the planner community.

How Learning Styles Can Help Your Homeschool

Amy Milcic

Do you ever scratch your head in wonder when you think about how your kids can be so different when it comes to your homeschool? Is it hard to understand why one approach or curriculum might work for your oldest while it fails miserably with a younger sibling? Do you perhaps find it difficult to teach your children because they learn so differently than you do?

Let me ease your concerns, dear homeschooler. You are not alone in your confusion about differences in learning among children. There is a valid reason for your befuddlement: Everyone learns in their own unique way.

Before we look at what learning styles are and how to use this information in your homeschool, I would like you to remember one thing: Your child is unique. Each child will have a unique approach to life and learning. While it can be helpful to have awareness of learning styles, a progressive understanding of your children and their individual perspective on life will be of the utmost help.

Let's explore learning styles and how to use this information with the notion that we can use it as a tool to better know our kids and ourselves. We can take note of our discoveries and add them to our parenting/homeschool toolbox. Use this tool to cultivate custom educations for your children while you are creating an environment of acceptance and understanding.

What Are Learning Styles?

A learning style can be defined as how one prefers to learn and the ideal environment for such learning. It is how one takes in, processes, understands and applies information. Learning style relates to what an individual attends to and how that person demonstrates understanding of a concept.

Learning styles stem from educational theories that became popular in the 1970s. These theories have never been proven, yet continue to have a major influence on teaching philosophies, approaches and requirements. Several theories exist to explain differences in learning styles.

We will look at two of the more common theories associated with learning styles. For more information on the different theories of learning styles, check out the resources listed at the end of this chapter.

VA(R)K Theory of Learning Styles

The VA(R)K model of student learning was created by Fleming (1992) to describe noted differences in learning. VARK is an acronym for each of four styles, which are:

- Visual
- Auditory
- Reading/Writing
- Kinesthetic

(Some educators omit the use of Reading/Writing as a style and adhere to VAK theory. They contend that the Reading/Writing style is part of Visual learning.)

These four learning styles are relatively well-known, especially in educational circles. Many curricula and lessons are designed to address these styles of learning. Differentiation of teaching approaches and activities based on learning styles is a common practice in the world of education.

For each learning style, individuals focus on different components of presented material. Attention is placed on specific features according to the person's mode of thinking. Here is a closer look at each style, according to VARK theory:

- **Visual:** The individual attends to images, pictures, and graphics. These learners often form visual images in their head to organize, comprehend and use information.
- **Auditory:** The individual listens and speaks to take in and process information. These types of learners prefer lectures and discussions, as well as repetition and mnemonic devices.
- **Reading/Writing:** These learners retain information via words. Individuals learn best through reading or writing.
- **Kinesthetic:** Hands-on learning is how these individuals best retain concepts. Tactile experiences ("feeling" activities) provide concrete ways for these individuals to process and apply.

Multiple Intelligences Theory

Howard Gardner wrote about seven types of intelligences in his 1983 book *Frames of Mind: The Theory of Multiple Intelligences*. His theory of multiple intelligences has often been connected with learning styles. In 2013, Gardner wrote an article for The Washington Post that refuted this connection and why the use of his theory for learning styles was a misinterpretation of his findings.

Gardner explains multiple intelligences using an analogy that our brains are like computers. Each of us has seven different computers that function independently from each other. We each have a dominant computer that drives how we process and apply information.

Multiple intelligences theory proposes that humans have seven ways that they take in, process, and present information. Individuals tend to have a more dominant intelligence. One type of intelligence does not trump another, nor does a person only have or use one intelligence. We have all seven intelligences, just at different levels and experiences.

The seven types of intelligences proposed in multiple intelligences theory:

Visual/Spatial: These learners think in pictures, often creating vivid mental images to process and retain information. They are often good at puzzles, sketching, reading and writing.

Verbal/Linguistic: These learners think in words and are often good at listening and speaking. They thrive in storytelling, teaching, writing, listening and speaking.

Logical/Mathematical: These learners think in patterns, numbers and logic. They often ask questions to learn more about a subject and are often good at calculations, experiments, classifying and problem-solving.

Bodily/Kinesthetic: Movement, coordination and balance are how these learners make sense of the world. They are often good at sports, crafts, acting and dance.

Musical/Rhythmic: Sounds, patterns, and rhythms help these learners discover and process. They often thrive in singing, composing music and playing musical instruments.

Interpersonal: These learners tend to be intuitive, peaceful organizers who are good at verbal and nonverbal communication, empathy, counseling, cooperation and conflict resolution.

Intrapersonal: These learners often reflect upon their thoughts, feelings and dreams. Also, they are highly aware of their strengths and weaknesses and are good at self-analysis and reasoning.

It is interesting to note that these multiple intelligences overlap. Also, it is easy to see how a person may find they have learning preferences in a few of the types of proposed intelligences. Edutopia has a short quiz (edutopia.org/multiple-intelligences-assessment) on multiple intelligences that can be fun and useful.

How to Apply This Information in Your Homeschool

The big take-away from this information is not to let learning style or intelligence limit your homeschooling approach. Instead, use the information to gain a better awareness of your children and yourself.

Overall, staying in touch with how your kids are processing information will help you discover how to best cultivate growth and development.

It can be helpful to have information about learning styles/intelligences for one-on-one instruction, as well as for small-group work.

Adaptive measures to enhance learning experiences can be applied based on learning styles/intelligences information. This information can also be applied to help your kids discover an effective academic course of study and future career path.

Ideally, each learning style/intelligence will be considered and included in homeschool lessons. Incorporating each style will help engage all students. Also, exposure to different types of conditions, prompts and materials may help students develop underused styles or intelligences.

How to Incorporate as Many Styles/Intelligences as Possible

Video Lessons: These types of presentations, especially if they include music and movement, address all learning styles and most intelligences. Visual/spatial learners benefit from watching the images.

Auditory/musical/rhythmic learners gain from hearing various sounds and words. Kinesthetic/bodily learners can experience learning by getting up and moving along with the lesson. Interpersonal learners can benefit from listening and working with fellow watchers on processing the lesson. Intrapersonal learners can gain from analyzing the presented information in terms of how it relates to themselves.

Logical/mathematical learners may enjoy breaking down the lesson into patterns and asking questions about the information.

Storytimes/Read-Alouds: The reading aloud of a book and presentation of its material is a fantastic way to include a variety of learning styles and intelligences.

Kinesthetic/bodily learners benefit from the use of props.

Musical/rhythmic learners may flourish with songs and fingerplays (great for kinesthetics, too!). Auditory learners benefit from hearing the book spoken aloud. Visual learners can enjoy picture books, posters or story cards.

Logical/mathematical learners can be encouraged to discover the sequence and patterns within a story, as well as to ask questions.

Interpersonal learners can gain from organizing the information and relating to characters. Intrapersonal learners can absorb the message within the story and use that for self-analysis and inner reflection.

Games: A variety of games can be helpful in addressing learning styles/multiple intelligences. Different players can participate in different ways. Think outside the box (and the rules!) and adapt games according to your children's preferences. Examples of games that can work are Scene It!, Pictionary and charades.

I would like to send you off with this reminder: Any tools, tests or information gathered about your kids and yourself can be used in a positive way to cultivate a love of learning. You are by no means required to use all of the information, nor must you limit your homeschool lessons in any way. I encourage you to take your enhanced awareness and use it to develop ways in which you can better understand and serve each other.

Amy Milcic is a mental health therapist turned homeschool soccer mom to five boys. She loves to share positive and creative ways to support learning at home on her blog at rockyourhomeschool.netShe can be found on Periscope @AmyMilcic weekday mornings for Rock Your Homeschool! She is also co-owner of plannersquad.com, a site dedicated to uniting the planner community.

Have Fun with Board Games in Your Homeschool

Christia Colquitt

One of my favorite parts of homeschooling is the freedom to make learning FUN. Games are the perfect way to add fun to learning, memorizing and practicing. Board games (and card games as well!) can be rich in learning opportunities.

Here are just a few of the skills that can be mastered with board games: number and shape recognition, grouping and counting; letter recognition and reading; visual perception and color recognition; eye-hand coordination; and manual dexterity.

Games don't need to be overtly academic to be educational. Just by virtue of playing them, board games can teach important social skills, such as communicating verbally, sharing, waiting, taking turns and enjoying interaction with others.

Board games can also help lengthen children's attention span by completing the game. Maybe you are ready to add a few board games to your homeschool day. Let me share with you some of my favorites for different age groups.

For Preschoolers

Zingo - This game puts a twist on bingo. No reading is necessary, so it is a great game for preschoolers to play. Beyond preschool, it still has learning value as kids take notice of the words that match the picture.

Hoot Owl Hoot - This is a cooperative game where preschoolers work together to get all the baby owls back into their nest before the sun comes up. This game is great for working on colors.

Cheese Dip - This is there perfect game for letter recognition and fine motor skills. Games are a great way to work on many skills at the same time. Each child takes turns using mouse tails to fish for the letters in their word.

Memory - This classic game will always be a childhood favorite. But... expect to be beaten. I have yet to beat my 4-year-old. Seriously. Kids have a crazy memory!!

Fish a ree - This is a combination of memory and measuring. Once you pick up your fish, you have to measure it with the provided tape measure to see if it is a match.

For Elementary Ages

For my elementary-aged kids, I LOVE to surprise the kids with game days for certain subjects.

This breaks up our school day and gives the kids a way to practice their new skills.

If you have a child who is having difficulty with a particular subject or concept, games are the perfect way to practice, practice, practice without the kids even realizing it!

Elementary Math

For math, repetition is key.

I also love using math games because they allow kids to use their skills outside of worksheets and textbooks.

Learning Resources Sum Swamp Game - This adorable game requires kids to add and subtract their way across the swamp. The Sum Swamp game makes adding and subtracting an adventure.

tri-FACTa Multiplication and Division Game - My two boys have struggled with math fact fluency in multiplication. I try to play at least two multiplication games a week to build fluency and encourage math fact memorization.

Head Full of Numbers - I love that this game can be used for all four operations: addition, subtraction, multiplication and division. This is a game we can play even with our younger kids, but use different operations to come up with correct answers. Plus, it is always fun to shake up dice.

Elementary Reading

Pop for Sight Words - Oh, sight words! Sometimes they make me want to pull out my hair. Just like with multiplication facts, repetition is key! This game works on 92 sight words.

Get the Picture Reading Comprehension Game - I love this game because it helps kids figure out the main idea and point of the story in game form and with a puzzle.

Wordplay for Kids - This is THE GAME to get for elementary reading. Everything rolled into one: word building, vocabulary, spelling and concentration. Worth every penny. Seriously. You need this game in your homeschool.

Elementary Science

Science Explosion Board Game - Two games in one, brought to you by the Magic School Bus. We love following the Magic School Bus science subscription activities and this game is a great complement to our homeschool. If you have children who love science, this is a great game for your family.

Elementary Geography

Ten Days in the USA - I love that this game has helped my kids become familiar with West Coast and East Coast states. We live in the Midwest and this game has helped my kids learn the states that are on the different coasts of the USA.

Ticket to Ride - This game is for ages 8 and up. But younger students can play with an adult. If you have boys who love trains, this is a MUST.

I would highly encourage you to check out some of these games and find a way to incorporate them into your homeschool day.

Whether you choose to have a certain game day every once in awhile, or you incorporate games into your day throughout the week. do not underestimate the power of games in your homeschool.

The right games can provide powerful educational opportunities.

 *Christia Colquitt is a homeschooling mom to five children. She is the proud mommy of four boys and one girl! Her house is loud, fun and filled with laughter, and, of course, super sticky floors! Yet, this was not always the plan! After receiving her degree in biochemistry from the University of Tennessee, she planned on going to dental school. God had other plans, and Christia has never looked back. Christia is married to 11-year NFL veteran player Dustin Colquitt. They make it their life mission to inspire and help others from all walks of life. Christia wants to share her triumphs and struggles in parenting, marriage, homeschooling, and how to make it all work on her blog FaithFilledParenting.com.*

How to Stay the Course (or Not) When the School Bus Looks Tempting

Ginny Kochis

I fought homeschooling. I'm four years in, and there are still days - many, in fact - where I'm on the ledge and seconds away from jumping. My house is always a mess. My to-do list is five miles long. I'm never on time for anything, and some days it feels like all I do is yell.

Those are the days when I stand by the window, teacup in hand, and peer through the rising steam. A whispered prayer ascends with it, like a burnt offering at the altar of the neighborhood school bus.

What if my children went, too?

I'd get more writing done.

I'd spend more time with the toddler.

My husband would come home to a clean house (not that he cares; I do).

I'd get the storage room cleaned out. The family photos in albums. The basement organized.

What if my children went, too?

Would I be a better mom? Would I be happier?

The truth is, my happiness lies in doing what I am called to do, in raising my children and being the mother they already have. At this juncture in my life, that means homeschooling. It means stepping back from the ledge, steadying my nerves and taking the steps necessary to recommit myself.

Below you will find the five steps I take when I'm ready to call it quits. But before I go on, I feel it's important to say that for some women, the answer to all of this might actually be to let go. You don't have to homeschool forever. If you consider the points below and determine it's time to move on, you are not a failure. You are making the decision that is right for your family.

When the school bus looks tempting...

Rest and Regroup

We homeschool moms are Type-A, driven people. We work the equivalent of three full time jobs: mother, teacher and counselor. Some of us might even carry another career, one that extends outside the home. Doing all of this without proper self care is a recipe for disaster.

I know, because I live it. I'm a homeschooling mom to three beautiful (mostly feral) children, with a busy tutoring business and a growing writing career. I don't have office hours, unless you consider them midnight to 11:59 p.m. In the fall of 2015, I was 10 months postpartum, teaching kindergarten and third grade at home, carrying a full load of clients, and suffocating under the weight of untreated postpartum depression. My heart knew I needed help. My head insisted I needed a tighter grip.

My life was a Chinese finger trap. I needed to rest, regroup and take care of myself for a change. I sought treatment for the depression, then made a list of questions to ask myself when I feel like I'm at my breaking point:

- What are three things I can do every day to make sure I'm taking care of myself?

- What is my favorite way to unwind, and how long has it been since I engaged in that activity?

- In what areas do I need help? To whom could I go for help?

- Who has offered to help in the past? Did I take them up on the offer? Why or why not?

The answers to these questions were eye-opening, so much so that I try to sit down and answer them once a week. They identify areas where I might be lacking in self-care and remind me that I don't have to do this alone.

Reevaluate

Once I've regrouped and taken time for myself, I find it helpful to reevaluate my homeschool. I focus first on what's working well, then identify the areas that cause the most stress.

- Curriculum

  o Which areas are the most successful? Why?

  o Which areas cause the most strife? Why?

  o What can I do to relieve that stress? Should I hire out? Find an online resource? Switch to a different curriculum? Use a hands-on (or hands-off) approach?

- General upkeep

  o Who is doing the bulk of the chores? Could the rest of the family help out more?

o   What systems can I implement to make life easier? (Zone cleaning? A token economy?)

- Mother/child relationships

    o   What are my mothering successes?

    o   How have I connected with my children?

    o   Is there a child with pressing needs?

    o   What are the stumbling blocks in my relationships with my children?

This is my list for reevaluating; yours might include entirely different topics. The key is to create a set of benchmarks by which you can measure the areas of strength and growth in your homeschool, then form a plan to capitalize on what's good while addressing the challenges.

Prioritize

I am not a "one thing at a time" mom. I'm not even a "one thing at a time" person. Separation of tasks and their delegation is difficult for me, so you'll often find me running about the house like a mad woman, complaining about the items on my to-do list.

Aside from ensuring I bear an unflattering resemblance to Chicken Little, this behavior is fruitless. It only serves to further frustrate and paralyze me, and I spend most of my day wringing my hands instead of taking action.

This is where I remind myself to prioritize.

- What school tasks should be completed today? By the end of the week? By next week? By the end of the month?

- What tasks around the house should be completed today? By the end of the week? By next week? By the end of the month?

- What self-care items should be completed today? By the end of the week? By next week? By the end of the month?

- What child-related issues need to be addressed today? By the end of the week? By next week? By the end of the month?

- What are my work goals for today? The end of the week? Next week? The end of the month?

Once I identify my priorities, I am better able to separate them into manageable tasks. Some tasks are entered into my planner, while others are delegated to the appropriate individual. Looking at one thing at a time keeps me from "catastrophizing" and significantly reduces my stress level.

Switch your Approach

My husband's Texas roots are fond of saying "a square peg don't fit in a round hole." He usually gets the side-eye when he uses the phrase with me, but it's true. It doesn't matter how forcefully you try to work a curriculum (or lesson, or technique, or schedule, or activity) into your homeschool: If it doesn't fit, it has to go.

Now, this is not an all-or-nothing solution. Sometimes it's simply a matter of switching things around for a week or two until everything has settled. If the current situation has worked in the past and you'd like to use it again someday, go right ahead. But if you find yourself straining against rough seas in a boat built for quiet creeks and rivers, consider changing things up:

- Flip the classroom and let your children do the teaching. This was a favorite technique of mine when I was a classroom teacher. I'd give the students a topic, then ask them to find a creative way to teach it to the rest of the class. This encouraged researching, reading, thinking, writing and synthesis as they processed the information and presented it to their peers.

- Try looping. This is a technique coined by Sarah Mackenzie of the blog Amongst Lovely Things. Sarah makes a general list of items she needs to accomplish, then goes through the week and checks them off. I've started treating my homeschool this way, and for the most part, it's reduced much of my schedule anxiety.

- Try doing a little bit from each subject each day. Watch a science video one day, then write about it the next. Do an experiment on the third day, then go on a field trip on the fourth. Breaking things into chunks can make bigger topics feel more manageable (and meltdowns less likely).

- Or, try devoting one day to a subject. Maybe do math on Mondays, history on Tuesdays, science on Wednesdays and reading and writing on Thursdays. You don't have to limit your school day to those subjects alone, but you can make them the main focus and spend shorter amounts of time (15 to 20 minutes, perhaps) on the others. This is especially good for days when you might have a larger project to tackle.

Finally, Go Ahead and Quit

I don't mean permanently. But maybe you just need a week off? Leave the books and papers at home and take a week to explore local museums. Go camping or take a hike. Immerse yourself in the arts for a few days. Just walk away and do something different.

This doesn't have to be impromptu. If you're a planner like me, schedule weeks of downtime throughout the year. As a homeschooling mom, I'm sure you know that learning can take place anywhere - even when you've taken a week off from school.

Homeschooling is not an easy calling. We carry a great deal on our shoulders, not the least of which is forming the young minds who will one day be in charge of this crazy, beautiful world. It's OK to feel like quitting. It's OK to feel like taking a break. It's OK to feel like you need to throw the baby out with the bathwater and start from the very beginning.

Really, it's OK. Take a deep breath. Look at your children. Know that whatever choice you make, you are doing what's right for them.

And then move forward, confident in your path.

Ginny Kochis is a former high school English teacher and adjunct professor turned homeschooling mom to three gifted, twice-exceptional kiddos. A Teacher Consultant for the Northern Virginia Writing Project and owner of The Writing Well Educational Services, Ginny supports families in their efforts to think critically and write effectively. Ginny writes about family literacy, mothering homeschooling twice-exceptional children and Catholicism on her blog, NotSoFormulaic.com. She can also eat an entire carton of ice cream in one sitting, but only if no one is looking.

Model Lifelong Learning and Inspire Your Children

Heather Weller

Moms are doing so many amazing things in the world. But sometimes we feel at odds:

- How do we find what we love?

- When do we pursue our passions?

- What time commitment can we give to our own learning?

- Where do we find inspiration when we are being buried under the pressure of mothering?

I bet if you are anything like me, a homeschool mom, a mom of littles, a mom of bigs, you are a little tired. Absolutely grateful to be mothering, sure, but perhaps you too need time to reflect on your needs and discover or rediscover your interests - to renew and realign yourself.

Before we have children, our lives are usually ours for the taking; we make our own schedules; we typically make decisions based on our wants and needs; and our time is ours to schedule as we like. Sure, we might have a job or other commitments, but before motherhood, we have more time of our own and can decide what we want to pursue in our free time.

Not so in motherhood. And certainly not when we add in homeschool.

What Lights You Up?

We come to find, as we grow, there is a time in life we might begin to feel dulled. We're not bright and shiny. We have lost our attention. We have laid aside those interests that used to light us up.

Sometimes we lose ourselves.

We lose ourselves and think we should sacrifice our own passions for those we love. But that doesn't make for a happy mom. And we want to be happy moms, don't we?

What if you could blend those two seemingly opposing ideas? What if you could serve the needs of your family as well as pursue your own interests? And what if doing so would benefit everyone?

You see, you can better serve your family and your homeschool when you are happy. You can find happiness when you find that which lights your fire. We need to find our awesome and get fascinated. Because then we become more fascinating!

Not One More Thing...

I know, believe me. I know how hard it is to try to maintain the energy to pursue an interest - or even discover what we are interested in. When you are already tired and have so much on your plate, it is a challenge.

Let me offer some encouragement: Let's model some adult happiness and joy to our kids! This might mean slacking off on housework or homework and slipping your fun into the slivers of time in your day.

Your Attention

Do you notice how we can seldom find time to concentrate on anything because a child finds us? And then, if you are anything like me, you have a few immediate feelings:

- **Guilt:** Uh-oh! I need to stop this to pay attention to them.

- **Resentment:** Argh! Why can I never do anything for me?!?

- **Putting It Off:** Oh, I'll just wait until they are in bed / preoccupied / not sick / napping / independent...

If we wait for those moments, they never come. Our lives as mothers are not set up to be compartmentalized. We must blend our passions into our life as mothers.

By showing our children what catches our fancy, what takes up our time and what we pay attention to, we are teaching them how to be interested and how to become interesting.

Our children seek to understand.

Why is mom interested in that? What makes it important to her? How can she do it for hours? Doesn't she hear me? What is keeping her from hearing me right now?

How Do Our Own Interests Build Better Homeschools?

When we model how to be interested in a subject, when we live the adage "lifelong learner," we show our children what we hope for them in adulthood.

Too many of us mothers are unhappy, or, if not unhappy, then tired and dulled, living lives without verve and brightness. By showing our children how seeking out and growing in knowledge and curating skills that enrich our lives makes us happier, they learn to do it for themselves.

It gives our kids an invaluable model of healthy adulthood.

Model being a fully alive and engaged adult so your children will know how to do it, too!

And do you know what that will do? Many positive things:

- Your kids will see you interested in something outside the realm of family. This will encourage them to pursue their own fascinations.

- Your kids will see you excited and happy and fulfilled. They will begin to understand that you are an interesting person, and that, while you're passionately focused on them, you also have interests you love beyond that.

- Your kids will see a less stressed person, because when we contribute to the world by building on our own fascinations, we share a vision of healthy self-care.

Tell Me How!

If you don't know how to even begin, start with these small steps:

- Read a book because YOU want to.

- Practice some self-care.

- Begin to pay attention to what pulls you. Seek out information on that interest using podcasts, YouTube, magazines, Periscope or social media.

- Share it! Talk to your kids about it. Let's face it, we have lengthy conversations about Minecraft and Shopkins with them... so they can hear about our fashion challenges or bullet journaling!

Still Stuck?

Answer these questions and start journaling:

- What are you so interested in that you get totally keyed up any time you think of it?

- What topics of conversation or books or YouTube channels do you never tire of?

- If you were faced with an entire weekend free from your normal, everyday responsibilities, what would you do?

We are the greatest example to our children of what it will look like to be a grown-up.

Let this be an inspiration to you: Lifelong learning serves us best when we find time to do it. Taking care of ourselves and pursuing our passions does more for our kids then nearly anything else. You know they already want to grow up so badly; show that how awesome it can really be.

Heather Weller is a former middle school teacher with a master's degree in education, a current homeschool mom of three and the creative voice behind wellermommablog.com, where she shares creative learning ideas, STEAM projects, nature study treasures and literature-rich book collections. She maintains her cheerful demeanor through writing, bullet journaling and running. When she isn't hanging out with her kids

at home or at local hotspots, she can be found outside in her garden, snuggled up inside with a book, on the phone with her mom or contemplating life's big questions - like what to make for dinner - with a cup of coffee or a glass of wine. She seeks to bring simple, effective learning opportunities to her kids - and yours, too - while remaining focused on healthy self-care, connection and creativity. Her husband calls her Happy Heath, and she likes to look on the bright side of life!

Making Flashcard Learning Fun

Kathy Gossen

Trying to help your child learn important facts such as multiplication, dates in history, or a new language? Struggling to get through those flashcards one more time?

Flashcards have been proven to improve retention, speed, recall, comprehension and more. But that doesn't mean they are necessarily fun. In fact, there was a time when I would have said they were anything BUT fun.

Last spring, my girls and I had been working on Spanish, addition and subtraction flashcards when we reached a dead end. Learning was a challenge, and progress seemed like a distant memory.

That is when I decided it was time for something different. We started to use flashcards as the base for all sorts of games, and learning became fun as a result!

Why Flashcard Games?

As a public school teacher, I used to incorporate flashcard games with my students. Why I never thought to use them with my own children, I don't know, but when I did, wow! The change was almost immediate. I heard words like "That was fun!" and "Can we do that again?" and "That game is my new favorite!" No joke!

These days, we play flashcard games at least a couple times a week, and the results have been astounding. Speed games and tests used to cause my oldest to flip out in frustration.

Now, she gets excited about seeing if she can improve her time. The memorization of new facts used to be daunting. Now, new information is motivating as it adds new challenges to a game.

Ready to give flashcard games a try in your home and see the results yourself?

Here are five of our favorite flashcard games that make learning fun at our house! Have fun playing them with your own children, and watch their eyes light up as they enjoy learning all over again.

Speed

Number of Players: 2

Objective: To have the least number of cards when the timer goes off.

Items Needed: Timer

Instructions: To begin, divide the flashcards evenly between two players. Set the timer for 1 minute. Start the timer. At the same time, the players should read the top card on their pile and state the answer (which is on the other side). They should then check their answers. If they get it correct, they place their card in their opponent's discard pile, next to the opponent's initial flashcard pile. If a player answers incorrectly, the card goes to the bottom of that person's own flashcard pile, and the game continues. If a player discards all the flashcards in the initial pile, that player may start to go through the discard pile that has been placed by the opponent. When the timer ends, players should count the total number of flashcards in both their initial and discard piles. The player with the fewest cards wins.

War

Number of Players: 2

Objective: To gather the most cards.

Items Needed: Nothing.

Instructions: Place the two players side-by-side. Show them one flashcard at a time. The first player to answer the flashcard correctly gets to keep that card. The game continues until all cards have been used. The player with the most cards wins.

Reward Road

Number of Players: 1

Objective: To make it to the end of the flashcard road

Items Needed: A toy car, toy animal or other small object and a few rewards (candy, pencils, stickers, etc.)

Instructions: Place the flashcards in a line to create a road. Assign progressive rewards along the road at different checkpoints. For example, the fourth flashcard could be a sticker, the eighth could be a Tootsie Roll, and the last flashcard could be a quarter. Make the rewards something the player would be motivated to win. Place the car (or other object) at the beginning of the road. The player should take the car down the road one card at a time. If that student answers the card correctly, the car or object may pass to the next card on the road. If the player gets to a card with a reward and answers that card correctly, the player gets to keep that reward. The game ends when the player answers a card incorrectly.

Basketball

Number of Players: 2 or more

Objective: To be on the team with the most baskets made

Items Needed: Something for a goal and a basketball. It could be an actual basketball and basketball net. It could be a miniature basketball and door net. It could be a sock ball and laundry basket. All work.

Instructions: Divide the players into equal teams. Have a player from the first team approach a line about 6 feet from the goal. Show the player a flashcard. If the player can answer the flashcard correctly, that player can take two free-throw shots for the first team. If the player makes a basket, that team gets one point. If the player makes both baskets, the team gets two points. Continue rotating players from opposite teams until all cards have been reviewed or until a pre-determined time has elapsed. The team with the most points at the end of the game wins.

Stack-the-Blocks

Number of Players: 1 or more

Objective: To build the tallest tower

Items Needed: Wooden or cardboard blocks

Instructions: Divide players into teams if playing with more than one player. Take turns showing a flashcard to each player on each team. Every time a player answers a flashcard correctly, that person may add a block to their team's tower. The game ends when both towers come crashing down. The team who had the tallest tower before it fell wins. If playing as an individual, play the game twice and see if the second tower can be built higher than the first.

Kathy L. Gossen seeks to encourage others to live for Jesus every day, no matter what the occasion. She is the owner of CornerstoneConfessions.com and author of several books. including Encompass Preschool Curriculum and And the Word Became Flesh: A 90-Day Chronological Study of the New Testament. If you are looking for more flashcard games, check out Kathy's latest eBook, 40 Fun Flashcard Games for Any Subject.

Determining How and When to Outsource Homeschooling Subjects

Pat Fenner

Are you paralyzed by the thought of teaching physics? Does the concept of tutoring high school chemistry cause your palms to sweat? Does teaching upper levels of math cause your mind to race in fear and panic?

If so, my friend, know that you're not alone .

But also rest assured: You don't have to do it all yourself!

In recent times, I've actually begun to refer to homeschooling using a different term. I find that the image portrayed by the term "homeschooling" is usually quite different than what actually transpires. This revelation has birthed a transformed understanding and approach to our own homeschool, as well. Let me explain.

The Dream

The kids sit around the kitchen table, quietly completing worksheets and checklists while Mom hovers about, teaching and reviewing when needed, and otherwise tending to a range of domestic arts.

While there are times this happens, it is not the norm.

The Reality

Many homeschool families I know have a full calendar of co-op classes; music, art and/or dance lessons; sports; volunteering and/or job responsibilities; and the like. Domestic arts are typically accomplished only when considered part of the curriculum. Additionally, there are often more days spent away from home than at the kitchen table.

As kids get older, they, too, begin to add things to the family "plate" - and having a teen driver in the house doesn't necessarily lighten Mom's load!

Nevertheless, moms often feel like they have to know whatever subjects their children are studying, as if simply by benefit of assuming the title of "homeschool mom," years of study and knowledge of all levels of math and science and history and English have been dropped into their heads.

Is it only me, or does that sound at the very least unreasonable, and, ultimately, a bit crazy?

The answer, of course, is "Yes, yes it does!" And this leads to the new term I use for and a new understanding I have of homeschooling.

The Result: Parent-Directed Education

So I propose we start using the term "parent-directed education" and stop trying to be a "jacks of all trades, masters of none."

The plethora of resources today, both online and offline, offers options to those of us who hold the above fears and limitations (please don't ask me to teach calculus!). The adoption of this concept of education, directed by Mom and Dad but not necessarily carried out by them, will help these same parents implement those external resources.

So how do I know when – and what – to outsource?

Of course we parents have our children's best interests at heart, but we also need to know our own limitations, and how they will affect the format of our efforts.

Factors that might indicate it's time to outsource some learning might be:

- A major family change, such as the arrival of a new baby, a serious illness or death, or Mom needing to go back to work

- The determination that your child has a learning disability or special needs

- The determination that your child has a special skill or ability that might lead to scholarship recognition and require coach-led team training

- Advanced classes that may benefit your academically advanced children as they prepare for college

- Mom feeling overwhelmed at the thought of teaching a particular subject

Now, you might laugh at that last one, but please don't. Being able to humbly seek and ask for help provides valuable character training and is an important life skill. Seeking alternative learning sources teaches our kids how to creatively find solutions for those times that life throws us a monkey wrench or two.

Outsourcing Options

Fortunately, these days, there are many ways to outsource your homeschooling efforts when and if the time comes.

Ask other homeschoolers you know in your area. They may know of classes at the Y or library, or small co-ops in your community. Ideally, your own homeschool support group may have weekly or bi-weekly classes – our family participates in two different co-ops, each of which have unique characteristics that led to our decision to commit to them.

Online classes vary from the "public school at home" type to the more creative "online unit study" type. This option will definitely incorporate knowledge of your child's learning style and age, the vision you have for your homeschool and the goals you have set for your child in order to make a good decision.

The math program that we use with our middle- and high-schoolers does not even require me to correct papers or maintain grades – I get a weekly progress report (which I do review to assess progress or lack thereof) and grades at the end of the semester. Again, find one or two more seasoned parent educators who are willing to share their wisdom with you, or consider short-term coaching to get over this hump.

- It may be possible to **hire a tutor to oversee your child's work** (check your state's homeschool laws). This will require a bit more work setting up, and you may have to use a textbook or curriculum that you are unfamiliar with, but with which the tutor is comfortable. However, this option will allow your child to work independently at home in between tutoring sessions with a real, live person.

- Finally, when high school rears its lovely head, check to see if the local college has a **dual-enrollment program** in which your teen can participate. This is an excellent opportunity for your high-schooler for three reasons. First, it allows teens to take advanced classes taught by college professors, and this totally removes the burden from Mom. Second, it's a great transition for college-bound home-educated children, enabling them to get a bit more familiar with both a classroom environment and the greater college environment before shipping off to parts unknown as a freshman. Finally, it enables them to graduate high school with a few college credits already under their belts – less for you to pay for at a most likely more expensive institution. A true win-win!

So in the end, feeling that you can't teach it all is not a sign of failure, nor is it necessarily a sign that you need to throw in the (homeschool) towel!

Outsourcing parts of your child's education when necessary is a valid call when the whole family is truly engaged in parent-directed education and a lifestyle of learning.

Pat Fenner has been homeschooling her brood of five for more than 20 years. With a passion for encouraging moms as parents and home educators, she shares experience- inspired wisdom with her friend Candy at PatAndCandy.com. Sign up at their site for immediate access to free printables to help you find joy and creativity as a mom and in your homeschool.

Homeschool Educational Methods to Consider

Renee Brown

Trying to understand educational methods can seem overwhelming when you are first starting out, as many might appear to be identical at first glance. But if you look closer, you'll start to see differences and nuances with each type. There are several educational methods common to homeschooling, but there are some you might not be familiar with.

There are many ways to go about choosing a method for your homeschool. For most, it comes down to the preference of the parents, usually the one doing the teaching. Others may choose a method best suited to their students. In fact, it's entirely possible to have a different method for each child in the homeschool setting. However, it might be burdensome for the parent/teacher to keep track of.

The truth is, there is no right way or wrong way to choose a method or educational approach. The right method is whichever works for you, your family and your children.

Classical

The Classical, or Trivium, method is an approach born in ancient Greece and Rome that found its way to Western Europe and eventually America by the 16th century. This is the approach that was used to teach most of the founding fathers of America. Many private schools and homeschools are using this approach because of its simple and natural learning structure.

Generally speaking, the child learns through exposure to a wide array of ideas, from the earliest stages of life. It is based on the Trivium method, which posits students going through three stages of learning: Grammar, Logic and Rhetoric. The Grammar Stage is the memorization of facts, the Logic Stage the age of argument to test those facts, and the Rhetoric Stage is for critical thinking and defense of that knowledge.

Many Christian homeschooling families believe that this approach is also a Biblical model of education, and therefore have adapted it to their homeschools. I suggest if you are considering the Classical approach you read *Teaching the Trivium* by Harvey and Laura Bluedorn.

Charlotte Mason

Charlotte Mason was an educator around the turn of the 20th century. She believed that education centered around three areas of learning: atmosphere, discipline and life. Her approach to education centered on reading using living books, narration, dictation and copywork, utilizing short lessons with great content.

This method incorporates core educational subjects with a strong emphasis on the humanities, like classic literature, art, classical music and poetry. The central theme of this method is that lessons are presented in "living books" made up of classic literature containing lessons surrounding the core subjects.

Delight-Directed

Delight-directed learning takes into account the individual needs, learning styles and interests of each child in the family. The teacher works to gather resources for each child to inspire them to learn. Using those resources as well as core subject curriculum, the teacher structures the child's day and lesson plans. This method incorporates specific core requirements and covers all subjects.

Often delight-directed learning is used in conjunction with another method or approach. It is giving the child a measure of freedom to learn what they want in a way that will be of greatest benefit to them by utilizing their learning style and life interests. While delight-directed learning allows for inspired learning, it does not focus solely on the delights of the child but is more of an asset to the full scope of an educational structure.

Eclectic

The eclectic method incorporates two or more methods to encompass multiple learning approaches into one cohesive form. This is not just a haphazard approach to education, but instead choosing one's own philosophy of education based upon established methods. One might agree with a portion of one philosophy while understanding that what works for one child may not work for another. The Eclectic method brings together styles and philosophies in a way unique to the teacher and student. This allows for a truly customized education to meet a child's needs.

The eclectic homeschool might use traditional textbooks for some subjects of learning while pulling together unit studies for others. One might like the philosophy behind a particular method, like Classical, but find that their student approaches learning better in a Charlotte Mason environment. Therefore, that parent might incorporate a lot of reading into the day while being mindful of the philosophy that he or she wants to use to guide the child.

Homeschooling affords flexibility at its best. An eclectic approach means simply determining what areas you want to teach then choosing a method for each of those areas that you feel best fits your teaching style or your student's learning style.

The Eclectic method may work best for teachers who are able to easily adapt and change course to suit the need. This approach requires one to be flexible and open to thinking outside the box. The parent/teacher has specific educational goals in mind, and makes deliberate and purposeful choices to meet those goals. Students who need to explore in their preferred pace and interest might thrive in an eclectic learning environment.

Montessori

Dr. Maria Montessori (1870-1952) was an Italian educator who believed that, for children, play is work. They learn best when presented with real-life scenarios and have an opportunity to work through their challenges at their own pace to help them to build skill levels.

The Montessori method is a multi-aged, child-centered and self-directed method that places developmental challenges within a child's learning scope. The teacher creates the learning environment and the child — through individual choice — works with what is presented in it. The teacher observes the child and determines when they are ready for additional challenges and subsequently places those challenges in their path. It is up to the child whether to select the challenge.

The Montessori method is based upon her philosophy that there are four planes of learning. Plane One, the time from birth to about age 5, contains three subsets of concepts: the Absorbent, Sensitive and Normalization periods. Plane Two covers from about 6 to 12 years of age, and is the stage where the work of the child is to form intellectual independence, morality and social development. Plane Three is the adolescent stage, where the work of the child is to form and determine their own self in relation to society. Plane Four is an early-adult stage regarding the beginning of independence as an adult in society.

The Montessori method may be best for children who are independent-minded as well as those who are kinesthetic (physical) learners. This approach encompasses language development and hands-on math through sensory processing as well as daily life practical learning.

Montessori schools operate under the umbrella of the International Montessori Foundation. The method can be adapted with materials you have at home or can be found in most educational supply stores.

The Principle Approach

This approach to education is based upon an American Christian history and government philosophy. The approach is grounded in a Biblical Christian worldview and the historical documentation that the American government was founded upon the same worldview. The Principle approach models two philosophies of education, one being the Hebraic philosophy that places the teacher in the role of mentor, and the other the Colonial American Christian heritage, in which Christ and a Biblical form of government are taught in every subject.

The Principle approach places the teacher as the mentor of the child and acknowledges that the parent is given this mandate within the Biblical model for education. The teacher is expected to be a living example for the student to model. This method holds students accountable for their learning, while at the same time valuing the dignity of children so that they can develop to their fullest potential in Christ.

This educational method focuses on the Bible and its teaching in all instruction, applying the principles of Biblical reasoning, Christian character formation and self-discipline as self-governing. This approach incorporates seven principles into the method, with each building upon the other.

- God's Principle of Individuality
- The Principle of Christian Self-Governing
- The Principle of Christian Character
- Conscience is the Most Sacred Property
- The Christian Form of Our Government
- Planting the Seed of Local Government
- American Political Union

Thomas Jefferson Education, TJed

This educational philosophy was written by Oliver and Rachel DeMille. It is based upon seven principles of education and allows for delight-led learning. These seven principles are incorporated over the educational life of the child through four phases. The four phases are the core phase from birth to age 8, the loving learning phase from ages 8 to 12, the scholarly phase from ages 12 to 16, the depth phase from ages 16 to 22.

Following the last stage, each individual sets out in the application phase, where they fulfill their life roles and missions.

This is more of an educational philosophy than a method, but it is gaining in popularity among homeschoolers. It is grounded in a classical reading program and seeks to reflect an education that guides students to become leaders.

Traditional

This is an approach found in most public and many private schools today. This method uses traditional textbooks and workbooks. Generally, lesson plans are formulated by professional educators and included in the materials. Parent teachers can simply follow the lesson plans to instruct students at home. It is ideal for parents who want to see a lot of structure with lessons that are guided by professionals for classroom development.

Unit Studies

Unit studies pull all subjects of learning, or at least as many as possible, together into one topical unit of study. Unit studies are often found in other methods of education, specifically Charlotte Mason, Montessori and Waldorf. These units can be adapted to any style of learning as well.

For example, a unit study about apples might include literature related to apples, vocabulary words related to apples, history related to apples such as the history of Johnny Appleseed, and science about how apple seeds spread, germinate, grow and then redistribute. The lessons could even be expanded to study soil and water, farming, industry and even the economy.

Often teachers who adopt the unit study method will use either notebooking (for journaling), or lapbooks, or both, to document what the child is learning. Notebooking can be done in a variety of ways, but generally a child documents their work by writing, drawing or pasting into a notebook. A lapbook is generally made of a file folder folded in thirds, to which the student adds mini-books made of folded paper. On each of the mini-books, the student presents areas of knowledge they have learned in their study. Both methods are similar, and in many instances some crossover can occur.

With unit studies, the direction and depth of scope are both at the teacher's discretion. You may find that your student becomes so interested in the unit that they continue their research and learning even when school is not in session.

The unit study method may best be suited for students who are kinesthetic learners and who like to be hands-on in their learning style. Children who learn in small amounts might also do well with this approach, since they document small bits of information at a time.

Unschooling

Unschooling is a method that allows for natural learning. This method seeks to allow children the opportunity to learn in their own ways, and at their own pace. The goal of this approach is to let children seek and take ownership of their knowledge in a natural progression from birth through life. The philosophy is that the child, by their natural curiosity, will seek answers to questions, explore the world for understanding, and obtain knowledge through experience.

This approach does not mean that parents cannot teach to their children or that children must only learn on their own. Parents remain active in the lives, education and development of their children. They do this by seeking and fostering the interests of their children and filling their lives with experiences that reflect those interests. In doing so, the children are exposed to real-life learning.

The family suited for the unschooling approach to education is one seeking to provide an organic learning style. They want to provide opportunities to experience life through the arts, books, museums, travel, nature and daily life. There really are no limits to the depth of learning that can be explored in this way.

There are no specific curriculum options for this method.

Waldorf

Developed by Rudolf Steiner in 1919, this method emphasizes the arts while teaching the students through a spiral approach to learning. A student of the Waldorf method may study one subject in depth over a long period of weeks. The scope of the curriculum covers all areas of basic subjects in order to give a base knowledge of experiences so students can choose what is of interest to them.

The Waldorf method also encompasses three stages of learning. These are identified as Imitation, Imagination, and Discrimination and Judgment. Each stage encompasses seven years of life. This method may be ideally suited for children who show artistic tendencies in art, music, dance, crafts or other artistic mediums.

Terms to Know

De-Schooling

This is not a method, but I feel it is important to note this term here. If you are leaving a public school setting and entering the homeschool environment for the first time, you may hear the word "deschooling." This is not to be confused with an "unschooling" method.

Deschooling is a brief period of time taken following a public or private school enrollment to allow children the opportunity to decompress from institutional learning. It gives them a chance to be kids without pressure, and to rediscover their own desire for learning.

At the same time, this gives parents a period of time to research, consider, pray and choose an approach to establishing their homeschool. Many parents rush out to buy curriculum only to find themselves frustrated because their homeschool doesn't function the way they thought it should.

Too often, parents want their homeschool to be a slight reflection of their former institutional school, yet the reality is, a home and family environment simply does not function that way.

During this period, no formal instruction is given. This time period may last several weeks or several months.

No matter the length of time for the break, know that the goal is to prepare heart, mind and attitude toward a different approach to learning and a long-term goal for life education.

Notebooking

Notebooking can be done in a variety of ways, but generally children document their work by writing, drawing or pasting into a notebook. It can be incorporated into a variety of methods. Using notebooks can simply be a tool in the homeschool teacher's toolbox that allows students to create a record of what they are learning. In some cases, it can become the children's preferred method for taking ownership of their learning.

Lapbooking

A lapbook is a simple, concise way to document what a child is learning on any given topic. It can be used as a lesson enhancement or as a central hub to keep you focused on the topic.

A lapbook is generally made of a file folder that is folded in thirds then the student adds in mini-books, which are made of folded paper. On each of the mini-books, students present areas of knowledge they have learned in their study. Lapbooking can be utilized with any method.

Choosing a Method for Your Family

If you are just starting out, don't get overly concerned with identifying your method right away. In fact, there is no real need to identify a method at all. These are simply offered as suggestions for methods that have worked for others. Having a method as a guide can help you to stay focused on achieving the goals you set for your family.

Take your time to try them on to see what fits best for your family.

My teaching method is eclectic. I like the simplicity and overall philosophy of the Classical method and keep it in mind whenever I am planning. Yet I like having the freedom to pull resources from many styles. I use traditional texts in science along with notebooking journals. I use unit studies incorporating the Bible, history, literature and art along with a traditional text as an overall guide. I also will gather from a variety of resources to provide a well-rounded English and language arts study. I will often add in hands-on lessons, as well as specific topic-focused research learning.

My son is an advanced learner who learns best in an immersion environment. That simply means he needs the freedom to flesh out a topic to its fullest until he understands every aspect there is to know about it. By using a variety of teaching methods, I can allow him to explore a topic until it is exhausted while still ensuring he is meeting state requirement for subjects covered.

That's just what works for me and my one child. It may not be ideal for a family with multiple children to approach their schooling in this way. Find what works for your family and, if necessary, you might adopt parts from multiple methods to achieve your objectives. Try not to become overly concerned with methods, learning styles and structure.

The goal is not to reflect a teaching method but to educate your children. You above all other people have their best interest in mind. Let your heart guide you to a path that is right for yourself as the instructor and the individual needs of your children. The structure and method you choose for your family homeschool may not look like any of the previously mentioned methods. The fact is, whatever works best for your family is the right method for you.

When choosing an education method for your children it is important to consider the type of learner they are as well as the style of teaching that you may be comfortable with. Be sure to read Amy Milcic's chapter on learning styles to explore this more.

 *Renée Aleshire Brown is a work-from-home wife of 25 years and mom. She homeschools one child who is currently in eighth grade. She began homeschooling in kindergarten and plans to continue through dual enrollment for college classes. Renée considers herself to be an eclectic homeschooler incorporating various methods into a comprehensive course of study for her son. In addition to homeschooling, she enjoys cooking for family and friends, teaching Bible class in her congregation and writing. Renée works from home as a virtual assistant offering services to other bloggers and small businesses. You can find more of her writing at her home on the web, GreatPeaceAcademy.com. She also has authored two books and co-authored several as well.*

Learning
Resources:
Language Arts
and Literature

Finding and Fostering Your Child's Reading Interests

Christia Colquitt

As an avid reader, I could not wait to share my love of books with my children.

You know those dreams you might have had before you had kids? The ones where you spent afternoons reading books together, a calm, quiet child on your lap, the sun streaming in through the windows, and a book read together out loud.

As a mom of five, I had this dream with each one of my children. I soon realized that each one of my kids has their own personality and tastes. And they are not so quiet and still as I thought they would be!

When teaching my kids to read, I soon found that teaching them to read was not the hard part. Getting them to sit down and read was much harder.

Over my eight years of homeschooling, I have learned that it is much more effective to allow your children choices and to not make reading so serious!

Children are much more interested in books and activities when they have a choice. As Frank Serafini says, "There is no such thing as a child who hates to read, there are only children who have not found the right book."

Let me give you a quick list that might help. Here are 11 ways that I have found to foster my children's reading interests.

1. Find the Perfect Series

Book series are an excellent choice for fostering reading interests. Series allow the reader to gain an attachment to the characters.

I have also found that my kids become more proficient at reading because of the author's style becoming more familiar as they continue reading.

2. Look on Pinterest for Book Lists by Grade or Reading Level

www.the-best-childrens-books.or g is my go-to search engine for new books. My favorites are the lists for guided reading levels, lists by grade, and the list for high interest, low readability books for struggling readers.

3. Read Aloud to Your Children Every Day, No Matter Their Age

Reading aloud is one of the best ways to foster a child's interest in reading. Reading aloud brings the story alive and fosters family time together.

4. Let Your Kids See You Reading

It makes sense that readers raise readers. When children see parents reading, they often want to mimic them. For reading, this is a great thing. It is also fun to swap books and recommendations as children grow.

5. Use Books for Grammar, Writing and English Lessons

Using books for school lessons opens up the world of reading even more. One of my favorite grammar and reading resources is called Daily Grammar Practice and Daily Reading Practice.

Each week, a new passage of literature is chosen. Students spend a whole week on that one passage. Grammar rules and grammar practice are introduced throughout the passage. Reading comprehension and literary elements are introduced throughout the series as well.

Writing about books is a great way to foster both reading and writing interests.

Looking for a great writing program? We love the Arrow program and Bravewriter. Both are wonderful programs focused on literature. Children enjoy repetition and mastering a concept. By using literature for writing prompts, kids can dive into the subject even further!

6. Let Kids Watch the Movie to Get Them Interested in the Book

I used to have the "read the book, then watch the movie" motto. It is what I prefer for myself!

But I soon learned that my younger kids do better at reading comprehension if they have seen the movie first. It helps them to paint the picture in their head by exposure to the story through the movie. It is also fun to do a movie/book comparison at the end.

7. Visit the Library or Bookstore Often

I have often found that these weekly visits to the library or bookstore jumpstart my kids' interests back into reading.

Maybe it is the quiet environment, the cozy chairs, or the smell of the books? Whatever it is, it is a good tactic to foster your children's reading interest.

8. Use Popsicle Sticks and Paintbrushes to Keep Focus

As a mom of four boys (my daughter and I are surrounded by boys!), I have found that they need just a little help staying focused.

This lack of focus used to frustrate me until I realized that this is just how God made little boys!

Using a Popsicle stick or paintbrush to use as they read can help kids stay focused on the words and chapters.

9. During Read-Alouds, Do Not Make Your Kids Sit Completely Still

- While I do make my kids sit, they do not have to be idle.
- Here are some ideas to get you started:
- Provide a snack
- Allow them to chew gum
- Make quiet jewelry, such as yarn jewelry
- Do cardboard weaving
- Thread beads
- Build with LEGO
- Do a puzzle

- Play Tangrams
- Build with Play-Doh
- Bend pipe cleaners
- Use Thinking Putty

10. Use Graphic Organizers

Graphic organizers can be very helpful for kids struggling with reading comprehension. As the story is read, they can write down sequential events or main ideas in the bubbles of the graphic organizer.

11. Do Not Be Picky About What Your Child is Reading

If you are only looking for one takeaway, THIS IS IT! Encourage your kids to read even if it is not a book that interests you. We have all been through the painful days of books that made us cringe. But remember we are raising lifelong readers. That is our goal. It is not our happiness, it is their love of reading!

If you find yourself wanting them to read something more classical than the book they chose, give them a chance. Provide all forms of literature. Over time, your kids will choose books that you both like, especially if you are not too pushy. You have this, mama! Get to reading with your kids and foster that love for books.

Christia Colquitt is a homeschooling mom to five children. She is the proud mommy of four boys and one girl! Her house is loud, fun and filled with laughter, and, of course, super sticky floors! Yet, this was not always the plan! After receiving her degree in biochemistry from the University of Tennessee, she planned on going to dental school. God had other plans, and Christia has

never looked back. Christia is married to 11-year NFL veteran player Dustin Colquitt. They make it their life mission to inspire and help others from all walks of life. Christia wants to share her triumphs and struggles in parenting, marriage, homeschooling, and how to make it all work on her blog, FaithFilledParenting.com.

Homeschooling through the Library

Emily Copeland

"There is more treasure in books than in all the pirate's loot on Treasure Island." – Walt Disney

It's no secret that many homeschool families love spending time at the library. We are one of those families, and we developed that love at the beginning of our homeschool journey.

It didn't take me long to see what a treasure we had in our local libraries. As a new homeschooler, our library visits gave us access to books I didn't know existed. They also kept us from using our homeschool budget on books that were only needed for a few weeks at a time.

Eight years of homeschooling later, I realize now how unnecessary it is to complicate our homeschool plans with lots of curriculum and overzealous ideas found online. I understand now that all we really need is to find the right books and let them be the foundation for our learning.

Using the Library as a Foundation for Homeschooling

We visited the library regularly from the beginning of our homeschool journey, but I was introduced to the concept of homeschooling through the library a couple of years later. For my son's kindergarten year, I used *Learn at Home: Kindergarten* for his curriculum. I also used *Learn at Home: First Grade* the following year. This is where I learned how to use the library for more than random books.

Learn at Home was a single book with clearly organized weekly lesson plans, teaching tips, and a few worksheets to complement the lessons. The series is no longer in print, and it's difficult to find unused copies now, but it was a great match for us at the time. This curriculum covered every subject through easy activities, play and books.

There were no textbooks, and there wasn't an additional list of required reading. It was simple, it was fun, and it was effective. It wasn't perfect – you know, because there is no perfect curriculum – but I learned some wonderful ideas from it that I still use today. That's where homeschooling through the library comes into the picture.

Our time learning through the library has changed since then, but the concept remains the same: Choose the topics and let library books do the heavy lifting. Here's how to make it work in your homeschool.

Start With a Plan

While you could certainly walk into the library and check out the books that seem interesting to your kids, having a plan is a better option. You need a plan or a goal to give you the direction needed to make this work for you. This plan could come in the form of Rebecca Rupp's *Home Learning Year by Year*, Jamie Martin's *Give Your Child the World*, Gladys Hunt's *Honey for a Child's Heart*, the Five in a Row curriculum or something similar.

These guides could all serve as the foundation for your homeschool days because they not only provide book suggestions, but they also let you know what those suggestions will accomplish. That kind of direction goes a long way, whether you're using the resources at your library to teach one of your homeschool subjects or all of them.

Get to Work

Find your library sweet spot. We have more library memberships than normal people ought to have. It's maddening to keep up with which books are due at each location and when they are due. It also gets to be a bit much in the way of late fees!

I put an end to those library struggles by coming up with a library log and by joining yet another library system. This membership was different from the rest, though. We paid a small fee to be members of a library system a bit farther away because of its huge circulation and numerous benefits. This new membership showed us the value of finding our sweet spot.

By going farther out, we've been able to find everything we need in one place. Finding everything in one place has streamlined my book searches and borrowing process. For us, the closest branches don't meet our needs as homeschoolers. You may find the same thing to be true for your library needs.

Know how your library works. You need to be familiar with book limits, checkout durations, request and renewal procedures and the general physical layout in order to maximize library benefits for your homeschool. It also helps to be aware of the library's extra offerings. Be on the lookout for programs for children, teenagers and families in general.

Research and request books ahead of time. Some libraries are a part of cooperative systems that allow them to share books with other libraries. For homeschoolers, that means the books we need may not be available on demand. That's why it helps to search your library database several weeks before specific books are needed and make any requests at that time. While it may not matter if you're learning about marsupials a few weeks later than planned, it won't be helpful to receive the Thanksgiving books you requested a week before Christmas.

Explore your borrowing choices. Don't forget that most libraries have a good selection of audiobooks, e-books, DVDs and CDs available for borrowing. We've even found educational games and manipulatives at the library before! No two libraries are the same, so it always helps to ask about these things at each branch you visit.

And, if you can't find the specific titles needed, look for an alternative. It's nice to be able to find exact recommendations, but chances are your library will have another book that will work to accomplish the same goal if you can't find a title.

Beyond the Books

While the access to a world of great books is enough reason to use your library for homeschooling, there's more to your library than books. The programs and resources vary from library to library and sometimes season to season, but if you stay informed about what's happening, it shouldn't take long to find even more reasons to love your library.

We've participated in wonderful library programs in all of the libraries we've used, from the big city library branches to the small town libraries, and the ones in between. Beyond the books, here are some ways we've put our libraries to work in our homeschool.

Weekly Story Time: Story time is usually designed for preschoolers and younger children, but we've enjoyed our share of library story hours over the years.

Summer Reading Programs: These reading programs are a great way to motivate your kids to read in the summer, especially if your homeschool follows the public school calendar.

STEM Workshops: Our favorite was a LEGO Robotics class we enjoyed – for free, mind you – through our library.

Animal Adventures: It's not every day that you get to hold a snake while visiting the library, but we've held all kinds of creatures through zoology programs at our libraries. This has been true for multiple libraries, too, even the small-town locations!

Online Classes: It's not uncommon for libraries to offer adult classes for anything from quilting to basic computer skills, but my library takes it up a notch. As a library patron, I enjoy free access to online art and music classes for the kids, continuing education for teachers and all kinds of business classes.

Family Fitness Classes: Need a change in scenery for homeschool physical education? No problem! Between yoga and the weekly read-and-dance get-together in our children's department, a trip to the library is anything but stuffy and boring!

Hopefully you can see that homeschooling through the library is easy and that it's helpful in building a lifetime love for learning. All it really takes is a good library, a plan and a stack of books to get started.

 *Emily Copeland is a homeschooling mother of two children and wife to a church-planting minister. She writes at TableLifeBlog.com, where she shares encouragement and ideas for homeschooling, family life, ministry and living with purpose.*

Family Literacy: The Secret to Raising a Writer

Ginny Kochis

I'm going to let you in on a secret. I'm a writing teacher, and I don't believe in writing curricula.

On the first day of my professional career, I stood in front of as many ninth-graders as I was years old, convinced that a solid curriculum and lots of practice were the keys to solid writing.

After almost two decades of teaching in classrooms, community colleges, private tutoring sessions, homeschool co-ops and my own homeschool, I've changed my approach. I don't have benchmarks; I don't follow a scope or sequence. Instead, there are opportunities for authentic discussion and an end to the struggles plaguing children who say they don't like to write.

Anyone can be a writer. Anyone can raise a writer. Here's how to make that a reality.

The Theory

I grew up surrounded by books. My father was a librarian, and we had an extensive library of titles across multiple genres. He would read to us or we would read on our own, sitting in the same room the way some families gathered to watch television. We discussed the books, too, challenging ideas and evaluating elements of style. One of my most treasured memories is discussing the works of Edgar Allan Poe with my father. I knew all about Poe as a master of Gothic literature before I reached sixth grade.

My parents raised us in a literacy-rich environment. I'm grateful, because such a home exposed us to elements of style, organization and voice we wouldn't have picked up elsewhere. When children are exposed to the likes of Shakespeare and Dickinson from the beginning, they develop an ear for rhythm. They learn to vary sentence structure through exposure to Fitzgerald, Hemingway, Silverstein and Sendak. Lewis, Tolkien, Nesbit and Potter offer a study of detail and description as a means to build character. And authors like Milne, Dahl, Cleary and Estes open a window into the mind of a child, offering insight into point of view.

So, like my father did with me and my sister, I talk to my children about the decisions authors make. We might consider the opposite point of view and argue it, or relate it to the hard questions and tough issues in current events. All of this is integral to building a writer. Kids who observe their parents thinking will become thinkers themselves, and this will translate into their writing.

The Practice

The application of this theory is a communal effort. In addition to reading and discussing ideas together, families interested in this approach should try the following: Write as a family. Strong writers recognize the value of sharing their work with others, and of developing an appropriate sense of audience and tone.

Writing as a family facilitates this, from making composition a communal act to exploring different forms and topics. It also increases the comfort level: If everyone else is doing it, then maybe I can, too.

How does a family write together?

Keep a family notebook. Put it in a central location and write messages to one another throughout the day. You can also add a family writing prompt; pick one out of a hat each morning or assign it at the beginning of the day

Use family photos to inspire writing. Display a photo, then ask your family to write what they remember about that day. How many details can you record? How would you describe that experience?

Write your own scavenger hunts, complete with riddle-like clues and an outdoor adventure. Tie it into your plans for the day (such as a nature walk for science or museum exploration for history) and you've worked in cross-curricular writing.

You can also **use nonstandard media**. The act of writing is still part of the process (and more approachable) even if the final product isn't typed and printed out. Need some ideas? You could make your favorite novel into a play or movie. Or write and perform a song about a topic in history.

This type of activity helps your child see writing as tangible, with ideas that live and breathe beyond the pen and paper.

Avoid empty praise. Phrases like "Good job!" and "This is great!" can communicate an unintended lack of interest. Celebrate accomplishments made through specific comments about what you like:

- You have worked so hard on this. I know it was a struggle and I'm proud of the poem/essay/project you've created.

- You prove your point really well. Tell me why you chose these examples as evidence.
- I can totally imagine what it's like to be in this magical place. Your description is perfect.

Comments like this not only reveal you've read the finished product, but also that you've paid attention to the process.

Challenge big ideas. Another way to offer support is through challenge. Encourage your children to consider what they think and question why they think it. What better way to strengthen your own belief systems (or maybe change your mind) than to consider the opposing view? Try asking the following questions:

- What would someone say who disagrees with you?
- How would you refute that opinion?
- What about looking at it from this angle?
- Have you considered exploring this aspect?

It's a bit like playing devil's advocate for an angelic purpose: Pondering bigger questions encourages deep thinking, and deep thinking feeds strong writing.

The Conviction

Raising a writer isn't about the curriculum you choose or the workshops you attend. It's not even about the quantity or quality of the writing assignments you give. Raising a writer is teaching your children to think critically about the world around them, then providing them with the tools to express those thoughts effectively, efficiently, creatively and uniquely. Raising a writer is raising a thinker, and the best part is - it starts at home, with you.

Ginny Kochis is a former high school English teacher and adjunct professor turned homeschooling mom to three gifted, twice-exceptional kiddos. A Teacher Consultant for the Northern Virginia Writing Project and owner of The Writing Well Educational Services, Ginny supports families in their efforts to think critically and write effectively. Ginny writes about family literacy, mothering, homeschooling twice-exceptional children and Catholicism on her blog, NotSoFormulaic.com. She can also eat an entire carton of ice cream in one sitting, but only if no one is looking.

How to Teach With Living Books

Jamie Erickson

When my homeschool days are boxed up and beautifully archived in family scrapbooks and digital iMovies, I know there will be certain bits and pieces of these years that stand out more than others. These are moments that are permanently etched in my mind, memories of learning and laughing together that not only molded the minds of my kids but also shaped the content of their character and helped to forge our relationship.

I know this because I can look back in the 10 homeschooling years we've already shared and can pick out a few of these very moments. Not surprisingly, so many of them are woven with one common thread: carefully selected living books.

From the beginning, we filled our days with them. We anchored all of our learning on them. We passed on those dry-as-dust history textbooks and chose real books instead. And why not? Living books are steeped in literary-rich language. They focus on the bigger picture, not just names and dates. They provide a third dimension to an otherwise two-dimensional study. In short, they're just more interesting, more enchanting.

But what exactly are living books, and how do you plan an entire education around them?

What Are Living Books?

Simply put, living books are true books; books that can be found at the library or a local bookstore. Living books would include biographies, historical fiction, engaging non-fiction, picture books or memoirs. They are books that tell stories; that paint pictures; that fill in the gaps between facts on a page and an authentic look at the people, places, things and events that shape the world.

The opposite of a living book would be a traditional textbook, the kind that most kids can't wait to toss aside come summer's eve. To me, discovering new information through a textbook vs. a living book is the difference between hearing a lecture and participating in a conversation. One catalogs black-and-white facts, while the other narrates humanity in a way that draws a reader toward a new thought, a question, a discovery or a conviction.

Why Use Living Books?

Living books encourage a lifelong love of learning. Once children learn to read, they can read to learn. Since living books are written by experts in a particular field and/or authors who use well-chosen words to craft engaging stories, they are interesting to read. They naturally compel a reader to want to read more.

Reading a living book is kind of an "If you give a mouse a cookie" scenario. Your child might read a biography about Robert E. Lee, which might propel him to want to learn more about the Civil War. A book about the Civil War could inspire him to look at the life of President Lincoln. While reading about Lincoln, he might grow a curiosity about the office of president, which might lead to a book about Ulysses S. Grant.

Books of General Grant will arouse more questions about General Lee. Mouse. Cookie. Exploration every time.

As an added bonus, living books pair perfectly with a homeschooling lifestyle, especially for large families. They are cheap and come at the low, low price of a public library card.

All kids, no matter their ages, can be learning about the same topic by reading a book at their own reading level. Living books teach children how to think, not what to think. By reading a variety of books about the same topic, children can consult the opinions of many authors and have a broader view of what they are reading.

This helps them to make better, more educated assumptions or decisions about what they have learned. They never have to fear that science has been editorialized or that history has been rewritten by any particular authors, because they have looked at the topic from many layers and perspectives.

Living books can be used across the curriculum and can be added to any method of education. So, whether you choose to homeschool with a traditional textbook approach, a unit study method, or with hands-on projects, you can always add a living book to enhance and add depth to the learning.

Finally, living books help to teach good writing and communications skills. If you want your children to become good writers, you have to introduce them to good writing. In other words, before children can learn to write well, they first have to recognize what good writing looks like, feels like and lays like on the page.

In the same way babies learn to speak by copying the sentence patterns, voice inflection and accents of those around them, children learn to write by copying the writings of others. Once they have developed a palate or taste for good writing and built up a storehouse of rich words and sentences, they can then begin to deconstruct all those words and sentences in order to form new ones of their own. In providing real books, books clothed in beautifully crafted words, you are helping to cultivate great communication skills within your kids.

How Do You Teach With a Living Book?

Truthfully, teaching from a living book can be as easy as picking out a book and handing it to your children to read. Or better yet, reading it with them. But, for the sake of a long-range education, there can, and probably should, be a bit more method than madness.

While I recognize there are many wonderful ready-made living literature curriculums, I have learned over the years that I'm more of a DIY kind of homeschool mom. I much prefer to cull resources myself in order to create a tailor-made education for my kids.

That being said, I'm just one mom with a finite amount of time and energy in my day. I can't be inventing the wheel for every subject and for every topic. So, I've developed a quick, just-add-water-and-stir system for learning through living books.

Because I am an eclectic homeschooler and use all different methods of learning, I don't necessarily use living books for every area of study. I typically save them for content-rich subjects like history, science, Bible, life skills, geography and world cultures.

With the exception of history, when beginning the planning stages of a living literature unit, I start by conducting what can simply be called a whatcha-wanna-learn-next-year brainstorming session with my kids. For the most part, content-rich subjects can be taught based on the natural interests and curiosities of the learners. In other words, there is no hard-and-fast rule that says kids HAVE to learn (fill in the blank) in any particular order. So, I let the natural curiosities of my kids drive my choices.

Our brainstorming session usually goes a little something like this:

Sit Down Together

TOGETHER is crucial because a discussion always evokes more ideas when there's more vs. less. (My idea strikes a chord with you. You toss out an idea based on mine. She throws out a thought that was birthed from yours. And he flings out a random notion that doesn't have anything to do with anyone else's suggestion, but strikes up an entirely new line of thoughts. And so on...)

I pose the following key questions to get the ideas flowing:

- What have you liked learning about most this year?
- Was there something that we learned that you'd like to explore further?
- Is there a question that you've always wanted to know the answer to?
- What was your favorite project that we made/created this year?
- What would you like to learn about in (insert subject name) this year?

I toss out the questions; I listen intently; and then I write. I jot down all of their curiosities, all of their I've-always-wanted-to-knows. And smile.

Because we've been doing this for a few years, they know that it is not possible nor probable for me to be able to cram all of their wants and wishes of learning into one year. But they know I've not just heard them, I've *listened* to them and will, to the best of my ability, design a course of study that has them and their delights in mind.

While this type of organic planning seems to work really well with non-linear subjects like science and geography, sequential subjects like history and Bible need to be a bit more premeditated and routine. For the most part, we just camp on the next era in the historical timeline and move forward with chronologically-ordered living books until we've exhausted that time period.

Consult a Spine

Once a topic of study has been chosen, it's time to whittle it down into logical subtopics. Again, for history this just follows the natural timeline of the major people, places and things in that era of history. For other content-rich subjects, the subtopics can often be organized in any order that I choose.

Since I'm not a knower-of-all-things, I consult a spine book to help me figure out which subtopics need to be addressed within the unit. A spine is just a encyclopedic or textbook-type book that paints a really broad picture of the topic.

For example, one year, I created a human anatomy unit for science. When planning the unit, I looked through the table of contents pages of a human body reference-type book and wrote down the subtitles for each major section of the book.

The subtitles were as follows:

- dermal system
- skeletal system
- muscular system

- nervous system
- endocrine system
- cardiovascular system
- lymphatic system
- respiratory system
- digestive system
- urinary system
- reproductive system

At that point, I could have written down sub-subtopics under each of the subtopics, but I chose not to do so.

When consulting a spine book, I don't necessarily read it. I just take note of the major sections and subsections within the broader topic of study to give me a general direction.

Make a Library List

After organizing the subtopics, I start my book search. I scan our personal library shelves, our public library's online catalog and my state's interlibrary loan system for books that relate to the subtopics.

Since I'm kind of a self-proclaimed book snob, I don't just want to use any old books in my unit plans. I want only the best. I want living literature... non-fiction books that captivate, biographies that inspire, fiction books clothed in beauty, virtue, and truth. I want language-rich reading.

For history, that means I usually consult my TruthQuest guides, a lengthy list of exceptional history series books that I've compiled over the years, or a few authors that I love, which include but are not limited to the following: David Adler, Jean Fritz, Ingri and Edgar Parin d'Aulaire, and Holling C. Holling

For science, that means I start with books from the following: Usborne, Answers in Genesis, my favorite nature study books and field guides, and any physical science books by David Macaulay

I choose from these, find others, and begin plugging the titles into my tentative plans for each subtopic.

Organize the Books

About two weeks before school starts, I begin requesting books from the library. I request the first few books on my list. A week later, I request a few more. Throughout the year, I'm continually looking one or two weeks ahead in my book list to request books that I will want in order to provide my local public library branch enough time to procure the titles before I need them. When books arrive at my library, I pick them up and consult my book list once again. This time, I use the list to organize the books chronologically or topically in a book basket, placing the first book in the front of the stack.

Since I have both older and younger kids, I preorder a mix of picture books and chapter books in my library requests. The picture books get placed in the basket to be read aloud to everyone, while the chapter books are divided. Some get placed in the basket and some are handed to individual children to be read as an individual assignment, usually a chapter a day until completion.

Read the Books

Each day when it is time for that particular subject, I take the next book out of the book basket and begin to read. In full disclosure, I usually save our content-rich subjects for snack time. With hands and mouths full of a tasty treat, my kids (even the youngest ones) are a captive and captivated audience. I can read longer portions of a book with fewer interruptions.

The length of our reading time varies from day to day. For the most part, I let my children's attention span, or lack thereof (ahem), determine when we stop reading. Throughout the reading, we discuss, consult maps and ask questions.

Often, our reading will lead us to watch a YouTube video or to do a hands-on project. We might finish with Charlotte-Mason style notebooking using a blank steno notebook or ready-made notebooking templates from my favorite resource, Notebooking Pages. Or perhaps we might do nothing but close the book and move on with the rest of our day. What we do not do is fill out a worksheet or answer comprehension questions. It's just not necessary to belabor and bog down the learning with any of those. The book and a simple discussion supplies a stand-alone education.

If we've completed the book, I make a note of it in a spreadsheet to be printed out for our end-of-the-year homeschool portfolio and then place the book in a pile to be returned to the library. But, if not, I put the book back in the front of the basket to be enjoyed more tomorrow.

A short explanation or segue is sometimes needed from one book to the next. This is where the original spine book comes in handy. I just read a short excerpt from the spine that helps connect one important topic to another.

The next day, it's just lather-rinse-repeat until we've read through the entire list of books or until I feel my kids have a firm grasp on the topic, whichever comes first.

Living book learning really is that simple. It's not rocket science. It's just pairing great books with great conversation. It's inviting a child to dig deeper by reading more. It's carving out time for togetherness.

How Do You Simplify Living Literature Learning?

While I love combing the library for treasures and compiling my list of books every year, I realize not everyone has the time or the desire to do so. But learning through books doesn't have to be overwhelming or time consuming. You don't have to invent the wheel to still use living books. There are several great, ready-made programs designed to point you to just the right titles at just the right ages and stages of your kids. While certainly not exhaustive, here is a list of some of the top living-book-based curriculums for home education. Whether you prefer a simple list of book suggestions or a more structured traditional curriculum complete with study guides and discussion questions, there's something for everyone.

Ambleside Online

Patterned after Charlotte Mason's original teaching methods, Ambleside Online is a completely free, online course schedule with suggestions for daily reading, narration and copywork assignments. Since most of the books listed are classics and time-tested, many are out of print and difficult to find. However, all the harder-to-find books can be read digitally on public domain websites. Yearly schedules are divided into three terms and include every subject except math.

Age Range: Kindergarten through 12th grade

Topics Covered: Full curriculum except for math

Worldview: Christian

Beautiful Feet Books

Beautiful Feet Books is one of the most time-tested living book curriculums on the market today. Designed to be more of an advisor than a schedule, the study guides include booklists, discussion questions, timeline and notebooking suggestions, and writing prompts for further research and independent learning. Unlike most history programs, Beautiful Feet Books does not teach history chronologically. The lesson guides purposely begin with American History and then cycle back to Ancient History.

Age Range: Kindergarten through 12th grade

Topics Covered: Ancient, world and U.S. History, history of the horse, history of California, geography, history of classical music, gentle science and character training

Worldview: Christian with an emphasis on Scripture and Biblical values

BookShark

Owned by the parent company Sonlight, BookShark is a complete curriculum. However, only their Reading with History and Science programs use living books. Don't let that deter you from adding BookShark books to what you are already using for language arts and math to create a one-of-a-kind curriculum that works for you and your kids.

Age Range: Kindergarten through eighth grade (4-day-a-week program)

Topics Covered: Full core curriculum, but living books are limited to history and science

Worldview: Secular

Five in a Row

The original Five in a Row is a literature-based unit study curriculum. Parents are encouraged to read a particular picture book (or chapter book, for upper grades) out loud to their child every day for an entire week and use the storyline of that book to teach the foundational concepts of math, language arts, history, science and art with hands-on projects.

Age Range: 2- to 12-year-olds

Topics Covered: Full curriculum

Worldview: Christian with an emphasis on character training

Heart of Dakota

Designed for use with multiple ages, Heart of Dakota is a Christ-centered history and science curriculum suited for large families. There are also additional elements that incorporate language arts and math exploration, but some homeschoolers would not consider this a complete program. Like Beautiful Feet Books, Heart of Dakota teaches American history to young children first and then transitions to ancient history.

Age Range: Pre-kindergarten through 12th grade

Topics Covered: History, science, handwriting, Bible, character, language arts and math exploration

Worldview: Christian with an emphasis on God's providence and Christian living

Illuminations

Illuminations combines course spine books (Mystery of History and All American History) with living books, notebooking and graphic organizers, and a completely customizable digital curriculum grid to create a hybrid living book program. The program is designed for family-style learning, allowing for multiple children to learn the same topic at different grade levels. The only thing not included in the program is a math component.

Age Range: Third through 12th grades (with suggestions for younger kids to join in on the family learning)

Topics Covered: Full curriculum except for math

Worldview: Christian

Living Books Curriculum

Known for its gentle and flexible schedule, Living Books Curriculum is designed for a 36-week school year divided into four eight-week terms, with a ninth flex week between each term for catching up on unfinished work. The teacher's guide contains reading assignments and activities with each lesson. Unlike most curricula, LBC includes study of both U.S. and world history each week. Sample lessons and book lists can be downloaded for free.

Age Range: Kindergarten through eighth grades, with suggestions for high school

Topics Covered: Traditional Charlotte Mason schedule including core subjects as well as nature study, picture study and composer study; math not included

Worldview: Christian

Logos Press

Using both a four- and a five-day scheduling plan, Logos Press provides a living book approach to science with a classical twist. The curriculum is designed for a three-year cycle so that students can repeat biology, chemistry and physical science at all three stages of the Trivium learning model. Living books and individual project kits can be purchased from the website. Full curriculum online classes with a classical model are available for students in junior high and high school.

Age Range: First through 12th grades

Topics Covered: Printed lesson plans are science only (elementary); online classes are full curriculum (junior high and high school)

Worldview: Christian with an emphasis on classical literature

Moving Beyond the Page

Moving Beyond the Page combines living books with project-based learning and unit studies. Lessons are taught through four nine-week units that each emphasize a particular concept. At the end of each concept, children are required to present a project that summarizes what was learned. In addition to living books and project kits, much of the learning comes from printable worksheets.

Age Range: 5- to 14-year-olds

Topics Covered: Language arts, science, social studies

Worldview: Secular

My Father's World

Designed with a unique family learning cycle, My Father's World is a living book curriculum combined with both a unit study and classical educational model. Geography and history are the two major components of the program as it has a missional and world cultures emphasis. All other subjects are woven in gently. The program is divided into three major age groups (pre-kindergarten through third grade, third through eighth grades, and ninth through 12th grades) so that families with multiple ages can be learning together.

Age Range: Pre-kindergarten through 12th grade

Topics Covered: Full curriculum except for math

Worldview: Christian with an emphasis on world cultures

Simply Charlotte Mason

Simply Charlotte Mason, which started as a website designed to partner with Charlotte Mason style homeschoolers, has become a place to purchase downloadable guides and lesson plans. The Bible is incorporated into much of the learning. Lessons use both living books one could find at the library as well as books specifically written for the program. Emphasis is placed on copywork, narration and dictation of books. The materials are designed for family learning, so grade levels are not indicated. Each level of materials provides book and activity suggestions for each age range. Once they have completed level one, a family can move on to level two, and so on.

Age Range: All ages

Topics Covered: Full curriculum

Worldview: Christian

Sonlight

Seeking to partner with families to raise globally literate kids, Sonlight approaches history with a geographic and missional emphasis. Oral narrations, timelines and history-centered read-alouds make up the core of the program. Lesson plans can be tailored to a four-day or a five-day schedule. Other subjects including Bible, science and language arts can be purchased and added to make a complete and rigorous program.

Age Range: Pre-kindergarten through 12th grade

Topics Covered: Mostly history, but can be expanded to include all subjects

Worldview: Christian with an emphasis on global missions

Tapestry of Grace

Tapestry of Grace could be considered a classical program that combines living books and hands-on projects. The entire course is divided into four large historical units. During the duration of their education, all students cycle through each unit four times, with everyone learning at the appropriate level. Each daily lesson features living books and hands-on activities for all of the four classical learning tiers, lower grammar (kindergarten through third grade), upper grammar (third through sixth grades), dialectic (sixth through ninth grades) and rhetoric (ninth through 12th grades). A separate Primer course is available for preschoolers.

Age Range: Pre-kindergarten through 12th grade

Topics Covered: Full curriculum except for math

Worldview: Christian with an emphasis on church history

TruthQuest

A self-paced program, TruthQuest provides an elaborate book list of both current and out-of-print titles arranged by grade level. All members of a family can be learning about the same era in history while enjoying books at an individual reading level. Book lists, historical background summaries and occasional narrations make up the bulk of the TruthQuest guides. Companion notebooking and lapbooking packs can be purchased separately.

Age Range: Pre-kindergarten through 12th grade

Topics Covered: History only

Worldview: Christian

A Final Thought

Charlotte Mason in her *Towards a Philosophy of Education* wrote, "To introduce children to literature is to install them in a very rich and glorious kingdom, to bring a continual holiday to their doors, to lay before them a feast exquisitely served. But they must learn to know literature by being familiar with it from the very first. A child's intercourse must always be with good books, the best that we can find."

While you could spend thousands of dollars buying the latest hands-on project kits, digital apps and critically acclaimed textbooks, none of those will inspire learning quite like the pages of a real book. Introduce them early. Have them available always. Step back and watch as your child opens the door to the great conversations of humanity simply by turning the pages of a book with life, a living book.

Jamie is the founder of TheUnlikelyHomeschool.com. She left her big city life to follow love all the way to a real-life Mayberry. After earning her bachelor's degree in elementary education, working for the nation's leading homeschooling curriculum company and teaching in a traditional classroom, she had babies, lots of them, and decided to point her gaze toward home. When she's not curating memories, hoarding vintage books or playing ringmaster to her own live-in circus of seven, she can be found writing, speaking and trying to stay warm in the upper Midwest.

How Memorization and Narration Benefit Your Child

Lara Molettiere

Memorization has gotten a bad reputation over the years from a focus on memorizing data for testing. However, memorization and narration are both incredible tools for learning and for developing excellent recall.

Memorization

Memorization has multiple benefits.

Starting at a young age, memorization of nursery rhymes helps children learn rhyming patterns and word patterns, and teaches word symmetry.

Memorization aids in neuroplasticity. That is, it allows the brain to form new neural connections and continue building new pathways on which information and recall can travel. This is something that benefits all ages and stages of life.

Memorization teaches your brain to remember and frees up brain power for other functions. If you know that 9 multiplied by 9 is 81, then you don't have to use brain power to calculate it and that extra bit of electricity can be used to make other connections.

Like logic puzzles and games, memorization helps keep your brain strong. The challenges of memorization are like a workout for your thinking muscles. And the more your children work those muscles out over the course of their lives, the easier it will be to keep their cognitive function up as they age.

Start the habit of memorization while they are young for lifelong benefits.

Some ideas of things your children can memorize are: nursery rhymes, Bible verses, quotes, historical dates, events, names, poems, hymns and songs, and sections of speeches and historical documents.

Narration

Narration is the result of an exercise in diligent listening. Narration is telling back, in your children's own words, of what has been read to them or what they have read on their own. Young children benefit from short narrations that are transcribed by parents, while older students can tell or write more detailed narrations of longer reading selections.

The benefits of narration are increased attention to material, better expressive language, broader vocabularies and increased retention of material. It is also an excellent method for students to clarify, for their own sakes, what they are learning from their studies. This valuable skill is an asset in higher education and in conflict resolution.

Narration is accomplished by telling the child that you are going to read a particular book or passage, and explaining that you want them to tell you what they heard after it is finished. Begin by first reading short passages to young learners, such as *Aesop's Fables*, and having them recite back from memory their own interpretations. Older children can be read more in-depth passages, poetry and classic literature, and can write out their narrations in notebooks for later review.

Narration is also a wonderful activity to spend time with your children intentionally enjoying their budding minds, fostering more in-depth conversations, and learning what details pique their interest. The discussions from narrations are often deeper and more meaningful than the piece they are taken from.

Here are some read-Aloud narration suggestions by age:

6 to 8 years old

- Aesop's Fables
- Where the Sidewalk Ends by Shel Silverstein
- The Wind in the Willows by Kenneth Grahame
- Stopping by Woods on a Snowy Evening by Robert Frost
- *Charlotte's Web* by E. B. White

8 to 10 years old

- Little House in the Big Woods by Laura Ingalls Wilder
- The Tale of Despereaux by Kate DiCamillo
- *Peter Pan* by J.M. Barrie
- Alice in Wonderland by Lewis Carroll
- The Lion, The Witch, and The Wardrobe by C.S. Lewis

10 to 12 years old

- *Tanglewood Tales* by Nathaniel Hawthorne

- The Green Ember by S.D. Smith
- *The Hobbit* by J.R.R. Tolkein
- Across Five Aprils by Irene Hunt
- Carry On, Mr. Bowditch by Jean Lee Latham

12 and older

- Shakespeare's comedies and tragedies
- The Constitution of the United States
- The Bible
- The Pilgrim's Progress by John Bunyan
- *The Valley of Vision* by Arthur G. Bennett

When your children are narrating, let them use their own words, but help them along with open-ended questions when needed. Facilitate deeper discussions and enjoy your time together learning in a conversational way.

Lara Molettiere is a writer and homeschool cultivator. Wife to John and mother to Mr. T and Mr. F, she shares encouragement, homeschooling ideas, printables and more at her blog Everyday Graces, laramolettiere.com.

Forming a Family or School Book Club

Ticia Messing

A few years ago, I went to a homeschool convention. I eagerly looked forward to attending a session on forming family or school co-op book clubs. I furiously scribbled notes as the speaker talked about the horrors of the boring required reading because it was "classic." Instead, he said, look at the books you loved reading as a kid. Look at the books that made you think, or gave you a new outlook on life, or made you so mad you threw them against the wall.

I breathed a sigh of relief as I heard this. I would not have to suffer through Charles Dickens' *Great Expectations* again.

I started brainstorming all of the books I wanted my kids to read. I thought of the boxes of books I saved from my childhood, and all of the ones I'd read for high school and college classes that I'd enjoyed.

And then I trimmed that list to a more realistic size.

I started thinking about the required-reading books that I thought actually led to a good discussion. *Great Expectations* was left off the list, as was *Hiroshima*, the only book in my school career I didn't finish (in my defense, I'd forgotten the due date, and I was having trouble keeping the characters straight). I added in *Animal Farm* and *Brave New World*. I contemplated which of Shakespeare's plays we would read, and which ones we would only attend at the local Shakespeare festival.

And I edited my list again.

After all of this, I looked at my kids, who were reading on roughly a third-grade level, and remembered the large number of children's books that have been made into movies. I also remembered how many of those books I had loved as a child.

I threw my initial list out. It's still nominally hiding somewhere in my mind, to be resurrected when we're tired of the method that we created, but we are loving it right now.

The Birth of A Book and a Movie

Ages ago, some book was made into a movie. This is so far removed into the dim recesses of time that I can't tell you what book it was. I *can* tell you that, like any good homeschool mom, I said, "You can't watch the movie until you've read the book." By the time they'd read the book, the movie was out of the theaters, so we sat down together and we brainstormed what snacks we would eat with our movie at home.

We came up with all sorts of themed snacks, and ideas to try out with it. In the end, our counters were filled with treats that would delight any foodie.

But I still needed to know they'd actually read the books, and not just said they had, so I challenged the kids to come up with a project to go with the book. They created complex Minecraft worlds, skits of favorite scenes or Lego creations, and it was clear they'd read the book.

And we talked.

We didn't follow a study guide (though there are plenty of wonderful study guides to be found if you want them). We just theorized why one character acted the way he did, or why some animals could talk and others couldn't.

I knew for sure I was on the right track when the kids were playing one day and the characters from the book showed up in their play, and I heard them using the words from the book.

As an ultimate culmination, we watched the movie. And we talked more. Which did we like better, the book or the movie? How did the movie change the book? Why did the movie make the choices it did? Why did they so thoroughly butcher the book?

Let's generalize this approach to your family.

Pick What You Want to Read

Let's go back to that talk I heard. What books are you dying for your kids to read? Maybe you don't like movies, and don't want to take my book-and-movie plan, but you absolutely loved *The Baby-Sitters Club* series as a kid (and there is a movie, in case you're wondering). You learned a lot about friendship and life reading those books. Pick a few to read and talk about with your kids.

If you're like my brother and hated reading as a kid, and proudly managed to graduate from high school without reading a single book, then look at some of the suggested reading lists and read some of those books with your kids.

The important thing is to pick books and get reading. You can get something from the most poorly written book ever, even if it's "Wow, how did that get published?"

How Will You Assess?

If this is just for fun, there's no real need to think about this part, but I'm assuming since you're forming a book club, you want to in some way assess what your children or the other participants are reading.

Do you want a traditional pen-and-paper test, or an essay?

Do you want a diorama or a book report?

Do you want a discussion?

Think through what you want from this. If you want a traditional report, you might consider looking at any of the many book study guides you can buy.

If you want a discussion, as you're reading the book, write down questions to talk about.

If you want a project, give the kids some kind of standard to work toward. I eventually had to outlaw skits for a time because watching three different skits on how a character died in *Johnny Tremain* was not fun. I had to do similar with Minecraft worlds because the kids turned it into an excuse to play, but did not really create something resembling the world.

How Often Will You Go Through a Book?

This is really going to depend on your children, and on how difficult the book is.

With some books, I thought they would take my kids a long time, and they flew through them in a few days. Others that I thought they would fly through, they dragged their feet.

 Ticia is a homeschooling mom to three elementary kids, twin boys and a little girl. She loves to make their learning hands on, and delights in making history fun. You can find Ticia at her blog adventuresinmommydom.org

Learning Resources:
STEM

science, technology, engineering, math

Hands-On Homeschool Geography

Ticia Messing

I have three very active kids. That means a paper-and-pencil geography program is not going to go over well at my house. For a very short time, I attempted a very highly recommended geography curriculum, only to be greeted by tears.

As you can imagine, it's rather disheartening as a teacher. Then I hit on a several better ways.

Geography Puzzles and Games

My kids are crazy for puzzles and games, probably because their mom also loves them. There are two different types of geography puzzles, and they serve different purposes.

Using Geography Puzzles with Pieces Shaped Like Countries or States

The most common geography puzzle has pieces in the shape of countries or states. We have one for each continent, and two for the United States (one wooden, and one in nice, thick cardboard pieces).

Some other things you can do with puzzles:

- Compare the relative size of states (this only works within the same puzzle).
- Put countries in alphabetical order.
- Find the major bodies of water in a country or state.

Using "Normal-Piece" Geography Puzzles

Normal geography puzzles are usually novelty puzzles. They're ones with cartoon drawings of a city, or stylized pictures of a country. Some are even three-dimensional, with extra pieces to add at the end.

Why use these puzzles? First, you can get some amazing information looking at these highly stylized maps. They'll tell you what that city is known for. We have one of London, and it spotlights the monuments and famous buildings quite well. There are also a few famous figures to be found on the map.

Raid Your Local Library and the Internet

My library has an amazing nonfiction section, and a fair selection of "everybody books" that are still useful for my junior-high kids. I sit at home in my pajamas and search the catalog.

I'll Google famous people or artists from the country in question and find all sorts of fun information.

When I get home with my library haul, I read through the books and let them inspire me. Ferdinand the Bull led to a pretend bullfight between my kids. We took turns being the bull and the matador. It was hilarious.

A book on Jacques Cousteau led to us brainstorming habitats for living underwater, one his fondest dreams.

Did your library fail you? My library failed me for Portugal. It had three books, two of which were the super-boring "Meet Portugal"-type books filled with facts, but not much for actually learning.

I turned to YouTube and made a quick geography playlist. Now, as we study a country, I add it to our playlist, and we watch a fun video with some facts on that country. We are currently working our way through Europe, so it's all Europe, but I think we'll be studying Asia next.

Cook Your Way Around the World

This can get expensive, depending on how authentic you want to be. I tend to limit the recipes we try to ones where I have most of the ingredients on hand. That way, I won't have to make trips to specialty stores, which can keep down costs. It does also make your recipes less authentic.

I do a few Google searches, browse on Pinterest a bit, and then pick something that I think we have a remote chance of making.

Now, I will freely admit, recipes found on the internet will be very hit-or-miss for authenticity. Especially if you try any of the recipes on my blog!

Recently, with the popularity of subscription boxes, there have been several geography-cooking-themed ones you can try. I haven't tried them yet, so I can't speak for how good they are. I am currently aware of Try the World, Snack Crate and Kitchen Table Passport.

If you don't want to cook, look up restaurants in the area. I live right next to our state capital, so we have a wide variety of nationalities represented. There are even a few fusion restaurants we can try.

Write Your Way Around the World

Want some primary materials from the source? I'd suggest trying Postcrossing, an international group where you write postcards and can get postcards in exchange from all over the world. I did find that we tended to get more United States postcards, but that worked just fine for us as we would then study the state from which we got the postcard.

The postcards can reveal a lot about the area the sender is from, and will often feature prominent local landmarks you can look up and learn more about. This can lead to a whole rabbit trail of fun new possibilities as you learn about the local customs.

You can study the stamp and learn more about who or what is on the stamp (though some recent American ones might be boring; my daughter just mailed a letter with a picture of a sunset, nowhere near as fun). Often, people from Postcrossing will talk a little bit about what their daily lives are like, or a particular favorite food.

Geography and Genealogy

On a separate note, if you're at all into genealogy, a great study would be to find out the history and the culture of where your family came from.

My husband's aunt has discovered all sorts of fun little stories about his family, going back more than 100 years.

But What About All Those Geography Terms?

One part of geography is just learning the terms. What is a hemisphere? What are fjords and plateaus? Things like that.

For these, I'd get a good globe. I'm partial to an inflatable globe, because you can deflate it when you're not using it, and you can play games with it as you throw it. With active kids, the ability to throw the globe is awesome.

Oh the other advantage of the inflatable globe is you can write on it with a Vis-A-Vis marker. You can draw labels for the northern hemisphere, southern hemisphere, equator or International Date Line. Your child will remember these things so much better if you use a globe than if you don't.

As to the geography terms, you just need some Play-Doh. I still remember making a salt-dough map in sixth grade with all of the different geographic features. I also remember the anguish of it molding later on and having to throw it away. That's one reason I'm partial to Play-Doh; your kids expect they don't get to keep their creations. My kids would keep everything if I let them.

So grab a few cans of brown, green and blue Play-Doh (or make your own), and start building a fjord or an archipelago. Challenge your children to name their island and have fun with the activity.

As you learn about habitats, build them out of the toys you have in your house (almost anything can be built with LEGO, especially in my house).

Ticia is a homeschooling mom to three elementary kids, twin boys and a little girl. She loves to make their learning hands on, and delights in making history fun. You can find Ticia at her blog adventuresinmommydom.org

Homeschooling Digital Natives

Beth Napoli

Have you ever seen the "Kids React to Technology" Youtube video series? A narrator gives kids a rotary phone or a Walkman or an old computer, and the kids need to figure out what it is and how to use it. I relate to these videos so much more than my girls do. They just sit there wondering, "What's so funny?" since they don't know what the items are either.

But, even without watching YouTube, I'm sure you'll agree that technology has come a long way in our lifetime. And it changes fast... too fast for us adults to keep up with sometimes. But guess what? Our kids are more immune to the technology changes because they don't know any different.

They don't know rotary phones. They don't know cassette tapes. They don't know 20-volume encyclopedia sets. They don't know a world where knowledge isn't just a click away. And because they haven't been educated pre-Information Age, our kids don't know how to learn like past generations did.

Our children are digital natives, yet we are digital immigrants. And that leads to a bit of struggle. We're the first generation of parents homeschooling digital learners. We're the first generation to battle the "too much screen time" war.

We're the first generation to guide children who have access to all the information in the world right in their back pockets.

We're the first generation with children texting and messaging and chatting with "friends" in an instant.

We're the first generation with our own mobile electronic "plugged-in" devices in our homes and cars and purses.

You see, we don't have an example from past generations to guide us. Think about it. We can go to any older, more experienced mother and ask, "How did you make sure your kids stayed healthy?" Or "What did you do when your child disobeyed?" Or "How did you manage your children's schedules?" But we can't go to a seasoned homeschool mom and ask, "How did you handle your children's screen time? How did you guide them toward developing healthy tech habits? How much technology did you include in your family's home education?"

Nor can we look to our childhood experiences for insight. Since the development of the Internet in the 1990s, things have changed drastically. And you have to admit that technological advancements have changed a lot of things in our world for the better.

I'm glad that my children have all the opportunities available in our tech-driven world. I consider how much more they can do than I could as a kid. I could have never discovered what to do about my sneezing guinea pig. Or edited a photo 50+ ways, then shared it with 50+ friends. Or played a word game with my aunt who lives 3,000 miles away. Or stayed home from school to learn whatever I want.

You cannot deny that today's digital learners can be better educated than previous generations. I don't mean that they have more knowledge and maturity. I mean that they are smarter about HOW they learn. And, as homeschool parents, we need to accept responsibility to guide their education, even though it seems unfamiliar to us.

The Needs of Digital Students Today

It is crucial that we understand the needs of digital learners, so that we can educate our kids in a way that truly benefits them. But what are the needs of today's digital learners?

Digital Learners Need a Learning Guide, Not an Instructor

Instead of feeding information to our children, we need to let them discover it for themselves. They know where to find the information, but they need guidance in how to process the information. They need to learn how to consider the large amounts of information available to them and discern truth from untruth.

Digital Learners Need a Challenge

They learn best by solving problems, using trial and error as they grow in knowledge. Rote learning and memorization doesn't cut it anymore. Today's learners want to know that what they learn is relevant and will benefit them in the future.

Digital Learners Need Opportunities to Take Responsibility for Their Own Education

Since they know how and where to find information, today's learners demonstrate more responsibility for their education. They no longer wait for someone to tell them how to do something. Instead, they take initiative to seek out knowledge, learning on their own.

Digital Learners Need to Apply What They Learn

21st-century learners are both "consumer" and "creator." They want to do something with the information they take in, whether it be creating a playlist, editing a photo or producing a video. They put their knowledge into action and share their creations with the world.

Digital Learners Need Integrated Learning Opportunities

Today's learners can't help but notice that knowledge is inherently integrated. Integrated means "combining or coordinating separate elements so as to provide a harmonious, interrelated whole" (Dictionary.com). Topics of study cannot be organized into subjects like education of the past. Digital learners expect and respond best to integrated, not segmented, education.

How Do We Meet Those Needs?

Despite the fact that many, if not most, homeschooling parents today are somewhat akin to "digital dinosaurs," there are a few concepts we can adapt to help prepare our children become adept at digital learning.

Here are six simple ways to get started.

Validate Techie Interests and Talents

Yes, it's very tempting to scoff at the dependence we have today on technology and to point out the limitations and negatives, but the fact remains: This is the method and mode of learning for the future. And just like children in the past (and still today) have artistic or science-related skills and talents, for example, children today might also have tech-related interests. Putting these interests down or trying to ignore them is neither kind nor healthy. It may feel a bit foreign to you, but make every effort to engage with your child and learn about them; you never know where it may lead to in their future!

Instill a Healthy Attitude About Tech

Granted, it is easy to get pulled into video games or social media threads, but that's no reason to throw out the baby with the bathwater. Sit down as a family to discuss and establish healthy tech habits and limits. If you feel your kids may be wasting time on their screens, try asking them some questions to discover what's going on. Remember, technology is a tool, not a toy, but you might find that you also need to change your attitude!

Encourage Digital Learners to Explore, and Teach Them Digital Literacy Skills to Find Answers

One of the most important characteristics of an enthusiastic learner is curiosity. However, many of us take the "it-must-be-true-I-saw-it-on-the-internet" approach a bit too far. Talk about what you see and hear with your kids. Ask them how realistic some news stories are and help them to develop a healthy amount of cynicism about unreasonable claims. Finding, evaluating and discerning online content is a necessary skill in this day and age; teach them how to sift between truth and fiction.

Stop Segmenting Education

Consider adding unit studies to your homeschool as a holistic approach to education. Unit studies allow students to pursue a particular topic or theme from a variety of angles, and are a delightful way to engage the whole family in learning. It is possible, for example, to choose World War II, and explore it through history studies (naturally!), but also geography, science, reading, art and music. Online unit studies best meet the needs of today's learners by incorporating digital projects. There are many prepared unit studies available, and if you're overwhelmed by choosing one, you may want to learn what issues are important to consider.

Create Projects with Web Tools

Even if you're still a bit intimidated by technology, you'd be amazed how comfortable your kids are with web tools! Creating a project to summarize or articulate the results of their learning is a great way for your students to "own" and internalize the process of learning. A wide variety of web tools to do just that are readily available, such as Emaze and Animaker.

Use Online Resources, Enroll in Online Courses

I'm not referring to "virtual academies" here (which are often simply public school curricula accessed online), but rather video courses, online unit studies, e-books, YouTube and other digital resources. Of course, I would never suggest that you merely turn your students loose on the computer, but there are many reliable and reputable products available.

Learning formats today are vastly different than in years past, and, as is the case with all progress, have both negatives and positives. If we are to prepare our children to be confident and capable adults in their tech-driven future, however, we need to teach them appropriately. Parents, model a love of learning and personal growth for your kids by discovering and using the tools and techniques necessary to enable them to become effective digital learners.

Beth Napoli shares wisdom gained from more than 12 years homeschooling her five daughters at techiehomeschoolmom.com. She inspires and equips homeschooling moms to meet the needs of 21st-century learners and incorporate more digital learning into home education. Beth is also the creator of Online Unit Studies, tech-driven internet-based thematic learning experiences, and hostess of the Techin' Your Homeschool Facebook group. Beth's not a computer expert; she's just a geek about cool webtools and online learning resources. She's passionate about encouraging others to discover and pursue the purpose God has designed them for and loves to connect with other homeschooling moms on social media.

Nature Study Opportunities for City-Dwelling Homeschoolers

Betsy Strauss

There is so much to learn from nature. It gets us outside, slows us down and causes us to observe something other than ourselves. However, not all of us have acreage and a creek in the backyard to explore.

Living in the concrete jungle, or even suburbia, you can't just walk out your back door and find a wealth of options for observing nature. While there are plenty of bugs, trees and birds to watch in my backyard, sometimes I'd like to inspire my little scientists with more variety. The good news is that there are so many wonderful places you can go to be inspired by nature even when you live in the city.

Where to Seek Nature Studies in the City

Aquariums and Zoos

With amazing animals to observe and beautiful landscaping to admire, zoos are a wonderful place to go for nature inspiration. Consider getting a zoo pass so that you can go and sit and watch one animal for a longer period of time, or over the course of multiple visits. When the weather isn't great, an aquarium can be a great indoor alternative.

Wildlife Parks and Nature Preserves

These parks put you in the center of the action. Whether you get up close and personal with a giraffe, or are sitting still and watching birds, parks and preserves offer an oasis in the midst of modern developments.

State and National Parks

Even though these locations generally require a couple of hours of driving outside of the city, when you arrive, you feel like you've been transported into a peaceful and serene destination. If you visit outside of peak times, the wildlife will be out and about to observe. The time and gas investments are well worth it.

Gardens

A beautiful garden is like a buffet for the eyes. With so many colors, shapes, sizes and smells, one could spend hours marveling at the diversity. These locations are also great to visit often, as the color offerings are new with each season.

City Parks

Even in big cities, there are so many local parks that have streams or ponds, and that offer great nature trails. These free options could be within walking distance from your home. Check your local city parks and recreation website or Facebook page to see a listing of all that they offer.

What Do I Do Once I Get There?

When you're not used to encountering nature, it can be a bit overwhelming to tackle nature studies. With a few simple ideas, you should be able to enjoy learning in nature with your kids.

Identifying Species With a Pocket Guide

Start with identifying what you see. National Geographic Pocket Guides offer great resources for figuring out the species of rock, plant or tree that you encounter. The more you practice identifying objects in nature, the better you will become at spotting them again. Additionally, it's fun to compare two of the same kind of thing. Simply look for ways they are similar, and ways they are different.

Nature Journaling

I love The Laws Guide to Nature Drawing and Journaling. While this book seemed pricey at first, the first few chapters made it worth every penny. John Muir Laws is very inspiring, but also very down-to-earth in his descriptions of how to get started in this great endeavor.

He encourages three basic ideas to spark observations along with your drawings:

- **I notice**: This makes you work on basic observations. This is something I really want to develop in my kids, and it is such a simple way to cultivate it.

- **I wonder:** Next, you cultivate curiosity with great questions. You don't have to be able to answer these questions, because these questions will drive your research later. Jotting down the questions can help draw out the wonder as you continue to notice more about the object/subject you're drawing.
- **It reminds me of:** I love this last notation. Children have beautiful imaginations. They can stretch their imaginations in this phase by thinking about what their subject looks like. Have they seen something similar in a movie or cartoon?

Help! I'm Stuck In the House!

It is possible that there are seasons of your life when these lovely ideals of soaking in nature are just not feasible. When you find yourself in this position, there are some simple ways to cultivate a fascination with nature from your home. It doesn't have to be fancy.

Grow Something in the House

If you don't have a green thumb, don't worry. Anyone can grow a potato in a Mason jar of water! It's pretty fascinating to watch. Pick a time each week to draw the changes in your plant. What if it dies? Take the opportunity to discuss what you think might have gone wrong, and try it again!

Bring the Nature to You

A simple bird feeder can bring nature right to your window. Choose a spot that you can easily see from inside to hang your bird feeder. Grab your bird-identifying books, and wait for the excitement that comes from watching the beautiful birds enjoy the free food.

Get a Closer Look

It's amazing what fascinating things you can discover about nature with a magnifying glass or a microscope. We have brought home fun items that we've found on nature walks to get a closer look at when we have more time. At face value, something might seem overly simplistic and uninteresting, but when magnified, complexities are revealed that fascinate even the greatest skeptic.

Even though living in the city poses challenges to nature studies, you can still find plenty of great ways to cultivate a love of the outdoors. In our busy schedules, a little time outdoors does the heart good, and might even provide a much-needed break from daily tasks.

Don't be afraid to get a little dirty every now and then. Your kids will thank you later, if not now.

Betsy Strauss is a wife to a deep thinker and a homeschooling mom of kids ranging from 8 to 16. Over the past seven years, she's been involved with Classical Conversations, which has blessed her whole family immensely. In her free time, she's a big fan of reading and collecting books. You can find her sharing her thoughts on becoming a family of lifelong learners at FamilyStyleSchooling.com.

Incorporating Fitness and Health Into Your Homeschool Routine

Brandi Jordan

Health and fitness weren't always an important part of our homeschool routine. In fact, they were pretty low on the priorities list when the kids were younger – which is, of course, awful to admit, but absolutely true. When you're working on only a few hours of sleep and have three small kids at home, the idea of doing anything other than surviving the day and getting lessons in is almost laughable. So, if you're new to homeschooling and you're in that place right now, I understand. Here's the little ray of hope that I want to throw your way, though:

Exercising is going to make you happier and healthier, and a better mom, wife, friend, sister and aunt. It's going to make you a better version of yourself.

So, the question becomes how to get to that place where fitness and health are a priority when there are so many other things competing for space in your already overwhelming day. That's when planning and routines become your very best friend. In fact, once fitness and healthy habits become part of the daily routine, you'll find it very hard to remove them from the schedule. They'll become a lifeline, because they'll make you feel so much better. Let's figure out how to fit them in and let me explain what exactly it is that I'm talking about when I say fitness and healthy habits. As always, consult your doctor before beginning any exercise routine to make sure that you and your children are healthy enough for exercise.

Understanding Fitness and Healthy Habits

When I'm talking about fitness in your homeschool routine, I really mean any activity that gets you and your children up and moving. It can be a walk around the block or playing in the snow. It can be playing chase in the backyard or throwing a Frisbee at the park. Fitness can also mean doing a workout video together or following a children's yoga routine from books that combine movement with the story inside. Whatever it is that you can do to move and get your heart rate up (even slightly) is wonderful. There's no pressure or expectation of 90-minute powerlifting workouts!

The term healthy habits encompasses everything from making nutritious food choices 80 percent of the time to making time for self-care. I am still trying to find those elusive "spa days" that moms are supposed to take, so if that's something that's not feasible for you either, don't worry – you're not alone! Self-care means getting a shower every day (even if it's only 30 seconds long), brushing your teeth before noon, and wearing something other than pajamas or yoga pants for at least one day out of the week. It's so easy to fall into a routine of comfortable casualness as a homeschooling parent, but before long we end up neglecting our own needs while taking care of others.

Self-care also involves our mental health. Taking time to relax and recharge is not selfish. There was a post on social media a few months ago that said something to the effect of "You can't fill someone else's bucket when your own is empty." That stuck with me, because I've seen many a dedicated homeschooling mom forget to fill her own bucket with the things that she needs to sustain her energy and mental health. Making self-care part of your everyday habit, and teaching your kids how to make it part of theirs, will result in a happier, healthier home life all around.

What happens if you don't have any extra time during the day to fit in a 30-minute workout or to plan elaborate healthy meals? That's OK, because we're going to work it into your already planned homeschool lessons. Come Shakespeare or algebra, fitness and healthy choices are going to be part of your daily routine by the time we're done. Now, what do you actually do to incorporate fitness and healthy habits? I'm glad you asked, because I have some ideas.

Nature Walks

No matter how old your children are, a nature walk is a great activity that serves at least two purposes. It gets your fitness activity in while offering you a ton of learning opportunities. You can take a walk to collect leaves in the fall, search for animal tracks in the snow, or hunt for flowers popping up in the spring. Break out the camera and take photos from unique angles or bring a journal or sketchpad and record what you see. Depending on your child's level of interest in science and walking outside, you can use the walk to justify science or science to justify the walk. Either way, the result is a science lesson and some fun fitness.

Roll the Dice

My kids love our set of giant dice that we found at a discount store in town, and we use them a lot for math. One of our favorite games combines multiplication and physical activity. The kids roll the dice and multiply the numbers. They then pick a physical activity challenge from a hat and do that activity for as long as the multiplication answer was in seconds. For example, if they roll a three and a four, they would multiply the numbers to get 12. They would then pick a physical activity out of the hat - jumping jacks, for example. Then, for 12 seconds, we would all do as many jumping jacks as we could. It's a lot of fun and results in great math practice, increased heart rates and a ton of laughs.

Chalk It Up to Balance

Grab a stick of sidewalk chalk and create your own long, winding path or maze. Practice walking on the line from one end to the other and then carefully walk the path backward. It's a simple fitness idea, but it's amazingly good for practicing balance and coordination. Don't just have the kids doing it either; balance is important to practice no matter how old you are!

Hula Hoop

When was the last time you used a hula hoop? If you had to think about the answer longer than three seconds, you haven't used one often enough. Hula hoops aren't only fun, they're fabulous fitness tools. When you're having a rough day in school or simply need a brain break, grab the hula hoop and start twirling. It's hard to be angry when you hula hoop and even harder not to break a slight sweat once you get it going.

Sight Word Catch

When my kids were working on sight words, I invested in some dollar-store beach balls and a Sharpie marker. I wrote sight words on the balls, and we used them to play catch in the backyard. When someone caught the ball, they had to say the words that their hands were touching. It was great practice and, since catching and throwing were also skills that were being developed in the game, we ended up chasing those balls around the yard when throws weren't quite accurate enough.

Homeschool Dance Party

Sometimes, you just need to turn on the music and get dancing. While listening to multiplication memorization songs or Schoolhouse Rock songs, we dance to the tunes. The movement helps the kids remember the songs better than when they hear a song without moving. Actually giving the songs life through dance helps build those brain connections and memory skills. Our dance parties still result in better learning and a lot of laughter. The fitness aspect is just a bonus!

What About Those Healthy Habits?

You've got the fitness idea down now and you're already thinking about ways that you can sneak activities into your everyday homeschool lessons, but what about those healthy habits? For those, may I suggest cooking and baking with your kids? Yes, even your toddler can mix a bowl of oats or put some carrots on a plate while you scoop hummus. Involving your child in the healthy food habits that you want to cultivate can help create a routine for both of you.

If you have older children, cookbooks are a great way to bring healthy food choices into your homeschool. Break out the cookbooks and discover math in recipe multiplication and the concept of following directions in the process of baking and cooking. Talk about ingredients and healthy options. Discuss sugars and artificial sweeteners. Learn more about honey and where it comes from. Cookbooks are a gold mine of learning opportunities – especially when it comes to teaching your children about healthy eating habits.

What about those healthy habits other than eating? Well, the best advice for those is to model them for your child. If you want your child to know that bathing every day is important, guess what? You need to shower every day. If you want your child to brush his teeth three times a day, you have to model that behavior. In your attempts to teach your children how to take better care of themselves, you actually get the added benefit of practicing self-care and healthy habits yourself. Remember, your children watch everything you do and if you want them to lead a healthy life, you have to lead one by example.

Practice Makes Better

It's not going to be an overnight transition to a healthier, more active lifestyle in your homeschool routine. However, the daily practice of small changes is going to lead to consistent routines that will result in big physical and mental gains. You'll discover that you all feel better, your moods are improved, and you can concentrate longer. Practice will make you and your children better at doing things that are good for your bodies and souls. You don't have to be perfect and, yes, you can still have ice cream, but you do need to start making the small changes now that will pave the way for a healthy life for the whole family. No one can give you a magic wand for a healthier lifestyle, but I promise you that it's worth all of the effort you'll put into it.

Now go exercise with your children and make some happy, healthy memories!

As a work-from-home, homeschooling mom of three, Brandi Jordan stays sane with the help of a lot of exercise, coffee and her wildly funny family. A former elementary teacher turned marketing manager and online instructor, she is also a NASM-Certified Personal Trainer and Youth Exercise Specialist. She blogs about homeschooling at MamaTeaches.com and about health and fitness at MamaExercises.com.

Making Science and STEM a Priority

Brenda Priddy

One popular buzzword in today's education world is STEM (or STEAM).

STEM is simply the interdisciplinary connection of science, technology, engineering and math (STEAM also adds art). The goal of STEM is to help children approach these subjects by applying critical thinking and problem-solving techniques to real-world problems.

Common STEM activities use the scientific process to create a solution for a problem. A typical STEM activity might work like this:

First, students think of a problem, perhaps how to waste less water at home.

Students will then use a combination of science, technology, engineering and math to solve the problem.

The students might complete the following actions to solve the problem:

- Determine how much water is currently used (math).
- Document where and how water is used in the house (technology and science).
- Make a hypothesis for how water could be saved (science).

- Create a plan to save water (technology and engineering).
- Implement the plan (science).
- Track the plan's success (all STEM topics).
- Adjust the hypothesis based on findings and repeat (all STEM topics).

Of course, such detailed projects take a lot of time and energy, which is why many homeschooling parents let them fall to the wayside in favor of other topics.

However, I believe STEM is important enough to be a main priority of homeschooling. Why?

Benefits of STEM

STEM studies provide value beyond simple instruction in science, technology, engineering and math.

- STEM studies encourage collaboration and working as a group.
- STEM studies show children how the "boring" subjects are used in real life.
- STEM studies prepare students for today's technology-driven culture and working environment.
- STEM studies in the younger years will make these topics easier in high school and college.
- STEM studies help children think independently and critically.
- STEM studies perfectly illustrate the scientific process.
- STEM studies show that, as is true in adult life, you can learn more through the process of

figuring something out than you can by just finding the "right" answer.

- STEM studies help encourage creativity and out-of-the-box thinking.
- Most careers use elements of STEM, even if you don't notice it.
- STEM activities bring hands-on fun into your homeschool.

These are not the only benefits of STEM. If you think about it, you can probably come up with a dozen more reasons to focus on STEM in your homeschool.

But, as stated before, STEM activities are time intensive and material intensive. So how can a busy homeschooling family work in these challenging projects and activities?

Every family is different, but we've made it work using the following tips.

Plan for a Weekly STEM Project

We don't do a STEM project every day. We try to do a big project once a week. We don't always do the full STEM project, either. Sometimes we do a hands-on math project, or a simple science experiment, or we do something with technology like completing a coding project in Scratch or making a stop-motion video.

However, we do try to stick to at least one project a week. Pick an afternoon when you don't have much else going on and make that STEM time.

Keep Activities Age-Appropriate

When my daughter Monkey was the age my daughter Bo is now (3 years old), I was overly ambitious of her skill level. I tried to do all kinds of complicated things with her. She wasn't ready, and the projects were mainly a waste of time.

Make sure the activities you do are challenging enough and at the current level of your children. Monkey is in fifth grade this year, and this is the first year we've moved beyond the simplest of projects and questions. Now, we are getting into chemistry, math, and detailed explanations of processes and experiments.

Bo, on the other hand, usually just plays with the activity materials when Monkey and I are talking. She is particularly fond of messy science experiments right now.

If you make things too easy, a child won't be challenged enough and will get bored. But if the activity is too challenging too soon, the child will get frustrated and may think that STEM includes all of the worst subjects.

Join a Science or STEM Co-Op (or start one!)

If you have a science class in your co-op, take advantage of it! A lot of co-ops around here offer science for older kids, but not as much for younger kids. If you don't see any science or STEM activities that interest you, start one!

If you're the teacher of STEM class, I guarantee you'll make it a priority.

Watch YouTube Experiments

If you can't do an activity due to time constraints (or if you're like me, it's because you forgot to buy the supplies), YouTube is an amazing resource. You can find videos on everything from the math behind chemical reactions to fun science demonstrations.

Use STEM Thinking in All Subjects

One of my favorite parts about STEM is how much the focus is placed on critical thinking, analysis and the use of logic to come up with an answer. When this thinking is applied to other subjects, children are able to think logically and creatively, even if they are answering an essay question on George Washington's journey over the Delaware River.

Use STEM-Friendly Curriculum

Not all curriculum is built around STEM concepts. Surprisingly enough, many Common Core curricula, however, are. I've been impressed with how the Common Core math, science, and even language arts materials focus on critical thinking, abstract thought and logic, and using technology for education, rather than just for watching Minecraft Let's Play videos on YouTube.

We currently use Building Foundations of Scientific Understanding as our STEM curriculum, which is not Common Core but which takes a systematic approach to science and STEM studies. We use this as a jumping-off place for our full-scale STEM activities.

Build on Previous Knowledge

What makes STEM activities so unique is that you can constantly build on new skills. Maybe you've done a baking soda and vinegar experiment every year, but each year, you can add more information about the process. Young kids can learn about the basic reaction between acids and basis. Children in upper elementary can start to learn about the chemistry behind the reaction. Children in middle school and high school could create a proposal for how to use carbon dioxide to benefit society in some way.

All of the information stems from one simple experiment or question.

Run Quizzes and Drills Frequently

I don't always have official "STEM class" with my kids. Instead, I try to get them to think critically throughout the day. While driving, we might talk about why it is raining, how it rains and what we can do to cut down on our environmental impact.

We might discuss weather patterns and how meteorologists track weather, what tools they use to do so and what math is involved.

Simply creating an awareness of how STEM is used everywhere and how it's a part of everything can spark further interest and study when children are alone.

Let Your Kids Create Their Own Projects

A large part of STEM activities is allowing children to work on their own. Children should be encouraged to come up with their own processes and solutions (and not to be afraid of failure, which is often not failure at all). When conducting a STEM activity, although there is often a "right" answer that an adult found at some point, there are not any "wrong" answers either.

I like to give my kids access to our STEM supplies so they can create their own projects. Monkey is currently interested in inventions and creating new tools, so she is often working on "inventions." She has invented a fishing game for her sister, ice skates for her doll, a dragon with moving wings, and many other things.

She was given a microscope for her birthday and, a few days ago, I caught her "researching" the slides with Bo. She had made various columns on a piece of paper so she could track the properties of each slide. She made note of things like texture, color, weight, and whether the specimen looked organic or non-organic.

She already knew what the materials were, as the slides had the name of the object already on them, but she told me she was just classifying the objects.

If I hadn't allowed her access to the STEM supplies, she would never have conducted this activity. I never would have thought of it myself!

Follow STEM-Themed Blogs

You'll find that a lot of educational blogs now write about STEM and STEAM-themed activities. However, not all sites offer quality projects. My favorite websites not only give the activity ideas but they also provide the information for the "why" of the activity.

While it can be fun to just do STEM activities for time-wasters, the best activities teach something along with the fun.

I happen to love the STEM activities on these blogs:

SchoolingaMonkey.com

We strive to provide easy STEM activities that aren't too complicated or expensive but that also provide real value. We usually try twists on classic science projects and STEM experiments that keep the activities fresh and fun. Our site was actually one of the first sites to focus on STEM.

STEAMPoweredFamily.com

Shelley is a fellow homeschooling mom and lover of STEM. Her site is full of fun out-of-the-box STEM activities that are a blast for kids to do.

FrugalFun4 Boys.com

This site is full of creative engineering projects and STEM challenges. I absolutely love how creative Sarah is. She frequently uses LEGO in her activities, which is an amazing tool for STEM projects.

LittleBinsforLittleHands.com

I love how Little Bins for Little Hands translates STEM thinking so that even the youngest kids can understand it. I am always impressed with the creativity and knowledge that Sarah can use to help even the youngest kids understand!

TheSTEMLaboratory.com

If you like printable worksheets, you'll absolutely love the STEM activities at The STEM Laboratory. Malia is not only super-smart (she has a master's degree in education from Stanford University) but she is also super-sweet! I'm always impressed with her STEM printables and activities.

How to Reduce STEM Costs

STEM activities and science projects often use weird (and sometimes expensive) materials like copper wire and high-powered magnets. But you don't have to break the bank to enjoy STEM activities.

Keep a STEM Supply List Handy and Stalk the Sales

I keep our costs lower by keeping a copy of our STEM supply list (which you can find in the Schooling a Monkey store) in my purse (or you could keep a list on your phone). When I'm shopping, I look for one or two items to add to my cart. This prevents us from having a heart attack when we shop for supplies and suddenly the bill is $150 for what is essentially Styrofoam cups and vinegar.

Additionally, if something STEM-themed happens to be on sale, I buy multiples. I have about eight containers of salt in my STEM closet right now!

Ask for STEM-Themed Gifts

Another way to not only focus on STEM but to also keep costs low is to ask for family members and friends to purchase STEM supplies as gifts.

We love science subscription boxes and STEM kits when Christmas rolls around. I'm thinking about asking for STEM-supplies myself for Christmas!

Don't be Afraid to Add STEM to Your Homeschool

Although it seems intimidating when you see chemistry terms and dizzying math problems, STEM does not have to be difficult.

If you stick to your children's current level, STEM activities will be fun adventures and may soon become the best part of your homeschool day. As children age, you can gradually make the challenges more difficult and challenging.

Above all, the STEM mindset is a constant quest for more knowledge about how the world works and how to make it a better place. And what better place to cultivate that environment than your home?

 *Brenda Priddy is a blogger, writer and STEM-lover. She has homeschooled her two daughters since 2010. She blogs about homeschooling, STEM and ADHD at SchoolingaMonkey.com.*

Incorporating Living Math Books into Your Homeschool

Jennifer

As a high school math teacher, I loved finding ways to make math relevant and engaging for my students!

As a homeschool mom, I now strive to come up with ways to make math fun and meaningful for my own children. I have created printable math activities. I have found math-related board games. And I have incorporated living math books.

What is a Living Math Book?

A living math book is a book that presents mathematical concepts in real-life context, which are relevant to the reader.

A living math book is not a textbook; rather it is a book... plain and simple, a book, with characters and a storyline, which happens to have math skills integrated within the story.

Why Incorporate Living Math Books?

Incorporating living math books in your homeschool is a great way to help teach and/or reinforce various mathematical skills and concepts. Utilizing living math books helps to make math meaningful and relevant, because they usually include real-life mathematical applications.

Children are able to see examples of how math is both used and needed in real-world situations.

While some children have a natural bent toward math, others do not. Introducing new math topics in a less intimidating form, using living math books, may allow for such children to grasp the concepts more easily.

Living math books, in contrast with textbooks and workbooks, can provide a gentle, non-intimidating approach to introducing new mathematical skills.

Living math books also help to encourage problem-solving and math literacy. Through reading the stories, children can learn to reason and analyze mathematical information because many times it is modeled within the books.

Essentially, living math books can be used to show children how to use numbers to solve real-world problems.

Needless to say, I believe incorporating living math books is a marvelous way to make mathematics meaningful, engaging, relevant, and, dare I say, fun for children.

How Can I Incorporate Living Math Books?

Incorporating living math books into your homeschool is actually quite easy. First, determine what math concept you want to address. Next, gather living math books about that specific math skill. Finally, read the books together, being sure to discuss the math topics found in the story and how those concepts relate to the action of the storyline.

How Can I Find Living Math Books?

By now, you might be wondering how to find living math books to incorporate into your homeschool. For your convenience, I have compiled a list of over 300 living math books, conveniently divided up by topic. My growing list of living math books can be found at LivingMathBooks.com. Simply choose your desired math concept and view a list of living math books addressing that specific topic.

Jennifer (aka Mama Jenn) is a Christian wife and homeschool mother of five, including one girl and two sets of twin boys! Find her online at MamaJenn.com, where she shares educational activities, crafty ideas, free printables and more. Jennifer is also the creator of the EducationCubes.com website, which features customizable learning blocks to help make learning interactive and fun.

Learning Resources: Training Hearts

Life Skills for Kids: What You Need to Know

Tonia Lyons

When I first started homeschooling, I was very worried that I would forget to teach something of vital importance to my daughter - and I did! I completely forgot about teaching her to tie her shoes. She loved Velcro and slip-on shoes as a child, so the need for learning to tie her shoes just wasn't there. It wasn't until she was older and wanted "real" sneakers that I discovered the lapse! Of course, it was an easy enough fix; she quickly learned and that was that.

I know that over the years, there will probably be other things I'll forget to teach; we just can't cover it all. But everyday "life skills" (like learning to tie shoes) are easily taught within the context of everyday life - no special curriculum needed!

What are "life skills," anyway? Simply put, they are the basic skills that are needed for living everyday life. Things like knowing how to tie shoes, sweep a floor or balance a checkbook are all daily skills that everyone should know.

Age-Appropriate Skills

The first thing to consider when teaching life skills to your children is age-appropriateness. For example, you can't expect a preschooler to know how to change a tire, but it certainly is at the top of the list for teens who are learning to drive.

How do you know if something is age-appropriate? I've found that most things I'd like my daughter to know come up in the course of everyday life. When she was small, she loved to help me empty the dishwasher, so it was easy enough to show her how to put away the dishes. As I took care of daily chores, it wasn't difficult to begin teaching her how to do those jobs herself. When she started getting a small allowance, we also started teaching about tithing, giving and saving. Money management was a normal part of earning.

If you think of life skills as basic knowledge acquired as you live life, you'll naturally discover those things your children need to know. Best of all, you can teach them within the context of everyday life.

The Importance of Life Skills

I know that homeschool moms are very busy, and it can often be much simpler to just do certain tasks yourself instead of taking the time to teach them to your children. But you must remember that these skills are an important part of life, just as necessary as learning math and grammar. If you look at daily chores as another way we teach and shape our children, you'll begin to understand the importance of teaching them to become independent individuals fully equipped for the future.

Don't forget the other benefits of learning these important skills: Increased confidence, stronger family relationships as you learn to care for the family home as a team, and the value of hard work are all natural by-products.

What if You Forget to Teach an Important Life Skill?

No worries! The beauty of homeschooling is that we are raising independent lifelong learners. As long as our children have the necessary skills for learning, they will be well-equipped for the future.

If you need a little inspiration for teaching life skills, I've included a list of basic skills divided by age group. This isn't an exhaustive list of skills, but it will help inspire you to discover more ways to equip your children for the future

Preschool and Early Elementary

- Pick up toys
- Dress and undress
- Comb hair
- Wash face and hands
- Make bed
- Put clean clothes away
- Dust furniture
- Weed garden
- Learn address and telephone number
- Learn how to contact emergency services
- Wash hair
- Fold laundry
- Wipe down table
- Set and clear table
- Clean windows
- Empty trash
- Sweep
- Water houseplants
- Make a sandwich

- Learn to swim

Elementary

- Use washer and dryer
- Load dishwasher
- Wash and dry dishes
- Mop floor
- Vacuum
- Clean countertops
- Operate small appliances
- Read a recipe
- Pack a lunch
- Boil eggs
- Make and count change
- Manage allowance
- Understand tithing and giving
- Use a cell phone
- Plant a garden
- Ride a bus
- Learn basic first aid
- Use the library
- Develop typing skills

Middle School

- Make hair appointments
- Purchase personal-care products
- Shop for clothing
- Clean fireplace
- Clean appliances
- Bake cookies and muffins
- Make a salad
- Make hot beverages
- Make a bank deposit

- Practice responsible cell phone use
- Use lawn mower
- Clean car
- Read a map
- Plan a party
- Hang a picture
- Paint interior walls

High School

- Install a lock
- Wax floors
- Use caulking
- Cook dinner
- Clean oven
- Plan and shop for weekly meals
- Operate outdoor grill
- Create a simple budget
- Write a check
- Balance a checkbook
- Pump gas
- Change a flat tire
- Fill tire with air
- Make appointments

Tonia Lyons is a homeschool mom to an only daughter. When she's not busy homeschooling or writing at TheSunnyPatch.ca, you'll find her in her favorite spot, reading a pile of books.

Helping Your Children Become Entrepreneurs

Amy Lanham

Like most homeschool moms, I try to find teachable moments in everything we do. So this past summer, when my kids wanted to have a lemonade stand, I tried to help encourage their entrepreneurial spirit.

They begged for weeks before I finally gave in. I mean, who wants to sit out in the 90-degree heat with the bugs and sunscreen to serve lemonade to strangers?

Well, apparently my kids did.

What Is An Entrepreneur, Anyway?

When I finally gave in to my children's pleading, I took the opportunity to help them learn a little about being entrepreneurs. An entrepreneur is a brave person who sees a need for a product or service and works hard to fill the need while hopefully making money doing so.

While many entrepreneurs are adults, homeschooled children have a great opportunity to create products and services that their peers in traditional schools might not have.

When I was a teenager, I babysat for several different families during times I would normally have been in school. Many teens offer services such as lawn care or pet-sitting. Some kids create and sell products, such as

317

crafts or lemonade. There are many ways to become an entrepreneur and there are great lessons to be learned.

Lessons Learned

While a lemonade stand or a pet-sitting service might seem somewhat juvenile, a kid can learn a lot from the process of starting and running a business, including traits like perseverance, diligence and integrity.

Not to mention, they are also learning business lessons like supply and demand, pricing and advertising. Kids who are able to catch the entrepreneurial spirit today will be the leaders of tomorrow.

How to Help Kids Have an Entrepreneurial Spirit

So how do you encourage your child to start a business and learn these lessons first-hand? Here are some principles you need to teach your kids to encourage them to become entrepreneurs.

There Are No Bad Ideas

Sometimes kids come up with the wildest ideas. They haven't quite learned yet that some things might be impossible. But that's a good thing when you are an entrepreneur. Maybe their ideas need some tweaking, but no idea is too crazy.

Reach for the Stars

Teach your children to set goals and work hard to reach them. Like almost any character trait, more of goal-setting is caught than taught. When they see Mom and Dad working hard to reach their goals, they will be excited to get started on their own.

Don't Go with the Flow

Entrepreneurs become successful when they fill a need. They have to do something that no one else is doing, or do it in a better way. Teach your kids to think independently from everyone else, and not to always be a carbon copy of their friends. Most people work a job, but entrepreneurs think bigger and make the jobs.

Here's Your Chance

Help your kids to find opportunities that need to be met. Maybe they notice the neighbor's yard hasn't been mowed in a while. That might be the opportunity to start or expand their lawn care business. There is always something that could be done better, so teach them to be on the lookout for the needs in their community.

Keep Trying

It's not really fun to try an idea just to have it flop. But that is part of the learning process. Thomas Edison said, "I have not failed. I've just found 10,000 ways that won't work." When an idea doesn't work, it's an opportunity to find a different way.

There are so many things to be learned from becoming a business owner. I hope you will encourage an entrepreneurial spirit in your kids. They are the business owners, inventors and leaders of the next generation.

Amy Lanham is a second generation homeschooling momma with a craving for excellent books. She juggles homeschooling, blogging, working from home, studying for the CPA exam and single parenting, all while trying to read "just one more chapter." She lives in wild, wonderful West Virginia with her three kids and one dog, but some days she wants to move to Australia. She blogs at LifeasLanhams.com, where she shares her passion for books, homeschooling and Jesus.

Raising Tomorrow's Thought Leaders

Betsy Strauss

Jobs are king in today's world. Everyone is looking for the magic formula for getting a job and keeping it. If you ask employers what qualities they keep an eye out for, the top response is "critical thinking skills." This makes sense. You would want your employee to be able to manage a problem in a way that benefits the company. Sometimes that person will have to problem-solve without leadership nearby. If the employee isn't skilled in solving problems, hiring them could mean a great risk for the company.

It seems pretty obvious that this would be a skill employers would look for, but why is it that they are struggling to find this quality among the thousands of applicants? The modern public school system generally teaches to a test. Each question has one singular answer. This is wonderful for unified thinking, but it's detrimental to critical problem-solving. If young people have never had an opportunity to express creative thought, their skills in this area will be inhibited.

Critical thinking isn't just valuable for job placement, it's a quality that will shape the future of our families which will shape the future of our nation. Those who can think can lead.

So where do we start?

Critical Thinking Skills in Elementary

There are many wonderful critical thinking workbooks and programs out there, but Martin Cothran suggests that math and Latin are the best tools for shaping thought. I agree.

When you work through math problems, you are continually practicing thinking about how to reach the answer. While there is one right answer in math, there are many paths to get to that answer. By trying several ways, your children will soon learn that one way is more efficient or effective than another. Every step builds endurance to make it to the answer. Checking your answer requires students to assess their work. All of these skills are wonderful for building critical thinking skills.

Latin is the same way. When you work to translate even a simple sentence into English, you are working through a multistep problem that requires problem-solving. As you add on the nuances of Latin and English grammar, you have the perfect recipe for training your students to think through challenging concepts on their own.

Critical Thinking Skills in Middle School

As students' ages increase, so does their ability to argue. Take advantage of this natural ability by giving them more tools to argue respectfully, while also combating propaganda that comes their way. The early preteen and teenage years can be a very challenging time for young people if they are not equipped to think in the world where they live.

In addition to your math and Latin studies, add in formal logic. A great place to start is with The Fallacy Detective. If they can identify faulty reasoning, they will have an advantage when they encounter opinions that differ from their own. These claims will come from the music they listen to, the movies that they watch, and the friends they spend time with.

Another great addition to your middle-schooler's toolbelt of thinking is Andrew Kern's Lost Tools of Writing program. It really should be called the Lost Tools of Thinking, because it equips students with tools to think longer and deeper about any subject.

In this curriculum, your student is introduced to "the five common topics." These topics are comparison, definition, circumstance, relationship and authority. Kern explains that the word "topics" comes from the Greek word "topos," which means place. This is where we get "topographical map." These five tools give us places to go hunt for more information when we get stuck solving a problem. If you know how to think *around* a problem to find an answer, you will quickly rise to leadership.

Critical Thinking Skills in High School

Once your students reach their mid- to late teen years, it's time to add some form of debate to their curriculum. If you would have met me five years ago, I would have laughed at this statement. I never had this course in my own schoolwork, and to tell you the truth, it scared me to introduce my son into the world of debate. It was due to my own fears, not his lack of ability. Formal debate cultivates problem-solving on the spot; it fosters compassion for opposing opinions; and it develops persuasive communication to others.

Since each round in a debate is timed, formal debate brings a heightened intensity to problem-solving by restricting your time. The first speech is the only prepared speech, and then the rest of the round is impromptu. This means that students need to come prepared by thoroughly researching their topics. Next, they have to practice processing information very quickly and responding with counter-arguments. These skills seem daunting at first, but with time become easier. Having this timed response experience is invaluable whether they go on to be professional debaters or not.

Generally, teens resist seeing an issue from both sides. They are so sure of themselves and the fact that their opinion is correct. As a debater, you're required to prepare to argue both sides, and often you don't know until the day of the debate which side you will take. Processing both sides of an argument fosters compassion for opposing opinions that will bless all people that they encounter in the future.

It doesn't do much good to have great ideas if you're unable to communicate them. In order to be a leader in thought, one must communicate opinions clearly and persuasively. Debate gives opportunities to practice both.

Challenges in Practicing Critical Thinking At Home

Homeschoolers can face unique challenges when it comes to developing sturdy thinking skills. It is tough to have a conversation about big ideas at home that brings about a great debate when you all share the same opinion. In addition, if they've only practiced presenting in front of your family, your students may struggle getting up in front of unfamiliar crowds.

If you're concerned that your child won't get enough of this type of interaction, join a debate group or a local homeschool group that discusses philosophy, worldview or current events. We've been a part of

Classical Conversations, and it's been a rich community for building these critical-thinking skills.

Sometimes your schedule or finances won't allow your family to be in a group like the above mentioned. That's OK! You can host a "worldview" night with some of your child's friends and their families. Pick a contemporary movie or song to enjoy together and then discuss. Use a guide like The Worldview Detective to ask good questions that spark a debate. Adding in adults to the mix provides greater depth to these conversations.

If you're looking for more opportunities to practice public speaking, host a recitation night. Invite your homeschool friends to come and share a speech, memorized poem or other oral recitation. When you have something to practice for, the results are so much greater.

Leaders In Thinking Are Free

Aristotle states: "It's the mark of an educated mind to entertain an idea without accepting it." If you are not enslaved by the tyranny of erroneous logic, you will be free to lead yourself and others.

Betsy Strauss is a wife to a deep thinker and a homeschooling mom of kids ranging from 8 to 16. Over the past seven years she's been involved with Classical Conversations, which has blessed her whole family immensely. In her free time, she's a big fan of reading and collecting books. You can find her sharing her thoughts on becoming a family of lifelong learners at FamilyStyleSchooling.com.

Stop Counting Raisins: Cultivating an Attitude of Gratitude at Home (Advice from the Trenches)

Caitlin Fitzpatrick Curley

"*Mom!* You gave her 26 raisins and I only got 22!"

Flabbergasted, I turn to meet his eyes. "Did you just *count the raisins?*"

"But you gave her *more,*" he whines, eyes filling with tears.

"You are crying about four raisins."

"But it's not fair!"

"What are you supposed to say when someone gives you something?"

He pauses for a moment, frowns, and grumbles a barely audible "thank you" before adding, "but it's still *not fair.*"

I take a deep breath and remind myself *this is not about the raisins.*

Sibling rivalry is a normal part of the parenting experience. Still, counting and comparing before uttering a thank you is not the kind of parenting experience I am looking for.

And I know I'm not alone.

These sibling squabbles always remind me of a quote by Louis C.K.:

"The only time you look in your neighbor's bowl is to make sure that they have enough. You don't look in your neighbor's bowl to see if you have as much as them."

We drill our children in manners, pleases and thank yous and excuse mes, but how do we cultivate true gratitude in our kids? How do we get them to look in another's bowl to be sure that person has enough?

How do we get them to stop counting raisins?

My little friends are in an ungrateful pattern right now, and I'm tired of it. While I certainly do not claim to have all of the answers (please see raisin-counting story above), I am happy to share the strategies we've been trying over here.

Simplify

Whenever our little world feels off track, I simplify. If you've been listening to The Homeschool Sisters Podcast, you already know that Kara and I are huge fans of the book *Simplicity Parenting* by Kim John Payne. This is one of a handful of books that I re-read regularly. It is a breath of fresh air and an easy way to reset our family life.

Do your children have too many toys sitting unused and unappreciated? Too many clothes? Books they never read?

Grab some cardboard boxes, fill them to the brim, and deliver them to someone in need... together! Sure, your kids might grumble at first, but you'll be teaching them important lessons.

Focus on Gratitude

Ever since I was a little girl, I've ended my day by focusing on a "highlight" for which I was grateful. These "highlights of the day" were often super-simple: a peaceful cup of coffee, time spent with a dear friend, a stranger's kindness.

I don't know whether I read about these highlights in a long-forgotten book or if I made them up myself, but I continue to pick a highlight to this day, decades later. (If you like this idea, be sure to stay tuned because Kara and I have added a new ending to our podcasts!)

Make space for gratitude in your day. In the past, we have maintained gratitude journals. During the holidays, we enjoyed a Just So Thankful Jar. Teach your children to write thank you notes early and often.

Model

Children are sponges. If you want to raise grateful children, you must practice gratitude yourself. Make sure you are using *your* manners. Serve others, give freely, say thank you. Share what you are grateful for with your children. Explain why you are thankful *for them!*

If you are deep in the throes of sibling squabbles and unkindness, give them a little incentive. Last summer, our family embarked on a simple yet effective Family Kindness Project and the results were amazing!

Teach Children How to Save, Spend and Give

This year, my husband and I read a thought-provoking book titled *The Opposite of Spoiled: Raising Kids Who Are Grounded, Generous, and Smart About Money*. It gave us a lot of food for thought about raising children who know how to maintain a budget and give generously.

Soon after reading the book, we implemented a weekly allowance system where one-third of the amount is for spending, one-third is for savings and one-third is for giving. The change in our children was immediate. They quickly learned the value of a dollar, and they have started to research and donate to their own individual causes.

Give together.

Donate to favorite causes.

Volunteer as a family.

If money is tight, give your time. When I was a college student, living on couscous and popcorn, I made it a point to donate blood every eight weeks. I continue to give regularly to this day; it is such an easy way to change a life.

More recently, our family has enjoyed gleaning together. We gather at local farms with other gleaning volunteers and collect leftover produce to deliver to local soup kitchens. It is a fun way to get involved in the community and lend a hand, even with active youngsters in tow!

If you are looking for more family-friendly service ideas, check out the website DoingGoodTogether.com!

Read Fantastic Books

There is so much power in a story! I rely heavily on storybooks as teaching tools. A carefully curated stack of read-alouds can serve as a stepping stone for fantastic conversation and learning. Over the years, our family has enjoyed read-alouds focused on being thankful, kindness, ordinary people who change the world, mindfulness and more!

Be Patient

This is probably the most difficult part, but remember how your mom always told you that Rome wasn't built in a day?

She was right.

It is normal for siblings to squabble. Developmentally, it is typical for children to focus on the self rather than others. Things *will* change. Keep up the hard work and teaching and modeling and giving and, with time, you will see a change.

Eventually, they will stop counting raisins.

 *Caitlin Fitzpatrick Curley is a school psychologist, a mom to three amazing children and an unexpected homeschooler. She loves nature, good books, board games, strong coffee and dancing in her kitchen. You can read about all of these things and more at my-little-poppies.com. Cait co-hosts The Homeschool Sisters Podcast and co-founder of Raising Poppies, an Facebook community for parents of gifted and twice-exceptional children. She is a contributing writer for Simple Homeschool and GeekMom. Her work has also appeared on The Huffington Post, The Mighty and Scary Mommy.*

Ten Ways to Volunteer Without Leaving Home

Mary Wilson

Volunteering as a family is one way to engage and support your community as well as the world around you. In addition to helping others, volunteering is a great way to build your children's self-confidence as they see themselves capable of tasks that help others.

Volunteering also allows your family to connect with your local church, community, and the world around you by meeting the needs of people outside of your home. Of course, volunteering is also a very concrete way to help your children develop compassion and a love for others.

Opportunities are plentiful, but finding a workable time slot or opportunities for the ages of your children can be tough. Other questions are also cause for concern: What do we do with our little ones if they are too young? How will this work with nap time? What if one child ends up sick on the day we offered our assistance?

Instead, have you considered the many ways you can volunteer without even leaving your home? Because, let's face it, we want to make an impact on the world around us, but sometimes we need to be able to do it from home.

Make blankets

There are lots of organizations that will accept homemade blankets to give to individuals in need or as a source of comfort. Project Linus is one of many organizations that will accept blankets. Call your local homeless shelter or hospital to find other places for blanket donation. Don't let a lack of seamstress skills stop you. There is the no-sew fleece blanket option, which only requires a knowledge of how to tie knots.

Make meals

Kids often love to cook with their parents! Meals can be made at home and delivered to friends who are dealing with illness or adapting to life with a new baby. Alternatively, ask your church or local homeschool support group to provide you with names of families who could use a meal prepared for them.

Make desserts

Bake your favorite brownies or cookies and deliver them to your local firehouse, doctor's office or police department. Many local rescue missions, homeless shelters and senior centers would love a delivery of homemade desserts, especially around the holidays!

Stuff envelopes

Contact your church or any local organization (political, community or religious) to see if they have a mailing you could take care of for them. Alternatively, ask for a list of summer missionaries you could support by sending out their mailings for them. Pick a time at home and teach your children the proper folding technique (half or tri-fold) and then how to prepare the envelope with labels and stamps.

Sponsor a child

Through organizations like Compassion International or World Vision your family can make a difference in the life of a child living across the world or in your own country. By writing letters and donating financially, your family will connect on an emotional and spiritual level with a child in need without having to leave your home.

Write your story

Did your family volunteer and it made a difference? Does your crew feel strongly about a particular organization? Organizations are often looking for testimonials and stories for their webpages and newsletters. Give them a call and see what you might be able to write for them and then use some time during language arts to cooperatively write a testimonial.

Vlog your story

Instead of writing your story, your family can create a short video to share on your own personal webspace, or email it to an organization for use on their space. Describe how volunteering for this organization has impacted your life. Share your passion for this organization on the video.

Make cards for the holidays

Create a stack of handmade cards with your kids. Deliver them to a local nursing home, senior center, local Rescue Mission or hospital. Many local places could use some holiday cheer to spread during the holidays.

Offer free childcare

Is there a neighbor or friend in need of childcare who doesn't have the budget for it? Perhaps your family could offer an occasional two-hour break for a mom in need of it. If you contact your church, they might have a person to introduce you to who is in need of this sort of help. Homeschooling families are particularly suited to this sort of volunteering because there are other children at home to help out and play with visiting children.

Call and ask

The best volunteer opportunity is often the one that is needed, so call and ask! Call your church, local nursing home, foster system, social service organization, Meals on Wheels, or whatever organization you feel passionate about serving and ask them if there is some need your family could fulfill for them from your home. You might be surprised what needs you could fulfill.

Of course, there are also plentiful volunteer opportunities for families that can be found outside of the home. Our family has enjoyed volunteering both in our home and outside of our home. Either way, I hope you feel inspired and equipped to volunteer with your kids.

Mary Wilson is a homeschooling mother of four children, ranging from 7 to 14 years old. She loves to share her experiences of homeschooling, parenting and adventuring on her blog, NotBefore7.com. When she isn't blogging you can find her hosting book clubs, traveling and running.

In But Not of the World: Helping Our Children Develop Strong Character

Rebecca Reid

Compared to past generations, today's world is not kind. Our society also praises success and expects it, even at the expense of integrity. There seems to exist a culture of expectation among the rising generation and their parents.

Please do not misunderstand. I am not a pessimist. I believe my community is filled with people who, more than not, try to spread joy and kindness. I believe in the goodness of the majority of the human race. Most people want to demonstrate a strong character of gratitude, honesty and determination.

However, bullying others, cheating and justifying rudeness are serious issues in schools and societies. Having a strong positive character is sometimes a feature lacking in adults as well as youth. It is our role as parents to help train the rising generation better than that.

What Character Traits Are Most Important?

I don't believe there is a simple fix or a curriculum for helping our children develop strong character. I cannot, unfortunately, list a "how-to" for such a subject. Each child and each situation is different.

One of the bonuses of being a homeschool parent is that, every day, I can help my children prepare to face this world. One of my priorities as a mother to this generation is to teach my children kindness, compassion, honesty and gratitude — and enough fortitude to be able to face the world on their own when the time comes.

Most of the strong character traits we hope our children develop are directly related to kindness. It all starts with that: kindness to self and others.

In Matthew 22:37-40, Christ taught,

> *Thou shalt love the Lord thy God with all thy heart, and with all thy soul, and with all thy mind.*
>
> *This is the first and great commandment.*
>
> *And the second is like unto it, Thou shalt love thy neighbour as thyself.*
>
> *On these two commandments hang all the law and the prophets.*

This concept of the "golden rule" is present in many cultures. And yet, people seem to have forgotten it. (A nice picture book to go along with the Bible verse is *The Golden Rule* by Ilene Cooper.)

If everyone in our community were to remember the golden rule, dishonesty and crime would go away (no need to lock things up, because no one would steal). Jealousy and greed would disappear (we would all be grateful for each other and happy for others' successes). Honor and determination would increase (because we all would be striving to do our best).

That said, it is not easy to impart these concepts to our children. Although I can't give a quick checklist of how to do so, I hope the following thoughts might help you as you ponder how to best reach your children.

Here is what I know: Teaching kindness and compassion must start with me, the parent. I must be an example. Similarly, as a parent, I help by teaching my kids to notice and use their words to communicate what we see. I can be their eyes until they can notice for themselves. Finally, I must be patient with them as I teach them principle upon principle. We can't learn anything all at once, and developing kindness is a life mission for all of us.

Being an Example

You've heard the saying, "Walk the walk, don't just talk the talk." Well, this is exactly what is needed when considering how to teach a young child what strong moral character is. Our ultimate example in our home is our savior, Jesus Christ. He lived a perfect life. His life is what we should all learn from.

Needless to say, I am not perfect. I have found myself yelling or berating my children when they are disobedient, slow or irresponsible. Yelling and berating is exactly what I do not want my children to do. If they are face-to-face with someone who is struggling, tired or confused, I want them to respond with a nice voice and a calm demeanor. I want my children to *want* to help someone who is upset. If I want them to do those things, then I need to do it first to be their example.

I have much to learn about showing kindness and compassion. I want to be better, and I try every day to aim to emulate Jesus. The only way my children will learn to react with kindness is if that is my own daily walk.

Here are things I've noticed help me show kindness and compassion to my children.

Say "thank you" as often as I can. Gratitude is a form of kindness.

Apologize sincerely when I realize I'm in the wrong. Let's face it, parents are often wrong. It's not always easy to admit, but it is true.

Lower my voice and get control of my own strong emotions before responding to a child.

Consider all sides of a situation before jumping to a conclusion.

What is your weakness? How can you better improve yourself so you may be a better example for your children?

Every Moment is a Teaching Moment

Even if we are being the best possible example to our children, it is quite possible they are oblivious to those around them. We all tend to see the world through our own eyes. I have one child who is naturally observant and sincere in compassion, and always has been, even since a very young age. A different child of mine is more self-centered, with different strengths of character and personality.

As the parent, I know my less-observant child needs help learning to be kind and compassionate. Here are some ways to do that.

Help your children find words for the strong emotions they are feeling. "You are sad because Ted took your toy! I wonder if Ted knows how you feel." As children learn to articulate their feelings, they will be better able to understand the feelings of others. I think it is super-important we never diminish the feelings of our children. ("Get over it! Your turn was over!") That teaches them that their voice does not matter, and may contribute to future rudeness on their part.

Help your children express gratitude for what they have been given. As they notice, they can better express kindness to others as well.

When others are upset and your children are not, direct their attention to the others. Ask them questions about how the other children are feeling.

Help your children consider how others feel while playing with toys or while not having toys. Encourage sharing and fairness, but especially point out the feelings of others around them.

When someone does something nice for your children, state what has been done and put a positive feeling with it. This helps the children notice what has been done and how they feel about it.

In a moment when the kids are receptive to learning, tell a tale of "walking in someone else's shoes" that they may relate to.

Children need to be taught to notice the everyday moments around them. When others are in need of compassion or are given kindness, then compassion and gratitude can become their natural reactions.

Walking in Someone Else's Shoes

My friend once told me a story. She was making a cake for a friend's reception. It took her hours of work. When it was time to take it to the venue, she carefully loaded it into the back of her car on a special tray.

My friend was very nervous about transporting the cake, however. She'd never driven with a cake of that size in her car. She really did not want to mess up the frosting after all the hours of work she'd put in.

Because of her care, she decided to drive extra-slowly. At each intersection, she braked early and came to a very gradual stop. At each turn, she moved at a snail's pace. Even in regular traffic, she ignored the others around her and went at a steady speed. She did not want to mess up that precious cake!

A few days later, she once again traveled the same route. As she waited at a stop light, she felt frustration at the slow car in front of her. Didn't the driver see the light had turned green?!

Almost immediately, she remembered her cake. Maybe the driver in front of her had a cake in the car! Her frustration melted away at the thought. That person deserved to get that cake to the destination without any smudged frosting. She could be more patient.

Road rage would not exist if we all controlled ourselves and showed kindness and compassion to others! Our kids learn from us. A tale such as this one helps us "walk in someone else's shoes." It can help our kids understand those around them.

What kind of analogy would relate to your children?

My children probably would not understand the cake analogy. But maybe my daughter would respond to a tale about a princess.

Accepting Imperfection

My prime exemplar is Jesus, who is perfect. But none of us are perfect. It is perfectly all right for kids to take years to develop an ability to show kindness and compassion.

As their parents, we are constantly showing them an example — good or bad. When we give kindness and express compassion for the very real feelings that our children experience, we improve our own lives. We are still learning. Of course it is OK that our kids are still learning.

For example, one day recently I mumbled a simple frustration about another driver as I drove. I was impatient. We were late.

My 4-year-old daughter quickly piped up, "Mom, Jesus does not want us to say mean things about people."

So yes, even though I am the adult and she is the child, we all can get a lesson each day. I love that I can learn to become better simply by being with my kids each day and striving to do so!

Life as a homeschooling parent is very hard. But the longer I do it, the more I think I'm becoming a better person myself. I want to be that good example for my children. God helps me measure up to the task.

Recommended Reading (for Parents)

Here are some books I've also loved that have influenced my views as I have navigated parenting and homeschooling. I've annotated the list with some explanations of how these books help you as you strive to teach your children to have a strong moral fiber.

It's OK Not to Share by Heather Schumacher. It emphasizes the need to teach kids to notice rather than to make them be nice, for example.

Teaching Kids to Think by Darlene Sweetland and Ron Stolberg. It helps parents nurture kids as the kids work on developing determination and grit. Kids need to learn to work through their own problems.

Awakening Children's Minds by Laura Berk. Although it is a bit more technical, Awakening Children's Minds has an emphasis on how to provide "scaffolding" to help kids learn concepts that are difficult for them. It is one of my favorite books for parenting and homeschooling reminders.

Raising an Emotionally Intelligent Child by John Gottman. Learning to regulate emotions and deal with them on one's own is essential to developing a strong character.

How to Talk So Kids Will Listen and Listen So Kids Will Talk by Adele Faber and Elaine Mazlich. This classic parenting book is nearly 40 years old. I find it to be a practical guide to helping develop open communication with my children.

How Children Succeed by Paul Tough, A look at why some children succeed while others do not despite their circumstances. He discusses how the ability to hang on (which he calls grit) is the defining characteristic and how parents can help kids develop it.

Rebecca Reid is a homeschooling mother of three: "Raisin," born in 2007; "Strawberry," born in 2012; and "Kitty," born in 2015. She loves creating games and hands-on activities for her kids. Homeschooling is the most difficult thing she's ever done, as well as the most rewarding. She blogs about homeschooling at Line Upon Line Learning, found at homeschool.rebeccareid.com and began blogging about reading classics, nonfiction, and children's literature at Rebecca Reads, found at rebeccareid.com in 2008.

Learning Resources: Unique Needs

Adapting Your Homeschool for Your Sons

Michelle Caskey

We all know that men and women are different. But did you know that God has made it so that men and women see differently, hear differently and even think differently? Because of this, boys and girls learn best in vastly different ways.

Many girls enjoy curling up on a window seat to fill out worksheets and read books. Ask a girl to write a story or to tell you about what she has learned and she will blossom. Ask most boys to do these things and you might find that they will rebel, especially if the worksheet is black-and-white and the book contains lots of long descriptions and little action.

Differences Between Boys and Girls

You might be amazed to learn boys and girls have more physical and mental differences than most people think. Dr. Leonard Sax has written some eye-opening books such as *Why Gender Matters* and *Boys Adrift*. These books include scientific evidence showing that boys not only behave differently than girls, but they also hear differently, see differently, respond to stress differently and think differently.

The things boys can learn are very similar, but the way they go about learning is very different. Boys require a different educational environment and teaching approach if we are going to help them reach their full potential.

Boys See Differently

When asked to draw a picture, girls will usually draw a picture such as a house with people and flowers and lots of pretty colors. Boys will be more likely to draw a tornado that is knocking down a house – and that picture will often look like a large black swirl.

Males have more rods in their eyes than they do cones. Rods help us to see distance and speed. Females have more cones than rods. Cones help us to see color and shape. Because of this difference, boys tend to draw verbs with little color variation in their pictures, while girls tend to draw nouns with lots of different colors.

Implications for Teaching Boys

Do not expect boys to draw something recognizable or to draw something with lots of colors. When we find fault in this way, boys begin to think that art is for girls and not for boys.

Allow boys to draw verbs, and to do it in a way that is fast and furious.

Don't hold eye contact with a boy unless you're disciplining him.

Boys Hear Differently

Baby girls can hear 10 times better than boys, and this difference gets even more pronounced as they get older. Boys can only hear every third word or so of soft-spoken teachers. When boys can't hear what their teacher is saying, they tend to drift off – getting some boys the incorrect diagnosis of ADHD.

Boys also tend to make little noises while wiggling and tapping pencils, which are irritating to girls, but they don't even realize they are making them.

Implications for Teaching Boys

Speak more loudly than you normally would, and be very expressive.

Use lots of voice fluctuation and hand motions to engage boys.

While working with your son, sit down next to him, spread the materials out and look at them shoulder to shoulder.

Boys Think Differently

We don't know all of the differences in how boys and girls think, but we now know that their brains are arranged differently. We've all heard that we use the left side of our brain for verbal activities and the right side for art. Actually, we now know that this is more pronounced in males.

Males who have a stroke on the left side of their brain lose 80% of their verbal ability. The verbal ability in females who have a stroke on the left side of their brain is much less impacted, proving that their verbal ability is spread across both sides of their brain.

Implications for Teaching Boys

Book learning is essential; however, without practical, hands-on experience, boys will have a hard time grasping concepts that seem simple to adults. They will disengage from their lessons.

Boys need real-world experiences in their education that engage all of their senses.

Boys also need plenty of time outdoors.

Boys have a hard time processing their emotions. Don't ask boys "How would you feel if..." questions. Ask them "What would you do if..." questions.

Boys like to have at least some control over their environments. Put each day's schoolwork into a folder and let them decide the order in which they will complete it.

When studying literature, try these tips:

Have boys draw maps based on clues in the book.

Assign articles from the daily newspaper.

Have them read books with strong male characters doing unpredictable things (e.g., C.S. Lewis, Hemingway, Dostoevsky, Twain, etc.)

Boys See Themselves Differently

Girls tend to underestimate their own abilities. Boys tend to overestimate their own abilities. Boys also enjoy taking risks much more than girls do. The more boys take risks, the more favorably they are seen by their peers.

Danger itself gives boys a pleasant feeling of exhilaration as opposed to the fearful feelings it causes in girls. Moderate stress also helps boys to perform better as adrenaline causes more blood to flow to their brain. Stress has the opposite effect on girls.

Implications for Teaching Boys

Boys respond well to a challenge if there are winners and losers.

A competitive team format works better than individual competitions for boys because they don't want to let their teammates down.

Participation in single-sex activities such as Boy Scouts or team sports is very good for your sons.

If your son seems to crave danger, take these necessary steps:

Give him lessons with a professional (i.e., skiing) to help him more accurately evaluate his own abilities.

Supervise your child. Their risk is lower if he isn't allowed to be alone with groups of peers because he will be less likely to try to "show off" for his friends if an adult is present.

Assert your authority – don't argue with your son. Don't negotiate. Just do what you have to do (for instance, lock up his bike.)

By the way, the optimum temperature for learning for boys is 69 degrees, while it is 74 degrees for girls. If you set the temperature so that it is comfortable for you, you may find your sons falling asleep or their minds wandering instead of focusing on their lessons.

Homeschooling Methods that Work Well for Boys

So now that we know about some of the physical differences between boys and girls, how should we homeschool our sons? Is it possible to help them love learning, or should we resign ourselves to the fact that most boys hate school, so they're probably going to hate homeschooling as well?

Fortunately, there are ways that we can teach lessons in our homeschools so that our sons will not only learn more but will also enjoy the process.

5 Ways to Adapt Your Homeschool for your Son

Consider letting him start later. Boys' language and fine motor skills don't develop as early as girls' do. If you notice your son is struggling, you may want to delay teaching reading and writing skills until he shows more signs of being ready. There are plenty of other learning activities you can do with your son that don't involve him having a pencil in his hand.

Let him move. Asking your son to sit still is one surefire way to tire him out and frustrate him. Rather than expecting your son to sit at a desk for long periods of time, come up with lessons that will allow him to move around. Physical play is essential for children's fine and gross motor development, and movement actually helps kids to learn better.

When you want your son to sit down, consider giving him a body ball to sit on rather than a regular chair. Believe it or not, chairs that allow him to bounce and wiggle will allow him to concentrate better on whatever else you're asking him to do as well. In his book *Spark*, John Ratey says that physical activity increases levels of the neurotransmitters dopamine and norepinephrine the same way that ADHD medications do. Both of these chemicals play a large role in increasing focus and attention in our kids.

Incorporate hands-on activities. Boys learn best with hands-on activities and those that incorporate their whole bodies. Building a bridge out of popsicle sticks will teach them so much more than merely reading a book about bridges. Also, when you want your sons to sit and listen, give them something mindless to do with their hands: allow them to doodle, or give them worry beads, Wikki Stiks or squeeze balls. Not having to focus on staying absolutely still will conserve your sons' energy for focusing on class lessons.

Choose books boys enjoy. Boys love books with lots of action. They often enjoy science fiction, mysteries and other fast-paced books. Rather than choosing books we remember reading when we were kids, us moms may need to mine the brains of our husbands to find books our boys will enjoy. There are also many lists on the internet of books that boys will enjoy. Also, feel free to let your son read his book up in a tree, down by the creek or snuggled in bed under a blanket with a flashlight.

Make it fun. Boys appreciate a sense of humor. Try not to be too serious while you're teaching your lessons. Inject some surprises. Laugh at your son's jokes. There is a time and a place for seriousness, but it can be easy for us moms to be so concerned about our children's education that we make their lessons dry and somewhat boring - especially in their eyes.

Remember, our goal is not to remove the maleness from our sons. It's possible to let your boy be a boy and educate him at the same time!

Homeschooling Methods that Don't Work Well for Boys

Unfortunately, many of us model our homeschools after the type of education that we received when we were kids, meaning we copy the local public school. This is a surefire way to make your sons hate homeschooling.

Families who have all daughters might be able to get away with educating them the same way that schools do. If you have boys, you should steer clear of certain types of learning.

7 Things to Avoid When Homeschooling Boys

Forcing them to sit at a desk with a pencil in their hand all day long. As I said above, boys learn best when they are moving. We should be allowing our boys to take frequent movement breaks as well as building movement into their lessons whenever possible. This is especially important for young boys. As they get older, they will be able to sit still for longer periods of time. You'll find, however, that even grown men appreciate being able to move around while thinking. This is one reason why stand-up desks are becoming so popular and why you'll see men pace while they are talking on the phone. Let your son move.

Handing them a pile of worksheets to complete all day. Most boys learn a lot more when they are actually DOING something vs. just filling out worksheets. Observe your son to find out how he learns best. Be willing to let him take apart your old alarm clock, build a tree fort in the backyard, collect bugs and dissect them, or wallow around in the mud to see for himself how pigs cool off.

Expecting lots and lots of homework to be completed every evening. Boys learn more with shorter, high-impact lessons than they do drawing out their schoolwork through the entire day. Don't feel like you need to drone on and on while talking with them. Make your point and move on. Some practice is good with subjects such as math. Once your son has learned something, though, he will appreciate it if you don't hammer it to death with piles of homework.

Never going on field trips. Real-life learning is so important for boys. Get them out into world and let them experience life. Learning about a battle by visiting the battlefield is going to be more memorable to your son than merely reading about it. Reading the details is also important, but don't forget to add in the field trips to make your son's lessons come alive.

Never getting together with other homeschoolers. Our boys need to learn how to support their families and get along in the real world. Getting together with other homeschoolers and discussing books, going on combined field trips or studying various subjects together is a great way for your son to do this. The more varied the people he's comfortable being around, the better he will be at getting along with future coworkers.

Never asking them what they would like to study. Each of our sons has been put on this earth for a specific purpose. God has put dreams and passions inside each of our children. Our job is to observe them and talk with them so that we can prepare them for whatever God has for their future. If we are set on following a rigid course of study and don't modify it at all to give our child an individualized education, we are missing out on one of the biggest freedoms that homeschooling has to offer.

Staying inside all day long. Fresh air and exercise are good for all of us. Try to get your boys outside as often as possible. Do your lessons on a picnic table in the backyard or at a park. Take nature walks. Go swimming. Encourage your boys to catch frogs and butterflies and worms. Let your boys explore God's amazing world and discover the awesomeness of creation for themselves.

By making a few simple changes such as the ones detailed above, we will make it much more likely that our boys will become lifelong learners. Remember, our boys require a different type of education if they are going to flourish. We need to keep the above points in mind so that we don't cause our boys to hate learning in our homeschools.

 *Michelle has been married to her best friend for 17 years. She is also a homeschool mom to her two wonderful (and tall) sons. Michelle is a Christian, a fan of simple living and a lover of chocolate. She loves her spicy chai tea in the morning and she has a hard time staying out of the snacks at night. You can find her blogging at homeschool-your-boys.com. Her mission is to encourage and inspire parents as they homeschool their boys.*

7 Things I've Learned from Raising A Gifted Child

Caitlin Fitzpatrick Curley

My son is gifted. When you read gifted just now, what popped into your head? Do you think I'm bragging?

Do you picture my son as a budding prodigy? Do you assume that I'm a Tiger Mom, and that my husband and I have hot-housed him since birth?

Do you imagine my son performing well in school? Do you assume he must be easy to parent? Do you think we're lucky?

My son is gifted, and it's not what you think. Gifted is a loaded term. The word gift implies that one has been given something; that one has a leg up over others. This couldn't be further from the truth. As the parent of a profoundly gifted and twice-exceptional child, I have learned so much about this population.

Gifted Children Are Asynchronous

When my son was just 2 years old, I entered his room one night to find him sobbing, unable to sleep. As I held him in my arms, comforting his trembling little body, he explained that he was afraid of extinction. "Mama," he sobbed, "The dinosaurs are extinct and the scientists don't know why. What if we all die, and become extinct for some unknown reason?!"

While the average child develops in a relatively uniform manner, gifted children are asynchronous. My son is many ages at once. Chronologically, he might be 7 years old, but intellectually, he is more than twice his age. His social-emotional development, however, is probably that of a 5-year-old. His little mind houses thoughts and worries that his emotions cannot yet process.

Gifted Children Are Emotionally Intense

When my son is happy, he's really happy. As in, overjoyed, literally-bouncing-off-the-walls happy. When he is sad, he collapses into a mushy mess on the floor. When he is scared, he is terrified. When we are out in public and he meets with frustration, he can throw a fit to rival that of any 2-year-old. I still have to underarm him out of public places on occasion. He tests my patience and keeps me humble on a daily basis.

Gifted Children Are Sensitive

My son is supremely sensitive. He was unable to watch television for many years; the themes were just too much for him to handle until recently. And I cannot recall the last time we watched the news in our home. He already worries about crime, poverty, endangered animals, global warming, and war without exposure to current events.

Giftedness and Achievement Are Two Different Entities

When my son was in kindergarten, his academic skills were 2 to 5 years above his grade level. He read Harry Potter on the bus ride to school, but did he perform well in school? Not at all. In fact, he floundered. He was the fidgety kid in the back of the class, tipping in his chair and singing the Frozen soundtrack in reverse order. He was the kid who brought his paperclip collection to school to fidget with, the kid who doodled on his neighbor's paper rather than listening to the teacher.

As the year wore on, the pile of behavior slips increased in height. At home, he was a joyful learner and yet, when I picked him up from school, he'd climb into my car and grimly ask, "Do I have to go to school tomorrow?" At only 5 years old, he was wholly misunderstood.

Gifted Children Can Have Learning Disabilities

My son's cognitive abilities are above the 99.9th percentile, but he struggles with sensory processing disorder and ADHD. He is twice-exceptional - gifted and learning disabled - and he is not alone.

There is an entire population of twice-exceptional students who struggle to have their needs met in a public school setting.

Gifted Children Need Intellectual Peers

When my son was 5 years old, we went out to breakfast with some of his friends. As we were leaving the restaurant, my son pointed to a garden trellis and shouted, "Guys! Look! Doesn't that latticework remind you of a portcullis?" His friends smiled and carried on with their play as I Googled portcullis on my phone. He was right; it did look like a portcullis. And then my heart sank because I wondered if he will ever have friends who truly get him and his unique thinking.

Gifted Is Not What You Think

My son is a funny, brilliant, creative, energetic, frustrating, demanding and exhausting little person. He is a joy to raise; however, parenting him has been the greatest challenge of my life. Over the years, it has gotten easier, but it's never been easy. He has taught me so much over the past seven years, including patience, understanding, grace and humility. He is my wisest teacher and for that, I am forever grateful.

Are you the parent of a gifted child, too? Welcome to the wild, wonderful, zany world of parenting poppies. Grab a cup of coffee and your sense of humor, and sit back and enjoy the ride! And don't worry... you've got this!

You are going to learn so much, mama. Children are our wisest teachers.

Caitlin Fitzpatrick Curley is a school psychologist, a mom to three amazing children and an unexpected homeschooler. She loves nature, good books, board games, strong coffee and dancing in her kitchen. You can read about all of these things and more at my-little-poppies.com. Cait co-hosts The Homeschool Sisters Podcast and co-founder of Raising Poppies, an Facebook community for parents of gifted and twice-exceptional children. She is a contributing writer for Simple Homeschool and GeekMom. Her work has also appeared on The Huffington Post, The Mighty and Scary Mommy.

Homeschooling Worriers

Caitlin Fitzpatrick Curley

Something happens every summer.

Somewhere between the sandy toes and the watermelon slices, the worry creeps in.

Usually after dark.

Summer is *supposed* to be an endless string of leisurely days filled with swimming and catching fireflies and eating popsicles and reading your weight in delicious books.

You're supposed to be *relaxed*.

How can one be worried when the days are so carefree? It seems counterintuitive.

As the mother of a worrier, I've thought about this phenomenon quite a bit.

Why now?

Why summer?

I think this whole summer worry cycle happens *because* we are more relaxed. It's kind of like how some people get sick on vacation. Your body lets its guard down. It's a worry sneak-attack.

And, when you think about it, summer is the perfect set-up for a worry sneak-attack. The days are longer and brighter, and it's often hot and sticky and hard to sleep. No wonder the worry creeps in!

Mothering a Worrier

I can remember, as a kid, sitting up in my bed on a hot summer night, listening to crickets, and freaking the heck out. I worried about *BIG* things: current events, war, poverty, global warming, killer bees, death and dying, and the sun burning out.

So is it any surprise that now, 30 years later, I am mothering a child who does the same?

I often describe our oldest son as a *World-Class Worrier*. In just eight short years on this planet, our son has conquered a multitude of worries. From mourning doves to television to global warming to mass human extinction.

I could go on and on and on.

I'd love to tell you that we've conquered worry for good, but we haven't.

Worry is tricky. It ebbs and flows and changes shape and sneak-attacks you just when you least expect it.

You can't make worry disappear completely, but you *can* manage it.

I can tell you this: Hindsight helps.

The more worry battles your child is faced with...

The more strategies added to his or her "Worry Toolbox"...

The more "Worry Wins" your child accrues...

Hindsight makes each new worry a bit easier to manage. Your family has been here before. You can do it again.

You've got this.

But sometimes that's hard to remember. When worry rears its ugly head, sometimes we freeze. We panic. We forget that we know how to do this.

Mothering a worrier can be exhausting. Believe me, I understand. When you are in the midst of a worry surge, it feels like all of your energy is spent fighting the battle. And then, suddenly, the fog clears... until the next time.

I have learned to think of these worry swells as teachable moments. After all, we *all* experience worry from time to time. Sure, some of us experience it more severely, and more frequently, but no one is immune to worry. It is a part of life.

Learning to manage difficult emotions is an important life skill. The sooner your child learns effective coping and calming strategies, the better. These coping skills will serve your child well in life.

Today, I am sharing a list of things that I believe every little worrier should know, plus a free printable that will help your child to remember past successes or *Worry Wins*. I certainly don't have all the answers, but these strategies have helped our family and I hope that they will help yours, too.

What Your Little Worrier Needs to Know

Worry is Normal

Worry serves an important purpose: protection. It plays a key role in the fight-or-flight response and keeps us safe.

You are not alone. Every single person on this planet has worries. *Every. Single. Person.* Worry is a normal part of the human experience.

Worry is Temporary

It certainly doesn't *feel* temporary, but it is. When it spikes, it is important to remember that worry ebbs and flows. And this brings me to...

Worry Can Be Managed

There are steps you can take to manage worry more effectively. You need to determine the coping and calming strategies that work best for you.

In our home, we call this our Worry Toolbox. I feel better if I do yoga, go for a run, listen to music or have some time alone with a book.

You might feel better when you go out with friends, go for a swim or meditate. Each person has a unique Worry Toolbox! Talk about your coping strategies with your child and then help your child to identify his or her own. Great strategies include, but are not limited to:

- Guided relaxation
- Meditation
- Distraction
- Humor
- Yoga
- Mindfulness
- Progressive muscle relaxation
- Deep breathing
- Music
- Art
- Writing

And don't be afraid to try something new! Lately, we have the most success with our calming doodle diaries. In the past, we had success with a calm-down spray at bedtime, and another time my son loved a calming play dough. But, what worked before may not work this time, and it's always a good idea to add more strategies to your worry toolbox!

Simplify, Simplify, Simplify

I cannot tell you how important simplifying has been in our family. Whenever our son's worry spikes, we cut back on everything else and refocus. We clear our calendars and make sure we are focusing on the most important things: family, quality time, exercise, quiet time, nutritious meals and sleep.

If your child is struggling with worry, cut back. You'll be surprised on how much better you all feel with this one simple act.

Talking About Worry is Super-Important

When you don't talk about your worry, when you avoid it, you give the worry more power. Talking about your worry is an important step toward winning the battle. Sometimes, worry can be difficult to talk about in the moment. In these cases, set up a date later to chat. Sometimes it can be easier to talk when you are moving, playing a game or riding in the car. It doesn't matter *where* you talk about it, just make sure you do it!

Your Worry Does Not Define You

Everyone has strengths and weaknesses. You have *oodles* of strengths! When the worry feels like it is overshadowing you, remember all of your gifts.

Being Sensitive is a Superpower

Sensitivity is a superpower. You care deeply for others and the world around you in a way that others do not. Your sensitivity allows you to be in-tune with the feelings of those around you and to treat others carefully. Sensitive souls make great friends and kindness attracts kindness.

Your Brain is Amazing

In our family, we have had great success through learning a little neuroscience. Did you know that if your amygdala is too sensitive, you can actually work to change it? You can exercise your brain just as you exercise your body!

Asking for Help is Brave

Sometimes, the worry is just too much. In these cases, it is brave to ask for help. If your child's worry is significantly impairing his or her daily functioning, or if there is a history of anxiety disorders in your family, it's important to seek help. The sooner, the better. Believe me, your child will be so relieved to have another supportive adult in his or her corner, cheering for those Worry Wins.

You Have Conquered Worry Before, and You Can Do It Again

Whenever my son is struggling with a swell of worry, I remind him of all the worries he's conquered in his eight years on this planet. The list is a long one. Reminding him of these successes helps him to remember that he's done this before. And not only has he done it before, he's done it a gazillion times! Listing all his past Worry Wins never fails to elicit a smile, even if he's deep in the throes.

I'll often make a Worry Wins list to hang in his bedroom, or on the bathroom mirror, to remind him daily that he's an expert at battling worries. This is one of our family's favorite strategies.

A Final Word

For the majority of people who suffer with worry and anxiety, it is *not* a one-time event. Anxiety ebbs and flows over time. One must learn to manage anxiety. And, unfortunately, our family has oodles of experience riding the anxiety waves and working to manage our son's anxiety swells. As a homeschool parent, it is important for you to realize that it is OK to pause and focus on this, right now. Coping skills are among the most important of life skills, and the sooner your child learns to manage strong emotions, the better!

Caitlin Fitzpatrick Curley is a school psychologist, a mom to three amazing children and an unexpected homeschooler. She loves nature, good books, board games, strong coffee and dancing in her kitchen. You can read about all of these things and more at my-little-poppies.com. Cait co-hosts The Homeschool Sisters Podcast and co-founder of Raising Poppies, an Facebook community for parents of gifted and twice-exceptional children. She is a contributing writer for Simple Homeschool and GeekMom. Her work has also appeared on The Huffington Post, The Mighty and Scary Mommy.

Homeschooling with Chronic Illness

Candy Reid

Illness strikes whomever it pleases, whenever it pleases. And homeschoolers certainly don't have an immunity against it.

My own family has lived through our share of illness. From our 3-year-old's diagnosis of MAE (myoclonic astatic epilepsy) to my own battle with a very aggressive form of breast cancer, we have learned how to "keep on keepin' on" despite challenging medical circumstances.

Yet I am here to tell you that chronic illness doesn't have to mean the end of your homeschool! With a little creativity, patience and teamwork, your children can still thrive at home.

Though every family's dynamics will be different, if you are suffering through chronic illness, you'll find the following concepts essential to continue learning at home through this time.

Be Willing to School Unconventionally

When my body was worn down from chemo, my little ones and I often "did school" on my bed. There's no rule that says school only counts if it's done in a school room or at a table. My littles actually thought it was fun. Remember, learning takes place in many forms, and the important thing right now is to get well. Concentrate on getting through the day, and do whatever it takes to do that. Each. Day.

Don't Be a Slave to a Schedule

Your body needs extra rest during times of illness. If you can sleep until 9 a.m., then, by all means, stay in the bed. Rest, mama! You can start your school day at 10:30 just as easily as you can start at 8. Schooling can also take place on weekends or in the evenings if needed.

Consider Outsourcing

If you have high school students or children who have special skills and study needs, this may be the time to outsource some courses. Check out the chapter called "Determining How and When to Outsource Homeschooling Subjects" in this book for some ideas.

Accept Outside Help with Household Duties

If someone says, "Let me know if you need anything," take them up on their offer. Seriously. Now's not the time to be concerned about their sincerity. Most likely they are sincere, but if not, they'll learn not to ask again.

Don't be Ashamed to Ask for Help

But if you're not getting offers of help, don't be ashamed to ask. Bear in mind, however, that most people have not walked a mile in your shoes, and may not even know what you need. So go ahead and be specific with your requests. Friends and family would likely be more than happy to wash a few loads of clothes, vacuum the floor, or cook a meal; you just need to let them know.

Incorporate Help from Older Children

If you've already taught your children the importance of working as a team to run a household, then this should be a fairly easy transition. If you haven't, well, then there's no time like the present. Older siblings can help the younger ones with schoolwork - handling everything from reading out loud and checking daily work to tutoring. All of the kids can do age-appropriate chores. Writing out a simple chore chart can go a long way in helping things run smoothly.

Be Willing to Accept a New Normal

Whether or not you like it, you'll need to get good at going with the flow. So start modeling this flexibility for your children and help them learn how to adapt to whatever life throws at them. Because no matter what y'all are going through now, there will be other stuff coming up down the line, too. If they learn today that "normal is only a setting on the dryer," they'll be less likely to develop either a sense of entitlement or a martyr complex tomorrow.

Keep the Lines of Communication Open with Your Kids

At the end of the day, remember that your kids are in this, too. While you might think that you're doing them a favor by keeping them in the dark about the situation, in reality you might be keeping them from some valuable real-life lessons. Homeschooling is so much more than the "three Rs." Character lessons such as tenacity, creativity, persistence, faith, and inter-dependency are super important. Practical skills such as housekeeping and shopping and cooking and even child care, perhaps, will be useful throughout their lives. Most of all, use this time to be real with them, and in the process, grow a solid relationship through honest communication. This concept of communication is probably the most important, and certainly one that can even influence their eternity.

I would never wish to walk through another life-threatening, chronic illness, yet I'm forever grateful that God used those times to teach me so many wonderful lessons. And I'm thankful that our family was brought closer together through the process.

If you find yourself in a similar situation, rely on God and seek Him throughout it all. He is gentle and loving and will most certainly provide for your family – everything from household management to homeschooling needs.

Candy Reid has been homeschooling for more than 20 years. Although most of those years have been good, many included journeys through serious illness. Nevertheless, she remembers the lessons she has learned through the hard times, and shares them to encourage others to stay the course on their own journeys. You can read all about her experiences in Who Turned Out the Lights?, available on Amazon. She continues to write about faith and family-oriented topics at PatAndCandy.com.

Learning at Your Child's Pace

Erin Brown

Children learn at different paces, and one of the beautiful things about homeschooling is that each child can work at an individual pace. Children who need more time can take more time, and children who are ready to forge ahead can forge ahead. It's just up to us, as parents and educators, to keep up with their pace. But it can be challenging to know where they are, what pace they need, and how to keep it all together.

Keeping Up with the Joneses

The hardest part of working at your child's pace is often judgment, or perceived judgment, from others.

There is a notion that all kids should be learning on the same level and at the same pace as other kids their age, but that is simply not reality. However, knowing that your children don't have to work at the same pace as everyone else and actually letting them work at their own pace and dealing with the judgment are two very different things.

Don't strive to have your children at the same point in their education as someone else just because their birthdays are close or they are the same "grade level." Even twins have different needs when it comes to education! Once we accept that all kids are unique, it is much easier to stop the comparisons.

Dealing with Critics

But what about when the judgment is coming from someone else? Sometimes other people feel it's their duty to let everyone know what they think. These might be parents, grandparents, other family members, friends, complete strangers or the clerk at the grocery store. It can be hard to stop the comparisons when someone feels the need to vocalize all those negative thoughts!

My recommendations:

- Ignore the remarks as best as you can.
- Redirect the conversations.
- Politely but firmly tell them to stop.

Your options will differ depending on who it is. As a last resort, avoid that person. Sometimes people aren't meant to be in our lives. We have no responsibility to continue relationships that are toxic. Taking a break from a relationship might be the factor that also saves the relationship.

How to Follow Your Child's Pace

First, **determine where your child is**. The method for this will depend upon what subject you are thinking about. For math, there are placement tests your children can take. Your best bet is to use a placement test from the curriculum you've chosen. Otherwise, there are multiple options online to determine placement for many different subjects. Other subjects work in other ways. Reading levels can be established with certain tests, too.

Second, **relax**. If you are a planner or a scheduler, you might need to just relax. Give your children a chance to set their pace and let you know how fast or slow they need to go. For my kids, it was a matter of finding the right starting point. Once we figured out where they needed to start, they zoomed through their lessons (for the most part). Had I tried to schedule the lessons and determine the exact pace, they would not have approached learning as enthusiastically.

Third, **encourage and motivate**. One of my goals in home education is that my children learn how to learn and feel motivated to learn. Learning should be a lifelong endeavor. However, I've found that when we have trouble with setting the right pace, they lose motivation. Sometimes going too slow creates boredom. Going too fast creates frustration. In both cases, they can quickly lose the motivation to learn.

We motivate in multiple ways. The best motivator is finding a subject they are interested in or relating a subject to an interest of theirs. For instance, my oldest has expressed interest in working in genetic research, so we explored science and math concepts that would be useful. He felt more motivated knowing that the concepts were related to genetics.

Achievement charts can be motivational to the right children. As my children get older, we stop doing immediate rewards and set one goal with one big reward. We typically don't set a goal that would increase their set pace, but we might set a goal like "Work on math 20 minutes a day." Every day that they accomplish that, they get a sticker. After a certain number of days, they get a prize. This isn't a method I would use all the time, but to get some of the magic back in learning, it can be a useful tool.

Finally, **adjust as necessary**. Once you find their pace, it'll probably change again. There are so many factors that can affect how children learn. By paying attention to their signals, we can adjust as needed and save ourselves and them from unnecessary stress.

Working Below Grade Level

Sometimes kids need to work below grade level. Perhaps they are not ready for the higher level, or they are behind in the course work.   I've found that sometimes, when switching curricula, it is necessary to go back a bit. When working below grade level, there can be a pressure to catch up. Some kids will go through the lower materials quickly and be back on grade level. Other kids will continue to work below grade level.

I have one child working below grade level in two subjects. At first, it was really hard not to rush him through the material. Once I relaxed and let him work at his pace, he actually started learning faster and gained a lot of confidence.

I would not suggest working through breaks in an attempt to catch up. Kids need breaks to reset and recharge! You know your children best, so keep in mind their needs in any attempt to catch up to grade level.

Working Above Grade Level

Working above grade level can be tricky because the higher grade levels are meant for older kids. In subjects where the material needs to relate to age, working above grade level can be a challenge. For example, when reading books geared toward 18-year-olds, the subject matter doesn't always hold the interest of a 10-

year-old. However, we don't want to hold kids back from their potential either.

Some people have to make decisions on whether to skip a year, or two, of a particular curriculum. This decision is a challenge in and of itself. When we are trying to figure out placement, we start at the lowest possible and work through, often skipping entire sections. For some subjects, like math, I want to make sure we don't miss anything. Once we've ensured we've covered everything in the book, I feel much more confident about moving on.

When Grade Level Matters

For many homeschoolers, the idea of grade level is a moot point. Their kids will never be in public school and won't feel the pressure to learn at another person's pace. For others, though, public school is a possibility or they might even have a plan to start public school in high school. In those cases, grade level is a little more important. You can still work at your children's pace and keep them close to grade-level work.

There are multiple ways to do this, but it's a delicate process. You don't want to speed your children up, obviously, as they wouldn't be working at their pace. Some kids work better with a goal, and others feel pressured. Know your child and determine if they would work better knowing that the goal is to be on grade level. If so, involve them in the process!

Set a goal date for when you'd like your child to be on grade level. Determine how much work needs to be completed in that time. You might separate it by unit, by concept, or in any way that makes sense to you. It might help to identify which concepts or units will be easy for your child and keep in mind that you might be able to spend less time on those. The more time you can take to catch up, the better.

Don't Do "Panicked Learning"

What I mean by this is, don't panic and try to rush learning in an attempt to catch up. It would be better to be behind than engage in panicked learning! Don't try to squeeze in extra learning on the weekends or by refusing breaks. Breaks are wholly necessary in the learning process. Instead, try to streamline the learning! If you can teach it in two lessons instead of three, do that unless it means extending each lesson! I've often seen curriculum that reiterates the same points multiple times. If your child has the concept down, skip the multiple reiterations or use them as a quick review.

Double Up

I don't mean do extra lessons. No, instead double up by adding a fun alternative to learn more. Khan Academy is fun and has easy-to-watch videos for math, science, finance, history and more. Many kids would find Khan fun. If not, there are other methods - books to read, documentaries, games, etc.

Kids will set their own learning pace, if you let them. Just relax and follow their lead!

Erin is a homeschooling mom to 3 beautiful little boys, Baloo, Royal, and Logi-Bear. Erin has BA in Psychology, and a passion in teaching her boys and making it fun and interesting. Find her blogging at royalbaloo.com.

Homeschool Planning Based on Your Kids' Personalities (and Your Own!)

Heidi Ciravola

One of the greatest benefits of homeschooling our children is the amount of flexibility it affords us. When you're homeschooling, you have the flexibility and freedom to choose when, what and how your children learn.

Now, I don't know about you, but when I started homeschooling, I was super-excited to lay out this spectacular vision I had begun to create in my head. It goes something like this:

Our day starts with everyone dressed, their rooms clean, ready to go at 8 a.m. We eat a fabulous breakfast together and hit the books feeling full and happy. There are tons of over-the-top science experiments and craft projects, all while beautiful music plays in the background. Afternoons are spent frolicking around outside and creating extensive nature journals.

Guess what? It hasn't quite gone like that, ever, in the 11 years we have been homeschooling! That isn't to say that we've had this miserable failure of a homeschool experience, it just hasn't gone as I had first envisioned it. Instead, we have sometimes struggled and, more often than not, reveled in the opportunity to write our own story, and it goes a little more like this:

The teenager is up by 7 a.m. to get an early start on math. (This is her sticky subject, and she does best to complete it first and without too much disruption.) The middle-school early riser rolls out at 8 a.m. (he is told he needs to wait until then to give his sister an hour to herself). Mom gets up between 8:30 and 9 a.m. The youngest sleeps until 10. Each child has their own planner or assignment sheet to follow. While we are not all gathering together for group lessons and hands-on endeavors every day, each one of our needs are being met in a way that works for everyone.

Here's the thing: Chances are, you and your children have different personalities and learning styles. For this reason, what works for one will most likely not work for all. The good news is that, despite it being more work, you can find a routine and a flow that suits all of you.

Let's walk through some things for you to consider, using my aforementioned family structure as an example.

Be Flexible With Your Times

In my mind, I would like to sit down at 9 o'clock or so and do our formal sit-down work until around 11. After lunch, we would have either an afternoon field trip or some sort of hands-on activity, or free time/quiet reading. As you might have already realized, that is not exactly what we do! Being willing to adjust the times in which one or more of us do things has become essential to planning homeschool days that work for all of us.

If you have an early riser like I do, you might want to allow them an earlier start time. My son gets up at 7 o'clock and does things in his room until 8 a.m., when he rolls down to the homeschool room.

What used to take my son multiple hours and an enormous amount of prodding to accomplish in the later morning hours takes him significantly less time and energy when he is allowed to work in the earlier morning hours. By being flexible and attuned to what would work best for him, we were able to create a much more positive and productive environment for him to learn in.

Consider Each Child's Learning Style and Needs Separately

I remember putting out what seemed like an exorbitant amount of money for curriculum with my first child. One of the reasons I used to justify spending the money was that I could use it for the other two. (Or so I thought at the time.) While there are resources and curricula I have been able to use for multiple children, there have also been many that only suited the needs of just one of them. Choosing curriculum according to their individual needs is an important piece of the puzzle when planning for your homeschool.

We found that my oldest daughter worked best with video-based programs. Therefore, I researched and sought out curriculum that would meet that need. In stark contrast to that, my youngest daughter loves to cut and paste. She loves learning through notebooking and lapbooking. The finished products she has from these endeavors are all cherished treasures in her eyes.

Compromise is Key

You may find that every little need of each person cannot be met simultaneously. This is a good time to work with our kids on compromise by giving a little to accommodate others.

For starters, I have an early riser. I am most definitely not an early riser myself! We had a rule in our home that the kids could not leave their rooms until 8 a.m. As our son has gotten older (and his older sister has graduated from homeschool) we have allowed him to move about even earlier than the 8 a.m. I previously told you about while talking about flexibility. My son is often up before 7 o'clock, with the stipulation that it is not gaming time, but focused work time. At times when we found him breaking that rule, he would go back to staying in his room until 8 for a period of time.

Allowing our son to rise and work during his peak hours has greatly benefited his ability to maintain focus and quality of work. This compromise on our part was beneficial to him, and still allowed me to have the quiet time I needed in the morning. During the previous years, while he worked in his room to give his sister some space, it was he that was learning to compromise.

Be Willing to Make Changes

Change is hard. Letting go of a plan is hard. But consider this: What if keeping your original plan is actually harder, and causing more stress, than it would be if you were to consider a change?

You may try something and find it doesn't work. The needs of one or more of you may change. Don't be afraid to drop something that isn't working in favor of trying something new that might have the potential to work out better.

Throughout our years of homeschooling, we have used many types of planners, curriculum, teaching/learning styles and schedules. One of the keys to a successful homeschool is being flexible and willing to ebb and flow as the needs in your house change.

Don't Forget to Consider Yourself When Doing Your Planning!

Mom, your needs and sanity are just as important, if not even more so, than those of the kids. They need you to be emotionally sound so you can guide and assist them.

My husband always says, "Happy wife, happy life." Or "When Mom's happy, everyone's happy."

While this might seem selfish or self-centered at first, it most definitely is not! You are the center of your home and your children's lives. If you are stressed and run ragged, you will not be at your fullest to assist your children in learning and growing.

So here's the thing: Homeschooling our children has afforded us an enormous amount of freedom and flexibility. Don't be afraid to stretch yourself and your children. If something doesn't seem to be working, change it! Your homeschool doesn't have to look like mine, and you don't have to answer to anyone but you! Work with your children to create a learning and home environment that works for all of you!

Heidi Ciravola has been married to her husband, Joseph, for more than 18 years. Together they have three children, and began their homeschooling journey in 2006 when their oldest was beginning second grade. Heidi is a mother, taxi service and homeschool parent by day and an avid reader, photographer and homeschool blogger whenever there is time left over. She is a member of the Hip Homeschool Moms team as well as an individual blogger. You can visit Heidi at her blog, StartsatEight.com, where she blogs about homeschool products, unit studies, homeschool organization and general tips, as well as homeschooling high school and middle school

Incorporating Special-Needs Therapies Into Your Homeschool

Kaylene George

When you have a child with special needs, it can quickly seem like your entire life is spent doing various therapies. At one point, I was taking two of my kids to five different therapies over three days every week. It can be overwhelming trying to keep up with that while homeschooling. When you combine homeschooling and therapies, you save yourself time and struggle. Two birds with one stone, right?

Beyond that, the actual therapy sessions are likely only an hour or two a week, so you need to do therapy activities throughout the week to help your child stay regulated and progressing. The good news is that it doesn't need to take up all of your time to add some simple therapy activities to your homeschool, or to add some homeschooling to your therapy activities!

Special-Needs-Friendly Curriculum

The easiest way to add special-needs therapies into your homeschool is to get a special-needs-friendly curriculum. There are tons of different ways to find such curricula, and they don't all have to break the bank, I promise! You can get a specialty curriculum, of course, for your child's particular diagnosis, but you can also just find curriculum that meets your child's individual needs. You can also adapt curriculum to make it more special-needs friendly!

If you're looking for a specialty curriculum, gather up your child's diagnoses. This is easier if your child has one and not more, but often, once a person has one disability, others are found and diagnosed.

Once you have them in mind, get your research hat on! Find a few iHomeschool Network bloggers who you trust who have children with the same diagnoses as yours and see what they're using. Keep in mind that specialty curriculum is often more expensive than typical curriculum, so if you're on a strict budget, you can check out the other options in this chapter!

The way that I tend to prefer is to find curriculum that meets your child's individual needs. This way, you can tailor it by subject and preferences. See, not every child with autism is going to have the same needs and preferences. My son can't stand picture schedules, while most autism experts recommend those for everyone. When you're looking for specific curriculum to meet your children's needs, here are some things to consider.

- How much movement does your child need throughout lessons?
- How much hands-on learning does your child need?
- What accommodations would your child be getting in a public school?

Once you have these questions answered, you can start looking for curriculum that meets those needs!

You can also take a traditional curriculum that you like and tweak it to fit your child's needs. If your child were in a typical school, accommodations would be provided, and this is really no different. If a child with dyslexia uses an audiobook for history, or a child with dysgraphia uses a dictation device, it gives them access to curriculum that could otherwise be a poor fit.

Adding Therapy Activities to Homeschooling

When you take activities that would typically be done in a special-needs therapy setting and you add them into your homeschool days, you help your children to start using the coping mechanisms that they're learning in their real life. Talk with your child's therapist(s) about what goals and activities they would like to see practiced on a daily basis, and find ways to add those in. We like to make sensory bins to go with our lesson topics, and lots of families can be found practicing math facts while jumping on the trampoline.

Adding Homeschooling to Therapy Sessions

On the flip side, you can add some of your homeschooling into your therapy sessions as well! Let your child's therapist know what goals you currently have, and they can help you make a plan to reach those goals. Our occupational therapist helps us with fine motor goals often, and the speech therapist will have some great tips on understanding language.

Final Tips on Homeschooling and Special-Needs Therapy

Be Flexible

As with everything homeschooling-related, you need to be as flexible as possible when adding special-needs therapies into your homeschool. There will be days when all you do is one therapy activity, and you can totally count that as school. There will also be days where you get school done but don't even look at your therapy goals. That's OK! The most important thing is that you have goals for homeschooling and therapy, and you understand how to combine those goals when you can!

Learn All You Can About Your Child

I know that we all know our children in ways that no one else ever really will, but you need to learn more than you ever thought possible about your child. Understanding your child's brain as best as you can is going to be invaluable when you're homeschooling a child with special needs. Learn about the different diagnoses that your child has and what the common accommodations and therapy activities are for each diagnosis. Learn your child's triggers and how to recognize good and bad days. The more you know about your child, the easier this will be.

Let Go of Your Picture of "School"

I know that this is probably the most common homeschooling advice you've ever seen. It doesn't have to look like school. It doesn't need to be textbooks, worksheets and 8 a.m. to 3 p.m. Monday to Friday. I'm going to take it a step farther, though, and say that we should also let go of our picture of homeschool.

Adding special-needs therapies into homeschooling means that your day will include sensory bins, audiobooks, noise-cancelling headphones, crash pads and trampolines. It probably won't look like quiet reading time under a willow tree. Learn to love your homeschool, and try not to compare it to what homeschooling "should" look like.

Bottom line, when you're adding special-needs therapies to your homeschool, understand your children and do your best to meet their individual needs. Know that every one of us special-needs mamas feels like we're failing roughly 87 percent of the time, and we'll all get through this. You can be the best teacher for your child, and I know that you can do this!

Kaylene is a homeschooling, work at home mom of 3 (almost 4) kiddos, two of which have special needs. Completely outnumbered at her house, she writes her blog, ThisOutnumberedMama.com, to offer tips, tricks, and encouragement to mamas out there in a similar season of life!

Synchronizing Curriculum for Asynchronous Learners

Lara Molettiere

What is an asynchronous learner? Asynchrony is a lack of concurrence in skills. A child who learns asynchronously learns different subjects, different social skills and different motor skills at different rates. All those developmental milestones are hit at varying levels of speed, so making a boxed curriculum work is often like trying to fit a square peg into a round hole.

The simplest way to create a curriculum for an asynchronous learner is to build one. There are many ways to go about creating a curriculum, and you can use the same curriculum for multiple ages and skill levels in many subjects. History and science both lend themselves to easy adjustments for multiple skill levels.

First, you will need to assess the level of your student in each subject area you want to cover. Having a solid baseline from which to plan each year will usually help prevent you from having to keep purchasing additional curricula to try. Sometimes a particular program ends up not working, or is too simple or too difficult, and you have to go back to the drawing board. It's a process of learning for everyone. Do not throw in the towel just because something didn't work. That doesn't mean everything isn't working or that it's your fault. It simply means that that piece of curriculum was a bad fit.

After you have assessed skill levels, the next thing to do is to consider how your child learns best. Visual, auditory and kinesthetic learning processes are different. You can incorporate the methods that work best for your child with most curricula, but you should always be aware if the curriculum you are considering will work well with the learning style needed.

There are many ways to pull together your curricula. Here are three of the most common.

Unit Studies

With unit-study schooling, you choose a theme and build materials around that. Choosing the theme based on your child's interests, a time period you need to study for state requirements, or a particular piece of literature are all viable options. Your history, literature, copywork, math and science can all be incorporated. The length of your unit study can be as long or short as you choose.

The beauty of unit studies is that compiled resources can all be chosen specifically for your child's level in that subject. If a student is doing sixth-grade math but is challenged in handwriting, then you can choose a primary-lined copywork set. If your child is a science whiz but struggles with reading, choose hands-on science projects with delightful literature and adjust reading accordingly. The options are all there for your choosing to create a thorough and lovely learning experience for your asynchronous learner.

Printable resources for unit studies can be found online at places like Homeschool Share, A Journey through Learning and many homeschool freebie websites. Your local library will also be a wonderful resource for gathering books for unit studies.

Do not forget other homeschool families. There is a wealth of knowledge and resources in communities. Veteran homeschool families are always willing to share ideas and often their own resources.

My personal favorites for purchasing resources are Amazon, ThriftBooks and Educents. Kits, books and audios that are very well done are worth purchasing to have around for many uses. Many asynchronous learners will latch on to a subject for weeks or months at a time and that one resource might get worn out, but the knowledge gained is well worth it. Choose your purchases carefully and you can still homeschool frugally and have excellent resources for your child.

Your unit study can incorporate some or all subjects, including:

- Reading
- Language Arts
- Poetry
- Geography
- Math
- Science
- Copywork
- Foreign language
- Spelling
- Bible

This is a very effective way to support your children's academically weak areas and help them flourish in their stronger areas.

Notebooking and Lapbooking

Notebooking and lapbooking are an excellent way to merge varying levels of curricula for your student. Because the students are able to record information at their own levels, this is a good method for teaching multiple ages the same subject at once.

Notebooking is basically keeping a journal-style record of facts, quotes, timelines and so on that coordinate with current studies. Nature notebooks are very popular among many homeschoolers as an example of notebooking. There are many printable notebooking resources available online, and a simple spiral-bound notebook works as well. Notebooking Pages and The Notebooking Fairy are both excellent resources.

Lapbooking is an interactive way of notebooking that results in a wonderful visually stimulating book that your child can enjoy putting together and reviewing. Like notebooking, lapbooking is easily adjusted for different ages and levels of skill. A Journey Through Learning and CurrClick are recommended sites for lapbooking resources. Traditionally, lapbooks are created with file folders and inserts of information with lift-a-flaps, folding books, coloring sheets and so on.

Some families love both these styles and combine them into lap-and-notes, or a notebook with lapbook elements included. You get the best of both worlds, and this method is very effective for older learners and proficient writers who learn well with hand-on activities.

Interest-Led Learning

This method can be delight-directed, unschooling, or combined with more traditional homeschooling methods. Chances are, your asynchronous learner has a few varied interests. This method allows you to build a curriculum around those interests to both fuel the flame of curiosity and to actually get schoolwork done, which can sometimes be a challenge with these types of learners.

Interest-led learning works well with lots of books and exploration time. Some studies may be done with video or online coursework, documentaries and even games. The library, local museums, zoos, colleges with speaker series, etc., are all enriching places for interest-led homeschooling.

Allowing your children to immerse in a subject of their own choosing may seem a bit frightening at first. As you develop your own methods of gathering resources and studying together, however, patterns will emerge that allow you to develop a comprehensive study no matter what subject your child is fascinated by.

As an example, if your child become fascinated with pottery, you might end up with a curriculum that includes:

- a Craftsy class on beginning pottery
- a historical study of pottery through the ages
- notebooking the history of pottery with sub-studies on the different markings used by different cultures
- mathematical studies of the volume different pottery pieces can hold, the ratios of clay and water to create different types of pottery, etc.
- a field trip to a local museum with a pottery collection
- living books like *When Clay Sings* to add depth to your studies
- science experiments including making clay, learning about archeology and how pottery is studied, etc.

All of these activities can be scaled to match your child's skill levels in each subject.

The important part of synchronizing your curriculum is making sure that you are enabling your child to flourish in strong areas and to grow stronger in weak areas. Building a curriculum takes time, trial and error, and patience. You are embarking on an exceptionally rewarding journey by homeschooling your asynchronous learner, and like all rewarding journeys, it is not without challenges. Together, you will learn and grow and thrive, asynchrony and all.

 *Lara Molettiere is a writer and homeschool cultivator. Wife to John and mother to Mr. T and Mr. F, she shares encouragement, homeschooling ideas, printables and more at her blog Everyday Graces, laramolettiere.com.*

When Your Child Doesn't Understand a Subject

Sallie Borrink

There are times when, no matter how carefully you have selected a curriculum and prepared homeschooling materials for your children, they simply might not understand the work you give them. When faced with this situation, there are a number of questions to ask yourself as you troubleshoot what to do and how to respond.

Is it Too Soon?

Just because a professional somewhere decided that a child should be able to do X at age Y, it doesn't mean all children will do it at that age. Children learn on their own timetables, and individual development can vary wildly. For example, some children learn to read at 3 years old, and some learn at 8. Both ages are perfectly fine, as is every age in between.

Math is a subject where you can create problems and future obstacles if you push children when they aren't ready. How many people hate math because they were pushed to do too much before they were ready for it? I think this is true of many adults. There are some experts who suggest children aren't ready for arithmetic until age 10, and yet schools have now pushed it down into kindergarten! Know your children and don't push beyond their true capabilities.

I'm of the opinion that, when a child is ready, learning is fairly effortless. Yes, it will take some work and concentration whenever a child learns something new. But it should not be laborious. It should not be overwhelming. It should not be confusing. Whether it is potty-training, tying shoes or doing multiplication, it will go much more smoothly if you wait until children are developmentally ready on their own time schedules.

Is it the Wrong Approach or Style?

Children truly do respond differently to various curriculum approaches based on their preferred learning styles. If you are trying to do a classical curriculum, using lots of memorization, with a child who is a visual-spatial learner, you are setting up your child (and yourself) for lots of frustration. If you are expecting a kinesthetic learner to do worksheets all day, you are setting that child up for failure.

If you don't know your child's preferred learning style, start by searching the internet for summaries of learning styles. Most of the time, it will be apparent from an early age based on preferences in how to play, read and do art. You can then create a learning plan that aligns most closely with that learning style.

Is There a Legitimate Learning Problem?

Sometimes there is a learning problem that requires expert help. For example, we gave our daughter time when it came to writing. We didn't push it because she was learning in many other areas, but she hated writing. It was very difficult for her.

After some time, we decided it might not be a maturity issue and we had her evaluated. As it turns out, she did have dysgraphia, which was then addressed by an occupational therapist. Sometimes it can be hard to know when to seek additional help, but I think if you observe your children closely, you will reach a point when you know you need to bring in an outside professional's opinion.

Are You the Problem?

I mean this in the kindest way possible, but sometimes, the problem is less about the child's struggles and more about the teacher/mom.

Most homeschool moms have a vision of what they want their homeschooling to look like and how it should function. If you are more committed to that ideal than to meeting your children exactly where they are, you can create some significant problems. If your child learns differently than what you want to do, you absolutely have to figure out another way to approach things.

Yes, you can "force" your children to do something that doesn't fit with their learning styles, but why would you? To toughen them up? To demonstrate you are in charge?

Yes, you can "force" your children to stick to the curriculum schedule you downloaded from the curriculum company or the state board of education, but at what cost?

The way I homeschool my daughter is not the way I would choose to homeschool if it were up to me. My homeschool ideal is at complete odds with the child I have been blessed with. I do what works for her. Homeschooling isn't about me. It's about her.

Homeschooling is about continually adjusting expectations. It's about observing and adapting. It's about starting over, ditching the things that don't work and finding something that does. Sometimes this means ditching our ideal and vision for what our child really needs.

Is it Time to Back Off?

I think it is always wise to err on the side of backing off and giving the child more time, especially in the elementary years. I have found with my daughter that if I wait until she is truly ready for something, she masters it in just a day or two. This is so much better than spending weeks trying to get a child to understand something and everyone ending up frustrated and upset in the process.

Backing off and seeking to really understand your child are the best ways to handle a child who doesn't understand a subject. In the vast majority of situations, the issue will resolve itself with minimal drama if Mom is willing to observe and wait.

Sallie Schaaf Borrink enjoys homeschooling her only child, Caroline, in beautiful West Michigan. As relaxed homeschoolers, they look at all of life as a learning adventure. Sallie shares her experiences, insights, and downloadable printables at SallieBorrink.com.

Homeschooling Your Child with ADHD

Ticia Messing

Does this sound anything like your day?

You start off your homeschool day with morning time. All of your children are sitting on the floor watching you. You turn to write something on your dry-erase board, and turn back around to find one of your children rolling on the floor. ROLLING!

Or, maybe it's not that extreme; instead your child has found several small bits of forgotten toys and is attempting to put them together.

You survive morning time and transition to working on math. The same child that was rolling on the floor then falls out of a chair.

If you're like me, you wonder how you *can* fall out of your chair, but apparently it's possible.

In the meantime, 20 minutes pass, and your child has only done two problems. Why? Because they were staring out the window at a bird. It's not like the child was loud or disruptive, or moving around, because you would have noticed that. No, they were just not working.

At the end of the day, you're wondering a couple of things: "Should I medicate my child?" "Should I just put them in public school and be done with it?" Maybe you even wonder, "Why did I sign up for this?"

Does this sound like a day you've had? It certainly sounds like a few days I've had.

I have three kids, and my boys are the super-hyper, can't-ever-sit-still type. When they're not paying attention, it's pretty obvious. By contrast, my daughter is more of the stare-out-the-window type, who will suddenly freak out when her brothers are all done with math, while she hasn't done a thing.

Both types have problems focusing, and both might be able to use the following strategies to help them focus.

First, Look for Distractions

I have ADD myself, there's some discussion among my friends if I also have ADHD. But, since I'm more or less able to function normally in my life, I don't really feel the need to fine-tune the diagnosis. Look around where you're doing school: What is causing the distractions?

Visual cues: Is it too colorful and stimulating? None of my kids can function with cutesy curriculum. If there are cartoon characters or lots of color, they spend all of their time drawing and creating stories for the pictures. Don't even get me started on math problems where they are asked to draw how they solved it.

Visual cues: Is movement distracting? I cannot have TV on or the blinds open when it's super-busy outside our window. I get distracted by the movement and stop to watch what's going on. Right now, I'm writing this at a restaurant, and every now and then I stop as I see a blur in my field of vision.

Audio cues: What level of noise does your student focus best with? My daughter wants absolute silence. We are working with her to get her to better function with some amount of noise, because silence is just not going to happen. By contrast, I work better with some amount of music going on behind me.

Environmental cues: What is your child's chair like, or their desk? While this might not seem like a big deal to you, it can be huge to a child struggling to focus. One time my computer had crashed and I had to use my husband's desk and computer for a conference call. I could not focus because his setup was different from mine, and the chair felt wrong, and any number of things.

Overcoming These Distractions

If your children struggle with visual distractions, consider making an office for them. All you need is a presentation board (I got a mini-board, so it fits better), and when they are working, set this up on their desk to block out extra stimuli.

Next, look at the sounds in your schooling area. Would earplugs or headphones help? Could they listen to music on their own as they're working?

How can you change your environment? Maybe let your children sit on exercise balls as they're doing their schoolwork, or just give up on sitting and let them lay down on the floor as they work (though my kids can't do this because their handwriting becomes illegible). Maybe you take your books to the park and let nature calm them. It's amazing how much calmer you can feel when surrounded by grass and trees, versus walls and the sounds of an artificial life.

The Boring Details You Might Not Have Thought of Yet

How long are your lessons? How old are your kids? If you have young kids, they might not be ready for long lessons because of their focus. When my kids were 5 years old, our reading lessons were a strict 10 minutes with a timer. They had to focus that long, and then we took a short break. It didn't take long to work up to 15 minutes, but it was a gradual change, and they always knew that when the timer went off, the lesson ended.

Timers are your best friend when dealing with a child with ADHD. In particular, look for a red-line timer, or an old-fashioned egg timer. These are ones where your children can specifically see how much longer they have to work. If they can look up at the timer and see "Only two more minutes," they will concentrate much better.

Once the timer has gone off, give them a short break. We have a 20-minute homeschool schedule. They work for 20 minutes, and then they stop. If they're not done, then we can come back to it later. After 20 minutes, they get a five-minute break. I set a timer for that, too, but that's more because I'll get distracted and not start lessons again for 15 minutes otherwise.

If your kids are getting extra-fidgety, don't be afraid to have them do jumping jacks or jog in place. I've been known to stop a lesson mid-sentence and tell the kids to run to the other end of the house and back two times before we continue.

Ticia is a homeschooling mom to three elementary kids, twin boys and a little girl. She loves to make their learning hands on, and delights in making history fun. You can find Ticia at her blog adventuresinmommydom.org

Managing Your Life: Unique Homeschool Situations

Family Learning: Combining Ages with a Multifaceted Approach

Sara Dennis

Once upon a time, I had my children each using separate curricula. One child was studying modern history. Another child was reading all about the Mayflower. A third child was exploring the Crusades, while my fourth child was diligently working through Roman history.

It was insane. I spent my day jumping around in history, unable to get my bearings. We weren't able to hold family discussions, watch documentaries or share a movie about the time period we were all studying. I thought I was losing my mind.

So, at the end of one summer break, a week before we were to start school again, I scrapped my plans for the school year and combined the children into one history and literature program. It was the best homeschool decision I've made.

Why Combine Ages?

Combining children into one curriculum or subject allows you to keep the family on the same page. It's the secret of those little one-room schoolhouses of the past.

Each child studies the same subject, but at an individually appropriate level.

You are no longer jumping back and forth between science topics or history time periods. Everyone can enjoy the same literature books, and it's easy to supplement your studies with field trips, movies, documentaries and family discussions.

There are several ways to combine your children's learning.

Multi-Age Curriculum

The first method is to find a multi-age curriculum that covers the age ranges of your children. These tend to be easy to use. Each age group has books, worksheets and maps assigned. However, you can complete the projects as a family, hold family discussions and give similar writing assignments.

The biggest disadvantage I've found is that many curricula will work with children from kindergarten through eighth grade, but leave you hanging in high school. As a result, many families will combine the younger children but have the high school teenagers studying independently.

My family uses Tapestry of Grace as our main curriculum for history, literature, fine art and geography. The assignments are divided between lower elementary, upper elementary, middle school and high school, so I simply give the assignments based upon my children's reading level and age.

Each child has age-appropriate worksheets, questions, reading assignments, writing assignments and activities. However, everyone is studying the same topic or time period. This makes my life easier as I plan supplemental activities.

We can have a family reenactment or a movie night, or plan field trips around our history studies. Often, family dinners will become long discussions.

Keep the Same Subject but Use Different Curricula

Since many curricula only combine kindergarten through eighth grade, it's difficult if you have high school students and want to combine your kids. In this case, keep everyone studying the same subject, but use a grade-appropriate curriculum for each child.

As an example of how this looks: Years ago, I had two high school teens, a seventh-grader and a fourth-grader whose studies I wanted to combine. My high school teenagers clearly needed a high school textbook, so I started there. Then I found a program I liked for my seventh- and fourth-graders.

I spent a few hours studying both the curriculums before I rearranged the units to correlate. For instance, I made certain we were all studying cells, plants, animals and the human body at the same time.

The children did experiments and projects together. Family dinners were a wonderful place for discussions about what we'd learned in science.

I could look over the younger children's reading for a refresher before sitting down with the high school textbook. It allowed me to stay on the same page with all the kids.

Use Spines

Spines are books that you use to cover a subject. For instance, you might have a history book or series you love, such as The Story of the World, or a science resource like Usborne's Science Encyclopedia. Use it as a jumping-off point for your studies.

This means you slowly work through the book in systematic fashion. Plan to read the biology sections of Usborne's Science Encyclopedia over the course of the year, or one volume of Story of the World. The beauty of the system is that you have time to explore topics you're interested in.

Rabbit trails are a necessity. If you read about Egypt and the kids are fascinated, don't hurry on. Instead, read other books. Do projects. Watch documentaries and movies.

The point for spines is to assign a spine for each grade grouping. The high school teens can all share a spine, but an elementary spine is not going to go into enough detail for a teenager. However, a high school spine will be well over the head of an elementary kid.

Do your best to align the spines to each other so the kids are all studying the same topic. Study Egypt and Mesopotamia as a family. Read about the Crusades together. Study bacteria and pull out the microscope. If everyone is reading about bacteria at their own level, you can all study the bacteria together at the same time.

Notebooking also goes along well with spines. Elementary kids can focus on writing a sentence or paragraph about their studies that week. Middle-school kids write a report about each week's studies or fill out a notebook page, while high school teenagers can write essays about their studies.

Spines and notebooking are a great way to keep the family on the same topic of study while giving everyone age-appropriate work.

Change Approach for Each Child, but Keep the Same Topics

You can always change the approach of study. My family uses Tapestry of Grace as the center of our homeschool. It covers history, literature, writing, fine arts, geography and more. However, the kids don't always do well with the assignments as given.

This simply means I've had to do a bit of adaptation. My oldest child loved the assignments as given. He happily read the reading assignments, answered the questions and did the discussions.

My second son, however, didn't care for answering the questions. He found them rather dull. Instead, I asked him to give me a written report each week covering something he found interesting in the readings.

That's precisely what he did. He'd read the books and then write a short report. I received reports on the Spanish flu and the battles of World War I. To be honest, I thought he'd have trouble with the discussions as a result. No, following his interests actually improved his discussions.

Currently, I have a third child working through Tapestry of Grace at the rhetoric level. This is a child who adores research. She follows rabbit trails at the drop of a hat, but she didn't care for the history readings. Instead, I've simply been giving her the list of accountability and thinking questions to research.

She's been happily reading the encyclopedia and searching the internet for the answers. While she's researching the answers, she also follows rabbit trails. Instead of hindering the discussions, it's actually expanded them. She's able to provide details and unusual tidbits that she discovered during her research.

Using the same curriculum for each child doesn't mean you have to assign the same work. Instead, adapt the curriculum to your child's needs, not your child to the curriculum's needs.

It's your homeschool, after all.

Combining your children's homeschooling doesn't mean that each child needs to be reading the same books, answering the same questions and writing the same papers. Instead, it means keeping the family on the same topic to facilitate discussions, field trips and hands-on activities.

Use spines to give each child appropriate readings at the right level. Use different modes of learning as needed. If one child prefers to write papers instead of answering questions, allow that. If another loves to research while yet another prefers to curl up with one book, don't worry about it.

Encourage your children to learn in the manner that's best for them.

Sara Dennis is a homeschooling mother of six children from 5 to 19 years old. After much research into homeschooling in 2000, she and her husband fell in love with classical education and use it as the foundation for their homeschool. Sara blogs at ClassicallyHomeschooling.com.

Co-Parent Homeschooling

Kaylene George

When you put on your dress and held your flowers, ready to walk down the aisle, you never thought you'd be here. Co-parenting was likely not even in your vocabulary, yet here we are. If you're new to this, I'm sending hugs and I promise you'll make it through.

No one goes into marriage expecting a divorce, and yet 40 to 50 percent of marriages end that way. Going through a divorce can be really scary, especially if you're a stay-at-home mom and homeschooling. Will you have to get a job? Will you have to put the kids in school? How can you go from spending all day every day with your kids to seeing them after school and every other weekend?

First, take a deep breath and know that you can do this. You can homeschool and co-parent if it's what is best for you and your kids. You can make it through this journey, and you and your kids will both absolutely thrive.

With that said, let's dive in to the nuts and bolts of co-parent homeschooling.

Why You Would Want to Co-Parent Homeschool

There are plenty of reasons to co-parent homeschool, and it can be a huge blessing to families who pursue it. Whether you were already homeschooling, you feel the call to homeschool and are making it work while co-parenting, or you chose to homeschool because you'll be co-parenting, there are tons of reasons to make that choice.

If you were already homeschooling at the time of the divorce, you might want to continue homeschooling to keep life as consistent as possible for your child. It's scary for children to change their lives so drastically, so keeping school relatively normal can help them cope.

Other parents choose to co-parent homeschool because they feel like they need to homeschool to give their child the best education possible and they have to deal with their co-parenting situation. Still others see the benefits of homeschooling after they're already co-parenting and decide that's what's best for their family.

One of the benefits of co-parent homeschooling is a greater involvement in your child's education, often from both parents. Homeschooling parents have to be directly involved in all education decisions, so it can often help co-parents communicate more effectively.

It also allows more flexibility in your parenting plan schedule. My ex works retail, so he will never have weekends off. Because we homeschool, his visitation days can work for him and the kids.

Co-parent homeschooling also helps your kids know that both of their parents are working together to help them, and that you will always work together when your kids need you to.

Talking With Your Ex

I know that talking with your ex-husband might be the last thing on the planet that you'd ever want to do, but it's arguably the most important step. This co-parent homeschooling journey will be so much smoother if your ex is on board.

If you homeschooled before your divorce, have this conversation as early as possible. If you want to continue homeschooling, make sure that he knows that and you can have some discussions about how to make that work. I would also recommend getting your agreement in writing in your divorce paperwork.

If you divorced before your kids were school age, or you planned to have your kids in school but you feel like you should homeschool them now, you need to talk to your ex about it. Just tell him that you need to chat about an idea and have the conversation.

Regardless of whether you homeschooled before, or you're talking about it with your ex for the first time, it's important to keep a few tips in mind.

First, it's a good idea to approach the subject gently. If you come at your ex-husband demanding to homeschool and threatening, you won't get anywhere fast. Try to start the conversation when you're both in a good mood and you have time to talk. Let him know that you need to talk to him and, if possible, do it without the kids.

I also highly recommend going into the conversation with an open mind. Really listen to your ex's concerns if he has any, and don't immediately start crafting your argument. Understand that the conversation is likely going to be a give and take, and you will be much better off!

Come to the conversation prepared. Your ex will likely have a lot of questions and concerns, and may not express those questions and concerns in the nicest of ways. Make sure that you're prepared to answer questions kindly to put your ex's mind at ease.

Some common questions you'll likely face are how you'll afford to homeschool, if your ex will be responsible for doing any schooling, what you'll do about socialization, why you want to homeschool, and how you plan to teach the children.

How to Make Co-Parent Homeschooling Work

Communication

Communication is absolutely key. If you plan to homeschool and co-parent, you need to have a lot of communication with your ex-spouse. Make sure that you are able to express yourself clearly and take your emotions out of disagreements as much as possible.

It's also really important to communicate clear expectations. Does your child have to bring "homework" to his visitation? Make sure that you, not your child, tell your ex what is to be done and what is expected. If your ex is teaching certain subjects, make sure you are both on board with teaching methods.

How to Afford It

This is probably the question that I'm asked most about co-parent homeschooling. How can any single mom afford to homeschool? How can you provide for your family while staying home to homeschool? How in the world can you afford curriculum?

I wish there was a one-size-fits-all answer I could give you, but like with so many co-parenting topics, it depends. I know homeschoolers who stay home full time, who work part time and homeschool around their schedule, who work from home, and who work full time and homeschool around their schedule. What I do want to tell you is that there is almost always a way.

If you plan to stay home full time and not work at all, you need to check with the laws in your state and take a hard look at your divorce paperwork (preferably with a lawyer).

In some states, as long as you've been a stay-at-home mom, your ex will need to pay enough in child support and alimony to allow you to continue. That said, many states don't have this option, and even if they do, it's often only for a year or two, so you should look into some of the options below just in case!

A great solution that many moms find is to get a part-time job and homeschool around that schedule. If your child support is enough that you could get by with only a part-time job, this is often a really great choice.

With a part-time schedule, you can work nights or weekends and school through the week, or you can do school in the afternoons and evenings when you get home from work. It's all about flexibility!

Another really popular option with single homeschooling moms is working from home. There are tons of real ways to earn money from home, but there are also a lot of scams. I would recommend really researching any opportunity that you look at. I work from home as a blogger, writer and virtual assistant, and I am in two direct-sales companies.

If you really want to work from home, you can definitely find a way to make it work!

And finally, there are some homeschooling moms who work full time. If you work a traditional 9-to-5 job, you could have older children complete some of their independent work while you are at work and then tackle the teacher-intensive subjects after dinner.

Some families have the babysitter homeschool a few days a week and they homeschool on the weekends. The exact schedule will depend on your job and work hours, but there are families who make it work!

Schedules

You are going to want to set up your schedule for success in homeschooling, and that schedule is going to vary from family to family. Some things to consider are whether your ex plans to teach lessons, your child will take a few things as "homework," or your ex won't have anything to do with homeschooling.

If your ex will have nothing to do with your homeschool, I would suggest creating a parenting plan similar to what you would have if your children were in public school. Your homeschooling time needs to be respected and it is as valid as a public school schedule.

That said, you can have flexibility. (For reference, many public school families have a standard schedule where kids go to their dad's house every other weekend and for dinner Wednesday nights).

If you will be sending your child for visitation with homework, or if your ex is planning to teach lessons, you have a lot more flexibility. My ex does a mix of homework and actual teaching (mainly homework) and because of that we're able to have visitation two days weekly.

I have the boys five days a week, and four of those days are school days. My ex has them two days a week, and one of those days is a school day. That's just our situation, though; you need to find what works for your family!

Compromise

Always, always, always be willing to compromise. Remember earlier in the chapter when we talked about really listening to your ex's concerns about homeschooling? This is where that is really going to come in handy! Because you now know the major objections that your ex has to homeschooling, you are in a great place to find compromises that work for both of you.

If your ex is really concerned with socialization, first you might have them read the chapters in this book on socialization (I'm kidding, kind of...), but then you can also compromise and agree that your child will attend a co-op, church group or sports team.

If he's concerned about you teaching the kids, offer to show him the curriculum. If his concern is how it would change visitation, show him your ideas for a schedule.

However, with all of your preparation, there's still a chance that you will need to compromise on bigger things. I know that you're passionate about your children's education, but understand that there are two of you making this decision and both of you will have to give something up.

Flexibility

Flexibility is incredibly important when co-parenting in general, but even more so when co-parent homeschooling. Trust me, I know that sometimes being flexible seems impossible. This is your child's education, and it's really important! Even still, sometimes you're going to have to let things go and go with the flow.

Some days your kids will get home from their dad's without even touching the backpack of homework that you sent with them. Ask me how I know. Sometimes your best-laid plans will completely fall apart and your schedule will be completely thrown off track. Your ex will get called into work unexpectedly and you'll have the kids on a day that wasn't planned. Or his mother plans a birthday dinner on one of "your" days, and you'll miss the day of school.

These things are OK, I promise. Your child will still get into college if they do their third-grade math lesson on Saturday instead of Friday.

Because if we're really honest with ourselves, homeschooling gets thrown off track all the time. Your child has a doctor appointment or you wake up with a migraine. We take random "life learning" days and go to the park. If we can be this flexible with ourselves, we should really be this flexible when co-parent homeschooling.

Kaylene is a homeschooling, work at home mom of 3 (almost 4) kiddos, two of which have special needs. Completely outnumbered at her house, she writes her blog, ThisOutnumberedMama.com, to offer tips, tricks, and encouragement to mamas out there in a similar season of life!

Homeschooling in Small Spaces

Emily Copeland

It's easy to get lost in the sea of Pinterest-perfect homeschool rooms while scrolling through your social media feeds. It's also easy to daydream about how much easier it would be to homeschool in those big, beautiful rooms. Trust me, I've been there.

You see, our homeschool journey started with a couple of workbooks and happened exclusively on the sofa. That house had a small eat-in kitchen, and there was no room to make it double as a school space. In hindsight, I'm glad Pinterest wasn't around then. It's probably best that I didn't have that steady stream of magazine-worthy schoolrooms in my face when we started.

Then we moved into a bigger home due to my husband being a pastor. It was still a small house, but bigger than the last. This home was a church parsonage that did, however, have enough space for a small bookshelf in the hallway near the bedrooms. That was helpful since our storage needs had grown by this point, but most of our homeschooling still happened on the sofa because our kitchen table was squeezed into a tiny dining area.

After that, we moved to another state and a larger home. Once again, it was still small, but bigger than the parsonage. Even though we added some square footage, it wasn't enough for a designated schoolroom. That's where I learned to homeschool with an open floor plan and make the most of our kitchen and dining area.

I learned over the years that the square footage of your home doesn't determine the success of your homeschool journey. Those Pinterest-perfect schoolrooms are nice to look at, but they come with their own issues. I also learned that homeschooling in a small space can be quite manageable with some evaluation and planning.

Before I share the tips I've learned for the day-to-day aspects of homeschooling in a small home, let's look at the importance of understanding our needs and wants.

Homeschool Needs vs. Homeschool Wants

It's important to evaluate your homeschool needs when homeschooling in a small space. Don't focus so much on what you have room to keep in your home or what you would like to have, but focus more on your absolute necessities for homeschooling.

Do you need a schoolroom? I learned quickly that a designated homeschool space is nice, but it's not needed for homeschooling. Many homeschoolers, including those with a separate schoolroom, find it preferable to school at the kitchen table, in the family room, in bedrooms and even outside. In fact, there are many cases where the designated homeschool space is used for storage and not so much for actual schooling.

Beyond a schoolroom, it's important to assess your homeschool storage needs. This will help determine how to make the most of your available space. Here are some things to consider:

Do you need to keep the curriculum you've used in the past or may use in the future?

Is it important for you to own all of the books you read?

Do your kids need an assortment of art and craft supplies?

How long do you want to keep your child's completed schoolwork and projects?

What are the best ways to document completed assignments for your state homeschooling requirements?

Does your homeschool space need to resemble a stereotypical schoolroom?

Once you have a good idea of your storage needs, you can organize your home with those things in mind. It might take some creativity and research to find the best storage solutions for your space, but you could even find that you enjoy the process!

If it turns out that you don't need all of the homeschool items taking up valuable space, start purging. That applies to non-homeschool items too! Reducing clutter is helpful for all areas of your home life, not just home education.

Doing More with Less

Ultimately, the key to homeschooling in a small space is disciplining yourself in the art of doing more with less.

Less Storage

We've never had an abundance of storage options available for our homeschool needs, so we've had to get creative over the years. There have been times where we adapted storage hacks found on Pinterest to meet our needs, but those don't usually help us for too long.

Here are the storage solutions that have proven effective everywhere we have lived:

Bookshelves: I've found that having one shelf apiece for each child is all I need for day-to-day homeschooling. The two shelves for my kids, plus the one I keep open to keep track of our borrowed library books, and one for the supplies we use regularly, are all the shelf space we need. I look at all other shelving as a bonus: It's nice, but not a true necessity.

Storage Baskets: Baskets and canvas cubes are perfect for storage in small spaces, and it's even better when you've got baskets that fit your bookshelves. We use the baskets on our shelves for school supplies, art supplies, chapter books, school-related DVDs and CDs, and other smaller items that need to be accessible, but out of sight.

Digital Resources: It wasn't easy to trade our physical books and curriculum for digital versions, but it's been a huge help in reducing our storage needs. Those storage needs have lessened considerably since we started using flash drives, cloud storage and e-readers.

Borrowing From the Library: This might not sound like a storage solution, but hang with me for a moment. When I borrow books rather than buy them, I avoid the need to expand my storage options. We still buy the occasional physical book, but we borrow them more often than not.

Less Curriculum

We're eclectic homeschoolers and use several different curriculum options each day. Add that to the fact that I've been a curriculum junkie for most of my years homeschooling, and you know that I understand how much this idea hurts. Nonetheless, when you're homeschooling in a small space, your curriculum choices need to work with your homeschooler and your home.

Consider a streamlined approach when possible. For example, a curriculum like Learning Language Arts through Literature combines all aspects of language arts. Since it covers reading, writing, spelling and grammar in one book, it frees up valuable shelf space for other storage needs.

Look into online or computer-based curriculum. This could work for all of your homeschool needs across the board or only a few subjects. Either way, approaching some of your homeschooling through a tablet or computer goes a long way in lessening your storage needs.

Sell it, donate it or throw it out. I know how tempting it is to view every teacher's manual and completed student book as a trophy on the shelf, but if you don't have room to display them, they need to go. Keep enough completed work to meet your state requirements and get rid of the rest. Don't get lost in the "we might need it one day" sentiment, either. If you didn't make it through the second chapter of that science book before switching to something else, it's doubtful that you'll want to use it with your other kids in later years.

Day-to-Day Homeschooling in Small Spaces

There's no one-size-fits-all solution for the day-to-day logistics of homeschooling in a small space. There might be times when it's easiest to have all the kids in one place working together, but at other times, they might do better to work independently in different corners of the room.

While we don't do all of our homeschooling around the table, I prefer for us to start there each day.

Everywhere we've lived, the small spaces and the not-so-small, our table has been visible from other areas. That means I can work on laundry or lunch, but still be close enough to help when needed or keep the kids from getting off track.

If there's no table or breakfast bar to work with, a living area or bedroom will work also. Even with our table, chairs, beds and sofa, there are plenty of days where my kids prefer to spread out in the floor to read and work. The same might be true for your kids.

For some families, it might work best to keep all the kids together for part of the homeschool day, but split them up when a quiet space is needed for concentration. That's the case for us on most days. My two kids are five years apart in age. That's why we start our days together at the table, but I move my kindergartener to another room to work individually with her. She needs more one-on-one time from me than my sixth-grader does, and the break gives him some distraction-free time for his more difficult work.

That kind of looking out for one another is crucial in a small space. For larger families, it might help to have a written rotation to organize who uses specific areas and when. If your family is smaller, like mine, you can probably deal with who uses what space on a day-to-day basis without much problem.

Be warned that there will be days where your small space will cramp your homeschool style. Don't be afraid to head outside on those days. A porch or picnic blanket can go a long way in providing breathing room and keeping peace in your home.

More Tips for Homeschooling in Small Spaces

Put it all away at the end of the day. Since your space serves multiple purposes, get in the habit of putting away your homeschool things at the end of the school day. That will help keep clutter at bay and keep your homeschool materials in better condition.

Close the curtains. Add a curtain to your bookshelves if you can't keep them from looking cluttered. This is also a great option if you don't have any closed storage.

No room for bookshelves? Under-bed plastic tubs work great for resources that aren't needed on a daily basis, while crates stacked under an end table or chair might prove better for daily work. On the same note, shoe hangers placed behind closet doors can help with storing school or art supplies when shelf space is lacking.

Don't overbuy. If you're not sure you need it, don't buy it. This is applies to school supplies, books, curriculum and any other resources. Buy what only you need, not what you want or might need.

Hold off on back-to-school shopping. There's nothing wrong with waiting until you need specific supplies to buy them. It's not a bad thing to stock up on the items you usually need throughout the homeschool year when school supplies are on sale, but if you don't have room to store them, skip the stockpiling and buy your supplies as needed.

Can't spare wall space? If there's no wall space for homeschool charts, posters and timelines, consider attaching them to tri-fold presentation boards instead. They can come out while you're schooling, but slide behind a sofa or dresser when the day is finished.

Don't be afraid to own it. You're homeschooling in a small space, and there's no need to apologize for it if someone stops by and, gasp, it actually looks like you're homeschooling. It may seem a little tongue and cheek, but we have a "Please excuse the mess, we live here" sign visible from our front door to make it clear that nothing on our table or in our floor at 11 a.m. should be too surprising.

In closing, remember that homeschooling in a small space doesn't have to be a big deal. Your space, whether big or small, is where great things are happening. Make the most of it and focus on what matters: pouring into those kiddos.

Emily Copeland is a homeschooling mother of two children and wife to a church-planting minister. She blogs at TableLifeBlog.com, where she shares encouragement and ideas for homeschooling, family life and ministry.

Academic Acceleration: When Your Child Moves Faster Than the Curriculum

Caitlin Fitzpatrick Curley

My husband and I are both products of public schools and, before having children, I worked as a school psychologist in an urban setting. I was passionate about urban education and had plans to return to my career once my children were enrolled in school.

I never imagined myself homeschooling. But I also never imagined a child could be so misunderstood in kindergarten.

It breaks my heart to think of all the misunderstood gifted kids who spend countless hours in classrooms all over our country waiting to learn.

Year after year, these children are told to wait. They remain bored, unchallenged, underserved.

These young minds who entered kindergarten bursting with ideas and questions lose their love of learning.

Meanwhile, the concerned parents of these children are told by The Powers That Be that acceleration is not only *not* an option, but that it would be detrimental.

We are holding back our country's brightest students. These are the children who will grow up to invent, to create, to solve problems and help the world. We need them now, more than ever before, and yet we tell them to wait.

The Research

The infuriating part of this is that we have research - years of research - that indicates academic acceleration is a highly-effective educational intervention that costs next to nothing.

In the past, I've shared our family's maddening experience advocating for academic acceleration in the public school system. At that time, I urged readers to read A Nation Deceived and to share it with their school systems. Since that time, the research from A Nation Deceived has been updated and is currently available in A Nation Empowered: Evidence Trumps the Excuses Holding Back America's Brightest Students. The goal of A Nation Empowered is to "inform educators, parents, and policy-makers of current research on acceleration, how that information has been applied to educational policy throughout the nation, and how educators can use the findings to make decisions for their brightest students."

A Nation Empowered lists 20 forms of acceleration for gifted youth, including early entry, subject acceleration, grade acceleration, mentoring, distance learning, telescoping, self-paced instruction, extra-curricular courses and more.

The National Association of Gifted Children (NAGC) also has a position statement on acceleration:

"Educational acceleration is one of the cornerstones of exemplary gifted education practices, with more research supporting this intervention than any other in the literature on gifted individuals. The practice of educational acceleration has long been used to match high-level student general ability and specific talent with optimal learning opportunities."

Despite this research, our nation's gifted children continue to be underserved. School officials tell parents that acceleration has negative outcomes. They ignore testing results and recommendations. They cite the child's behavior, his or her overexcitabilities, as an area of concern moving forward. They talk about social difficulties and the gifted child's asynchronicity.

Some of us, enraged by the system, opt out altogether. When I realized that the school was refusing to allow my child to learn, we walked away.

And do you know what? Once we removed the public school from the equation, he blossomed. His smile returned. He was our curious and joyful learner once more. One size does not fit all.

Academic Acceleration in Your Homeschool

Many confuse acceleration with pushing, but when you are the parent of a gifted child you know that the truth: If anyone is doing the pushing, it is the child.

Acceleration is not pushing a child to achieve, but rather it is allowing a child to soar. It is giving the child permission to move forward, to dive deep, to learn.

If you are homeschooling a gifted child, please know that it is OK to do things differently. It is okay to accelerate if that is what you feel your child needs. In fact, the research supports this path!

Acceleration in the homeschool setting may take a number of forms, including:

- Grade acceleration

- Subject acceleration
- Project-based learning
- Self-led learning
- Unschooling
- Finishing materials very quickly (speed of learning)
- Spending extra time on materials in order to dive deep (breadth of learning)

Academic Acceleration in Our Homeschool

Our family doesn't talk much about acceleration these days. There's no need to. Acceleration is a non-issue for our family right now.

I don't use homeschool curriculum in the traditional sense. I don't open chapter one and work through the resource until we have reached the end of the book. Instead, we pick and choose based on interest. We skip through entire chapters. We dabble in this and then lose ourselves in that. There's a lot of diving down rabbit holes and hands-on learning happening over here, and much of it is unplanned.

Homeschooling allows us the freedom and flexibility to meet our children where they are, regardless of grade level. Sometimes, my kids move quickly through the curriculum. At other times, they slow down and move deeply through the content.

My children are happy, and they love learning. To me, that is most important and a sign that we are on the right path.

(How amazing would it be if we could take this student-focused education model and apply it to the public education system so that all children can learn?)

Caitlin Fitzpatrick Curley is a school psychologist, a mom to three amazing children and an unexpected homeschooler. She loves nature, good books, board games, strong coffee and dancing in her kitchen. You can read about all of these things and more at my-little-poppies.com. Cait co-hosts The Homeschool Sisters Podcast and co-founder of Raising Poppies, an Facebook community for parents of gifted and twice-exceptional children. She is a contributing writer for Simple Homeschool and GeekMom. Her work has also appeared on The Huffington Post, The Mighty and Scary Mommy.

Homeschooling When You Have to Work

Amy Lanham

"I can't homeschool – I have to work!" I've heard it over and over. And I've thought "It might just be easier if I put them all in school" more than once. As a single mom, I have to work in order to pay the bills and keep food on the table. Sometimes it seems overwhelming to think about one more thing to do in my day.

For several years, I worked an 8 a.m. to 5 p.m. job at a CPA firm, and during tax time I even put in some overtime. I am blessed to have supportive family members who embrace homeschooling wholeheartedly. I would drop the kids off at my mom's every morning, and she did the bulk of the everyday homeschooling.

This year, I am working from home, and our schedule looks different than last year. Either way, it can be challenging to work and homeschool at the same time.

Should I Homeschool When I Work?

Homeschooling is a family's individual decision. I don't think every family has to homeschool, and maybe some families shouldn't homeschool. But I have been called to homeschool my kids. I feel like God has given me a responsibility to raise my kids in the nurture and admonition of the Lord. And for now, that means homeschooling them. Every time I have prayed about

461

putting them into school, I have felt like it would be the wrong thing to do. So until God leads me to do otherwise, I will be homeschooling my children.

So, if you feel like you are called to homeschool but have to work outside the home or are a work-at-home mom, I have some tips that might help you. And they might help you even if you don't work!

Pray and Rely on God

If God has called you to this job, He will be faithful to complete it. I can't tell you how many times I have been at my wit's end, and God has always provided. Whatever your needs are, God has the answer. Maybe you don't know which curriculum to use. Pray. Don't know how you are going to pay for the curriculum? He owns the cattle on a thousand hills; just ask Him. If you need a homeschool buddy, God can send one. When you don't think you can do this anymore, talk to God about it. I have had many, many heart-to-heart talks with God when I didn't know how I could go on, and I always feel better after taking my troubles to Jesus!

Find Curriculum They Can Use Independently

Many homeschool curricula require lots of teacher interaction. While I am sure those curricula are wonderful, I have to find things that don't require much work from me. I just don't have the time to sit with each kid for hours a day. This becomes easier the older they get. Until a child can read well, there will have to be someone to read the directions to them. Thankfully, usually younger grades don't require as much time to complete

.

Make Them Accountable

When I was working a regular office job, I sometimes felt like I didn't have a good handle on what my children were learning. Independent learning is wonderful, but they still need some accountability for actually completing the work assigned. So I started meeting with them every Friday evening when I got home from work. There were meetings that we had to skip or postpone, but I felt like I was more involved in their schooling and we could catch mistakes before they got out of hand.

I think this year will be a little different, since I will be mostly working from home and will be with them most of the day. I'll give you an update on that sometime soon, after we have gotten back into the swing of school again.

Find a Routine That Works for Your Family

Your homeschooling doesn't have to happen between 9 a.m. and 3 p.m. every day. Maybe you will do your homeschooling in the evening. You might work evenings and school first thing in the morning. Maybe the bulk of your schooling is done on your days off. There is no rule that says your homeschool has to look just like someone else's.

Be Organized

Everyone is busy nowadays, but as working homeschool moms we have to be even more mindful of the time. I try to set up our schedule by nine-week terms. It helps the kids to know what should be done by a certain time, but gives me a little wiggle room if I need to adjust things a bit.

Each week, I give them a checklist, and they are responsible to finish it before the end of the week. If they don't get it done by meeting time on Friday, they will have to work on "homework" on the weekend. They don't like losing their Saturday to relax, so it usually gets finished.

... But Be Flexible

In all of your scheduling and planning, leave room for flexibility. Maybe the whole family gets sick, or you have a huge project that takes more of your time than you think. You need to be able to change your schedule when something unexpected arises.

Simplify, Simplify, Simplify

This is something I am constantly working on. It's easier to keep the dishes washed when you don't have too many dishes. Toys are easier to pick up when there aren't a million of them. Laundry doesn't pile quite as high if everyone has fewer outfits. It is my goal to simplify this year. I'm working on it. I have a long way to go, though.

Acknowledge Your Limitations

As much as you want to, you can't do everything. Maybe the house won't be up to your normal specifications, or you don't get to do all of the Pinterest projects people are raving about, or you cut back your hours at work. As much as we want to be, we aren't superheroes. So don't take on too much, or you will find yourself overwhelmed. Just say "NO!" (Preaching to myself here! Been there, done that! Probably will again!)

Let Your Kids Help

My kids have always had responsibilities around the house. I feel like they need to learn how to work hard in order to become responsible adults. But after I went to work full-time, my kids had to learn to take on a little more around the house. There are jobs they can do that take a HUGE load off of me, so that I can do work that will be able to support us.

Find Encouragement and Recharge

I have been so blessed to have family and friends who have helped me since I became a single mom. It might feel difficult to find help, but you're not Superwoman, remember? If you don't have supportive family nearby, maybe you can find a homeschool family who will team up to do a co-op, or who would allow your kids to come to their house a few days a week. Or you might be able to find a group of homeschoolers that can encourage you when you want to give up. Even finding some encouraging blogs can help you when you are feeling down.

You can do this, dear working momma! If God has called you to homeschool your kids and you still have to work, he will help you be able to do it!

 *Amy Lanham is a second-generation homeschooling momma with a craving for excellent books. She juggles homeschooling, blogging, working from home, studying for the CPA exam and single parenting, all while trying to read "just one more chapter." She lives in wild, wonderful West Virginia with her three kids and one dog, but some days she wants to move to Australia. She blogs at LifeasLanhams.com, where she shares her passion for books, homeschooling and Jesus.*

Dealing With Anti-Homeschooling Family

Amy Dingmann

If you've made the decision to homeschool, chances are you've encountered someone in your life who doesn't agree with your choice. While some folks can politely agree to disagree, others can make family get-togethers a huge bundle of stress. I bet we've all heard some version of these anti-homeschooling comments:

- Just watch. Your kids won't be able to make any friends.
- You're not qualified to teach your kids.
- You're seriously going to ruin your kids.
- You'll do it for a while and they you'll give it up. Just wait.
- You went to public school and you turned out just fine.
- What are you? Some kind of hippie?
- What are you? Some kind of religious nut?
- All the homeschooled kids I know are weird.

We could go on and on, right? Since commentary seems to come as part of the homeschooling package, how do we deal with family members who are unsupportive of our decision?

I think the first thing to do is take a look at the list of possible reasons behind their comments and lack of support.

Possible Reason: They Don't Understand Homeschooling

When you get down to it, the main reason that I've caught flak for or been questioned about homeschooling is because the person questioning simply didn't understand what we were doing. In every single case, they were operating with a completely unrealistic vision of what homeschooling is.

In their defense, if the only exposure they've had to homeschoolers is on television or a news program, chances are they're going to need some truth talkin'! (Does it occur to anyone else that the media seems to latch on to homeschoolers on the extreme ends of the spectrum and very rarely talk to anyone in the huge middle ground?)

After almost a decade of warding off unsupportive commentary, I truly find that misinformation and lack of education is what's at the heart of most issues. When education about home education happens, I've almost always found that anti-homeschooling sentiment disappears.

Possible Reason: They Think You're Taking On Too Much

Sometimes people will say "You won't last," or "You'll never be able to handle it." Sometimes they make comments about how you'll go nuts being around your kids all day. Now, while some people can brush this off, it's worth considering for at least a moment — is this a valid concern?

Let's be honest. If out of one side of your mouth you announce you're excited to start homeschooling, but the other side of your mouth complains that parenting drives you crazy, you're going nuts without time to yourself, and you feel completely unsupported in your role as a mother, there might be some validity to their concern about you choosing to homeschool.

If there is no reason for their concern, thank them kindly and let them know they don't need to worry. But if there is half a valid reason for their concern, take an honest look inward and consider if homeschooling is really part of the path you want to travel at this time.

Possible Reason: They Think You're Judging Them for Not Homeschooling

When you announce you're planning to homeschool, some folks assume you're judging them for not choosing to homeschool — which immediately puts them on the defensive.

Unfortunately, the homeschool/private school/public school decision can drive a judgy little wedge right smack the middle of some families. Don't let it! Open those lines of communication and let them know homeschooling is a personal decision for your family and has nothing to do with them, their parenting, their children or your opinion about them. Be supportive of their kids and excited for the things they're enjoying in school!

Possible Reason: Family Drama

Can we be honest? Sometimes family members speak out about your choice to homeschool because they are simply tossing another log onto an ever-burning bonfire of family drama. In cases like these, their commentary actually has nothing to do with your choice to homeschool. You understand that, right?

We've all got "history" with family members. There are some people who will make snide remarks about homeschooling because they make snide remarks about everything. You can't please everyone, and it's not your job to do so. Make the choices that work for you, your spouse and your children... and don't worry about the rest. You can't win with these types of people. If your kids were in public school, they'd find something wrong with that, too.

Possible Reason: Some People Just Don't Like Homeschooling

Fact: Homeschooling isn't everyone's cup of tea. Some people just don't like it — much like some people don't like public school, watermelons or wood floors — and that's OK. Personal opinions are part of life. Might these people just need time to come around to the whole idea that homeschooling can be a fabulous amazing wonderful thing? Maybe. Be patient. Until then, talk about something else.

How to Respond to Anti-Homeschooling Comments

Now that you know some of the reasons people might react negatively to your homeschooling decision, you're more prepared to deal with discussions about it.

So how do you deal with it? What's the correct way to respond? Firstly, since most anti-homeschooling conversation stems from misinformation, I think it's our responsibility to educate the other person. (I know. We're always having to teach, right?)

Let them tell you why they think homeschooling isn't a good choice for you. Really have them talk through it, past the soundbites and all the "things they've heard."

Listen to them and acknowledge their concerns. If they've said things that are flat-out ridiculous, agree with them that if those things were true, you wouldn't want homeschool, either! (Humor always helps.)

Next, calmly and politely give them information that contradicts what they've just said.

Educate your unsupportive family in a way that will reach them, specifically. If spewing off numbers or statistics isn't going to impress them, don't do it. If they're more apt to listen to personal stories or examples, go that route. On the other hand, if your family would be convinced by your child's last test scores or what level they're reading at, there is nothing wrong with using that to your advantage.

Stay calm. Even though it's often our first natural reaction, try not to get defensive. The number one reason these discussions fail is because both parties hold so tightly to what they believe is right (and get defensive about it!) and they're simply not able to have a civil discussion. Keep the conversation as light as you can.

Test the waters. If it appears a real discussion is in order, great! Be willing to answer questions, as long as the purpose is clear. If the conversation seems to veer off track, it's worth stopping to interject, "Are you really interested in learning about what we're doing, or are you just waiting to tell me we're wrong?" If, after honestly assessing the situation, you feel that the other party just wants to complain or attack, it's time to change the subject. There are a lot of other things to talk about at the Christmas party, right?

Set your boundaries and be clear about where they are. I've always felt that people can question us about homeschooling all they want — and believe me, things can get heated — but at the point they get disrespectful to or about my kids, we're done. And honestly, if you're in a situation where you're dealing with someone who wants to drag your kids into a battle about homeschooling at a family gathering, the issue is not with homeschooling; it's an issue with the other person's attitude and behavior.

471

The bottom line is that you're either going to talk with the people who disagree with you or you're going to avoid interaction with them. Your method of how to deal with anti-homeschooling family will most likely depend on how closely related the family member is, how often you see them, and what happens when you're together. Your grandma who lives next door is a completely different story than your cousin you only see every other Christmas.

Something else to consider is that it's not necessarily our job to convince anyone about anything regarding homeschooling. Homeschooling is made infinitely more stressful when you feel like you are spending your time trying to prove its worth to people. Educate those who actually want to listen, but at some point, you have to go on with your homeschooling and let the chips fall where they may. Don't let a snarky, unsupportive family member get in the way of an amazing homeschooling experience.

A Note on How to Deal With Your Kids Being Quizzed

A common way for anti-homeschooling family to get under your skin is by quizzing your kids. Sometimes this is just to see if they are "learning" anything. Other times it's because they want to make your kids flub up in order to somehow prove that homeschooling doesn't work.

My oldest son came up with a great solution for this. Knowing that certain people in our midst had a propensity for these quiz-type questions, he told me, "I figure if they keep quizzing me, I'll just ask them a simple computer programming question. And when they can't answer, I'll take that as my cue the conversation is done."

In our several years of home education, I've seen homeschooled children get quizzed a lot... but I have never seen public school kids get quizzed. Weird, right? And let's be honest: How many people — homeschooled kids, public-schooled kids or adults — can even answer who the 15th president was or what the scientific name of a fox is without using their smartphone? So what's the logic behind quizzing homeschooled kids about these same things? (By the way, it's completely acceptable to bring this up when you're a victim of constant quizzing.)

Anti-homeschooling commentary can be a real struggle for homeschooling families. Use it as a way to teach your kids about the best ways to deal with people who disagree or believe differently. It's a life lesson! Stay calm, don't get defensive, and steer your discussions towards educating people about their misinformation. And remember, you can always change the subject. You can always talk about something else. And, if things get too heated, you can always walk away.

 *Amy Dingmann lives in Minnesota with her husband, where they have been homeschooling their two sons since 2007. Her hobbies include filling up her sons' bottomless pits, drinking a lot of strong coffee and smiling. Her least favorite subject is math. Her favorite subjects are everything else. She likes talking to other homeschooling parents and assuring them that even though they worry they're totally screwing things up, they actually totally and completely rock. Amy blogs at TheHmmmschoolingMom.com, and works as an author/speaker on homeschooling and parenting/family topics.*

Involving Dad and Extended Family Members in Homeschooling

Amy Dingmann

Ask any homeschool mom about the benefits of homeschooling and one of the answers will often be "it's brought our family closer together." Family relationships are a huge part of the homeschooling experience. The flexibility of homeschooling gives us time and availability to foster those strong bonds, both with Dad and extended family. So how do we go about ensuring that our family members are tuned in to our journey?

How to Involve Dad in Your Homeschooling

Dad's involvement in homeschooling is incredibly important! However, that involvement can be defined in many different ways. As homeschooling moms, we sometimes assume that Dad's involvement in homeschool should look like exactly like ours. For some families, that works out great! For others, it's practically impossible. Let's talk about the different ways that dads can be involved in homeschooling.

Before we figure out how to get Dad involved in homeschooling, there is an important matter we all need to get out in the open. Maybe it's not something you even discussed while making the decision to homeschool. Maybe you both operated on a lot of unknown assumptions as you embarked on the road ahead. But there's something you definitely need to get out in the open now, especially if it wasn't something you talked about then.

Here goes: When you decided to homeschool, what did your husband think his role was going to be?

Some of us were so excited that our husband agreed with homeschooling that we headed off into homeschooling bliss without knowing where our spouse stood regarding the day-to-day of the homeschooling life. Sure, your husband agreed that homeschooling was a fine choice, but were you both on the same page about the logistics of making that happen?

Through several writing projects in the past, I've spoken with many homeschooling dads. I've found that some of their most common complaints about homeschooling come from two very different camps in the homeschooling wilderness. So your first task is to have an honest discussion to determine which of these two camps your husband is currently tenting in.

Camp "I Want to Be Involved"

Sometimes it's easy for dads to be involved. They hop right in and get their hands dirty with whatever the day's lesson is. They're right next to you, team-teaching. Or they're graciously taking over the subjects that you don't want to teach or don't feel you understand as well as they do.

But other times, Dad has a hard time getting involved (despite really wanting to) and it's actually because of us. Sometimes Dad doesn't know how to be involved because his wife and kids are like a secret society. A team with a special bond. A club that he doesn't know the password for. When the kids and Mom are always together, he can feel like an outsider who struggles to fit in.

The unfortunate thing is that moms can sometimes see that as "he doesn't want to be involved" when really, it's that he doesn't know the best way to be involved without messing things up for you. He doesn't want to overstep his bounds. He doesn't want to get in the way of what already seems to be a good thing.

Let's be honest: Has your husband jumped into help at some point and been met with frustration from you? A friend tells of a time her husband tried to offer help to the kids with math and was teaching them how to solve a problem in a totally different way than she'd taught the kids.

Now, while it's great to have different ways to solve a problem, the timing of the husband's second solution wasn't optimal. The concept was completely new and everyone was struggling. The kids ended up more confused, she was frustrated, and her husband — who was trying to make things easier — wondered for quite a while if it was just easier to not help at all.

If we're honest, sometimes we homeschooling moms can be a little bit control-freakish about how things run. We think the experiment should be set up a different way or things should be done in a different order or we think the kids get too silly (or not silly enough!) when Dad is heading up the show.

Learn to relax. There is absolutely nothing wrong with Dad doing his own thing with the kids! Just because it's different than your style doesn't mean it's wrong.

Communication is the key! Talk in depth with each other about what your concerns and frustrations are. What makes homeschooling easier for both of you? What things do each of you do that make teaching or being involved more difficult for your spouse? Are you on the same page about what's most important in your homeschool? Do you both agree on the method of homeschooling that's been chosen?

If Dad is hanging out in Camp Want to Be Involved, for goodness' sake, let him be involved. Not only that, but get out of his way! Your kids will benefit from both of you being part of the show. Chances are, you're completely different in your teaching styles and the things you think are important for the kids to learn. You both have strengths and weaknesses. Give your children the opportunity to experience learning with Dad if that's how Dad wants to be involved.

Let Dad take the reins with subjects where he has interests and strengths. Also, consider that Dad might reach one of your children better, or be able to explain things in a way that you just can't. Everyone's brain works through concepts differently. Your husband's alternative ways of seeing things or explaining them might just be the ticket to help the light bulb go off.

Camp "Homeschooling is Your Gig, Mom"

There are two reasons your husband might be in this tent. One is that your husband's schedule simply doesn't allow him to be available to help. The other is that he's just not interested in the hands-on aspect of homeschooling.

Don't assume that because you're a homeschooling family that Dad wants to take on teaching courses, setting up in-depth experiments, or dressing up for Wizard of Oz Day. This occasionally causes issues in a family where Mom assumed that Dad would be up and at 'em, teaching and leading, and Dad wasn't aware that was plan.

Sometimes Dad just wants his contribution to be (1) a hearty thumbs-up to the idea of ditching public school (important!) and (2) funding for the stuff your homeschool needs to do its thing (important!).

Here's a secret, though: Even if he says he's not the homeschooling parent and that homeschooling is your thing, the kids are still learning a ton from him. Even if he's not sitting with them at the kitchen table doing an experiment on how to mummify a chicken, you can bet he's teaching them important life skills, as well as lots of things that have to do with his particular strengths, weaknesses, and interests. It's important that Dad sees this and knows that he's important in whatever capacity he's able to or chooses to be involved.

So how do you at least keep Dad in the know when he wants to be (or has to be) a little more hands-off in your homeschooling?

Make an effort to fill him in. When our kids were younger, my husband had a challenging work schedule and lived elsewhere during the workweek. We didn't have a lot of time with him, and I'm sure when he came home to hang with us after being gone for several days, he felt like he was walking into another world. We tried to make things easier by making sure we let him know what was happening while he was away. While he was gone during the week, I would take a few notes on what we'd done every day.

Maybe our oldest had worked hard on reading a book or our youngest had watched a show about dinosaurs and said something funny. Maybe we'd taken a walk at a park and spotted a salamander. Maybe we'd tried a new food or learned a new song. Writing a few things down each day helped us to share what he'd missed without forgetting what we'd done and leaving him wondering what was going on.

Post your schedule or plan for the day so Dad can, at a glance, know what you're up to. This can be something the kids are aware of or not. It gives Dad a place to start when he's looking for a topic of conversation with the kids. Asking "What did you do in school today?" will often get a blah response, no matter where a child attends school. But if Dad can instead say, "Electricity from a lemon? No way! I don't believe you!" chances are the conversation will get much more interaction.

Make it easy for your husband to be involved by giving him ideas for how to interact with the kids about their day. And who knows? You might hit on something he's excited about, and next thing you know he's got the kids in the garage working on a wiring project!

Every homeschooling family is different, and that means the definition of Dad's involvement will be different, too. Talk to your husband about what he feels is the best way he can bring his own bit of awesome to your homeschool. It might be teaching a class on music history at your co-op. It might be leading a discussion about current events at the dinner table. It might be providing the money for that amazing science curriculum you want to use.

All of these things are equally important to the homeschooling experience, and we should count ourselves lucky to have Dad as part of the team.

How to Involve Extended Family in Your Homeschooling

Homeschooling is wonderful because it gives us an amazing opportunity to build relationships with extended family members as well. Has your extended family ever asked how they can help you out with homeschooling? Or have you ever wanted to get your extended family more involved in what you're doing? Here are some ideas for how to make that happen.

Bring them along to co-op/park days/social group field trips. This is especially awesome if you have family members who are questioning the whole socialization issue. Inviting them to hang out with you at one of these events will give them a front-row seat to what your kids are doing and how much fun they are having. I remember the first time I brought an extended family member to one of our park days. Her comment afterward? "I had no idea there were so many homeschoolers in the area!"

Tap into their interests. What areas of expertise does a grandma/ grandpa/ uncle/aunt/neighbor have that you can take advantage of? It doesn't have to be a job or a career. It can be a hobby or an interest, too. When my oldest was much younger, he loved to sit with my dad and look at old coins. It was an interest they both shared, and my son learned so much about them from his grandpa. Is there something that an extended family member would love to share with or teach to your kids? Welcome their knowledge and willingness to get involved!

Hire them as a substitute teacher. Do you need a day off? Can your extended family take over for a day? I remember my mom serving as my substitute teacher on occasion. It was a nice break for everyone – me from the kids, and believe it or not, the kids from me. There were school-type things the kids would do for Grandma that they wouldn't do for me without an argument, and as it turned out, Grandma had a few tricks up her sleeve that I put into use that really helped things run more smoothly in our day-to-day.

Invite them to "school functions." Don't forget the events that your kids are involved in—invite extended family to see what's going on. One of the first co-ops we were a part of put on a medieval feast after a co-op wide unit on the Middle Ages. Our extended family is always attending other cousins' sports meets, choir concerts and similar programs — why did I not think to invite them to the medieval feast that showcased everything we had learned over the past nine weeks? The things your kids are involved in might not look like "normal" school functions — and that's OK! They shouldn't! — but ask if extended family is welcome to join, and then invite them.

Correspond with them. Do your kids need to learn how to write letters, either handwritten or typed? Are they working on their email skills? Do they need some safe people to text? Or do they need to (gasp) learn how to make an actual phone call? Extended family members will love hearing from your kids and helping them learn how to effectively communicate.

Let your kids teach them. When kids get older, they sometimes have knowledge that our extended family doesn't. You know how fast a kid can learn a computer/tablet/any piece of technology, right? Homeschooling is all about learning, but wouldn't it be great if your kids could learn to teach, too? When Grandma can't figure out how to put that app on her phone or Uncle Jim is having issues with new software he just installed, can your kids teach them how to remedy the problem? This is such a great experience because it helps kids to slow down and think through how to explain what they already know to others... and it proves to them how much they actually know! Kids shouldn't always be the students. It's empowering for them to know they can be the teachers, too. They've learned by watching you!

Use your flexible schedule to your advantage. One of the biggest benefits of homeschooling is having a flexible schedule, and perhaps you can involve your extended family in that by showing them the great things you can do with the flexible time you have. Can you volunteer together as a family? Is there a way you can help a family member out with your flexible schedule? Does your flexible schedule simply give you more time to be able to meet up with your extended family? Can you plan a field trip together? Stretch the minds of your family to understand that the lifestyle you've chosen to live means you're free to do things differently, and get them involved in that process!

Make an email newsletter/blog/private Facebook group. For family members who live far away, a great way to keep people involved in the happenings of your homeschool is to make a monthly email newsletter or blog. Kids will enjoy putting this together, and your extended family will love hearing about what's going on. It keeps them up to date with what's happening and opens the lines of communication. Another idea is to set up a private Facebook group for family members where you can post the things your kids are doing. Technology has given us so many ways to communicate; take advantage of them!

There are so many things we can learn from our extended family, and homeschooling gives us the flexibility to bring that right into our daily lives. Take advantage of this flexibility and use it help foster strong, healthy family relationships. Show off what homeschooling means to you and what your days are full of — you just might have some family members wanting to jump in and take part!

Amy Dingmann lives in Minnesota with her husband, where they have been homeschooling their two sons since 2007. Her hobbies include filling up her sons' bottomless pits, drinking a lot of strong coffee and smiling. Her least favorite subject is math. Her favorite subjects are everything else. She likes talking to other homeschooling parents and assuring them that even though they worry they're totally screwing things up, they actually totally and completely rock. Amy blogs at TheHmmmschoolingMom.com, and works as an author/speaker on homeschooling and parenting/family topics.